EXPERIMENTS IN MICROPROCESSORS AND DIGITAL SYSTEMS

SECOND EDITION

DOUGLAS V. HALL
Portland Community College
Portland, Oregon

MARYBELLE B. HALL
Clackamas Community College
Oregon City, Oregon

McGRAW-HILL BOOK COMPANY

New York Atlanta Dallas St. Louis San Francisco Auckland Bogotá Guatemala
Hamburg Johannesburg Lisbon London Madrid Mexico Montreal
New Delhi Panama Paris San Juan São Paulo Singapore Sydney Tokyo Toronto

EXPERIMENTS IN MICROPROCESSORS AND DIGITAL SYSTEMS, SECOND EDITION

2 3 4 5 6 7 8 9 0   SEMSEM   8 9 0 9 8 7 6 5 4 3

ISBN 0-07-025553-9

CONTENTS

PREFACE

Experiments in Microprocessors and Digital Systems, Second Edition, is intended to be a supermarket or smorgasbord of digital and microprocessor laboratory experiments. It has been designed to complement *Microprocessors and Digital Systems,* Second Edition, by Douglas V. Hall, and it has references to specific pages in that text. Included are experiments suitable for a wide variety of course levels, available time, and accessible equipment. We have attempted to make the experiments sophisticated enough to be realistic, yet straightforward enough for beginning digital and microprocessor students to follow.

Because schools vary widely in the number and length of lab classes, the experiments have been broken down into modules. Each module can be performed either as a complete lab project or as one part of the more comprehensive experiment. This allows flexibility in the scheduling of time, number of topics covered, and the depth and detail desired in laboratory study.

All circuits use readily available parts. The circuits can easily be built on any of the popular solderless breadboards using 22- or 24-gauge, color-coded, solid-core wire. Furthermore, the microcomputer experiments have been designed to be hardware and software independent. Thus, the experiments may be performed with any microcomputer on which the student has access to simple serial and parallel ports and, in one case, an interrupt line.

It is hoped that these experiments will suggest further projects to the reader in areas such as electronic music synthesis, robotics, and interfacing of various devices to personal computers. The authors welcome comments concerning the use of this book and would like to hear of any problems encountered or suggestions the reader has for improving any of the experiments.

The authors wish to thank Dr. William H. Murray, Professor, Engineering Science/Physics Department, Broome Community College, Binghamton, New York; Arthur H. Seidman, Professor of Electrical Engineering, Pratt Institute, Brooklyn, New York; and David M. Hata of Portland Community College, Portland, Oregon, for their helpful suggestions concerning the content of this manual. We also wish to thank Judith Seeger of Hewlett-Packard, Palo Alto, California, for her review of many of the experiments. Last, but certainly not least, we wish to thank our many students for their candid critiques of the labs.

Douglas V. Hall
Marybelle B. Hall

LABORATORY LOGBOOK DIRECTIONS

Electronics technicians often are required to record their technical work by writing in a laboratory logbook. This logbook is a running record of daily activities and is completed in chronological order as experimental work is being performed. The name *laboratory logbook* is probably the best descriptive title that could be selected because almost everyone realizes that a log is the official record for ships at sea. A log is a carefully prepared record of events, both large and small, that occur in a daily period. It is not as well known that a signed and dated laboratory logbook is also the official record for technical experiments that lead to patent applications.

The laboratory log should be recorded in a bound notebook, not the looseleaf type, to prevent removal or insertion of pages of unofficial data. The date and signature of the person who enters the information must also be recorded to make the document official. The person who signs the log is stating that the information recorded is the true information taken in the laboratory. Data copied from scratchpaper in order to keep the log neat is not official data, and this procedure does not follow the intent of the laboratory logbook. You must learn to record data in a form that can be read and interpreted as the experiment is performed. This procedure prevents you from making the laboratory log into an art project outside the laboratory.

The following procedures are used in preparing the laboratory log. Remember that this is an official record that must be read in your absence by another individual.

1. *Log-in.* To conform with patent laws, the technician's name, date, and experiment number must appear at the head of each day's work and at the top of each page. Remember, no pages should be left blank and no pages should be removed.

2. *Objectives.* At the beginning of each experiment, write brief statements explaining why the experiment is to be performed.

3. *References.* The books, magazine articles, and technical notes that are read in preparation for the experiment are listed along with relevant page numbers. If further references are used during the experiment or the analysis of the results, these are noted in the log, too.

4. *Materials.* Make a list of specific components, the quantity required, type or value, other materials, and supplies needed for construction of the experiment's circuits.

5. *Equipment.* The serial number, model number, or laboratory number of each piece of equipment used in the experiment is recorded. In some cases, the technician may be asked to repeat the experiment to show why unusual results have been obtained. The unusual results could be due to a faulty meter, which the technician can prove only if the meter which was used in the experiment is known.

6. *Wiring Diagrams.* Prior to building a circuit, schematic diagrams are drawn neatly and corrected as necessary to reflect any changes in circuit values. For each circuit you build and test, you must draw the actual circuit diagram to be used.

7. *Predictions.* Before power is applied or measurements are made, calculations of predicted voltage values, polarities, and expected waveforms, if any, are recorded. Predictions are based on nominal values of components.

8. *Procedure.* Short comments about what measurements are being made, by what instruments, or any special techniques being used are usually sufficient, and these may be included preceding and/or alongside the data (see item 9). The comments on procedures should be complete enough to allow another person to perform the experiment for verification.

9. *Data—Charts or Tables of Measurements, Waveforms, and Other Observations.* In most experiments a number of measurements must be recorded neatly. Charts are the most convenient method of recording this data, since all values are readily available for analysis. Regarding errors: Do not erase recorded data. Draw a single line through your possible error so it can still be read. Then record new data nearby or in another table if an entire set of measurements is being retaken, because of error or large discrepancies in circuits, measurements, equipment, and so on. Be sure to record the instrument used, scale, or magnification, and label all waveforms completely (frequency, attenuation, volts per division, and so on). As the experiment is being performed, and results are calculated, etc., be sure to write comments on unusual results, problems encountered, and measures taken to correct the problems or explore unusual results. Note any observations you feel are significant.

10. *Calculations.* Most experiments require a certain number of calculations before the final results are obtained. Formulas and sample calculations that are completely identified must be included. It is not necessary to show repeated calculations.

11. *Graphs.* Label axes, plot points accurately and neatly, and circle the points. Draw lines to show the general tendency of the data (do not connect the dots). Discrepancies and unusual results will appear off the line. Graphs should be large. Not all experiments require graphs.

12. *Conclusions.* Your conclusions summarize how your findings answer the objectives of the experiment. A good summary should list, tabulate, or otherwise describe all the specific characteristics of

the circuit or device under test that were definitely observed or measured. If possible, the circuit or device should be compared with preceding circuits or devices for similarities and differences. A brief discussion of problems, errors, revisions, and unusual results must be included. The statement of results and conclusions is very important. The entire experiment may be considered a failure if you do not understand the results and cannot decide what to express as a conclusion.

When you complete each laboratory experiment, your logbook must be reviewed, signed, and dated by your instructor before you begin the next experiment.

Note: If you are using "precanned" experiments, it is not necessary to be quite as complete in your logbook. The essential information to record might be as follows:

1. A schematic for each major circuit, with noted minor modifications and additions as required
2. Predictions of anticipated circuit responses
3. A record of:
   a. Voltages and signals applied
   b. Circuit outputs measured
   c. Waveforms observed
   d. Timing diagrams determined
   e. Problems encountered and troubleshooting techniques used
4. Any required calculations
5. Discussion of results for each circuit tested
6. Concise summary of experiment, which answers the stated objectives

Pages vii–x are sample sections of logbook pages which illustrate many of the above procedures.

NAME : M.B. Smith   EXPERIMENT #3   DATE : 3/1/83
                              page 3-1

Objectives :   To observe, measure, and graph the I vs. V
                characteristics of 3 resistors.

References :   Grob pg. 42-44, class notes, XYZ Lab Manual
                page 22.

Materials :   1K
        1   1K Ω resistor
        1   100K Ω resistor
        1   10 Ω resistor
        1   bread board
      asst   jumper wires

Equipment :   (Lab Station #1)
        1   Power supply, DC, 0-20V   Serial #302
        1   Data Precision DVM, Model 2480   Serial #23
        1   Simpson VOM Model 260 Serial #66

Wiring Diagram Schematic :

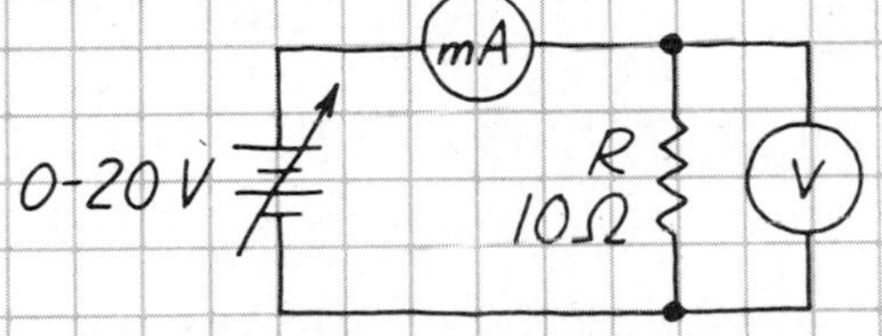

0-20V   R $\bigcirc{V}$ CIRCUIT #1
                        10Ω

Predictions :
        Voltage will be varied from 0 to 5V at 1 volt
        intervals. According to Ohm's Law, $I = \frac{V}{R}$, I
        predict (calculate) that I should observe the
        following set of values for current through
        the 10Ω resistor :

Predicted for 10Ω = R

V	I
0V	0
1V	.1A
2V	.2A
3V	.3A
4V	.4A
5V	.5A

sample
calculation (for 2V)

$I = \frac{V}{R}$

$= \frac{2V}{10\Omega}$

$= .2A$

$= 200\,mA$

I predict the graph
should be a straight
line (linear) with a
fairly steep slope
                similar to
                ← this

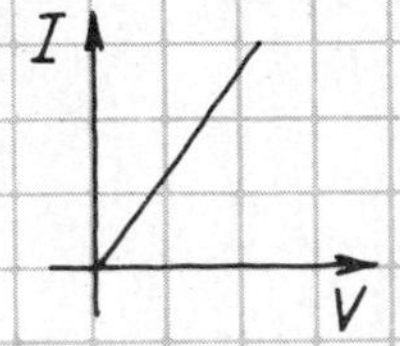

I
  ↑
  | /
  | /
  |/_____→ V

Procedure for CKT #1:

    Circuit built as drawn. Voltage applied, varying from OV to 5V in 1 volt intervals as measured by DVM. Current values measured on Simpson VOM and recorded in chart below:

Data table for CKT #1:

V	I
0V	0A
1V	98 mA
2V	1.94 mA
3V	~~274 mA~~ 290 mA
4V	386 mA
5V	485 mA

measurement seemed low, so rechecked measurement – Voltage wasn't set correct (c 2.9V) so reset voltage & made new meas.

Graph will be plotted after all measurements taken for all 3 resistors; then plot all lines on same graph for comparison.

M.B. Smith   (didn't finish yesterday – cont. today)   3/2/83

Procedure   CKT #2:

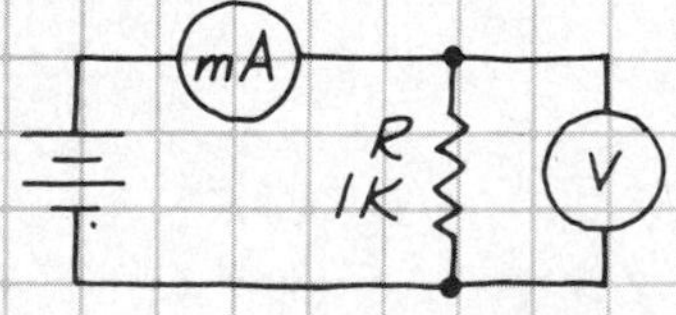

Now replace 10Ω resistor with 1K resistor and perform same operations as with 10Ω.

Predictions for 1K: Measurements

V	I		V	I	
0V	0mA	Graph should	0	0	Something wrong here!
1V	1mA	be linear	1	5a	
2V	2mA	but less	2	5a	Disregard this
3V	3mA	steep than	3	10a	~~graph~~ chart
4V	4mA	for 10Ω	4	11a	see page
5V	5mA		5	11a	following for new measurements

(Wrong part & reading)
(on wrong scale – rebuilt)

SAMPLE LOGBOOK PAGES

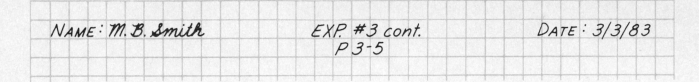

Graph:

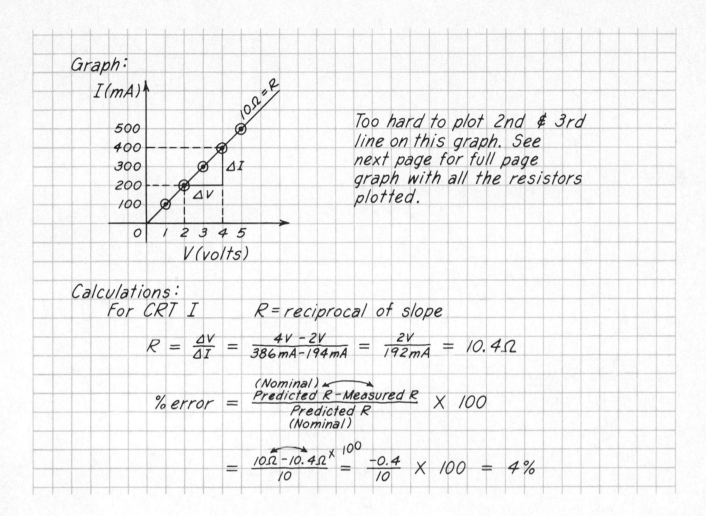

Too hard to plot 2nd & 3rd line on this graph. See next page for full page graph with all the resistors plotted.

Calculations:

For CRT I   R = reciprocal of slope

$$R = \frac{\Delta V}{\Delta I} = \frac{4V - 2V}{386mA - 194mA} = \frac{2V}{192mA} = 10.4\,\Omega$$

$$\% \; error = \frac{\overset{(Nominal)}{Predicted \; R} - Measured \; R}{\underset{(Nominal)}{Predicted \; R}} \times 100$$

$$= \frac{10\,\Omega - 10.4\,\Omega}{10} \times 100 = \frac{-0.4}{10} \times 100 = 4\%$$

Conclusions: My results show that a resistor is a linear device, & Ohm's law is verified. —Equal changes in voltage produce equal changes in current for a specific resistor. Larger resistance values allow less current for the same voltage. The graph....
... etc... reciprocal of slope should...etc... % of error

EXPERIMENT 1

FAMILIARIZATION WITH LABORATORY EQUIPMENT

REFERENCES

Hall, *Microprocessors and Digital Systems:* pages 4–16.

Operator's manual for laboratory oscilloscope.

Operator's manual for laboratory function generator.

Basic Oscilloscope Operation by Tektronix Inc., Beaverton, Oregon, 1977.

OBJECTIVES

It is assumed that you are familiar with or will familiarize yourself with the dc power supply, DVM or other voltmeter, ohmmeter, and current meter at the laboratory station. Depending on the sequence of previous courses and their supporting laboratory exercises, however, you may or may not have learned how to operate an oscilloscope or a function generator.

At the conclusion of this laboratory exercise, you should be able to:

1. Set the controls of the laboratory oscilloscope to obtain a visible, clear, stable, and calibrated trace.
2. Set the controls of the laboratory function generator to obtain a stable square-wave output of a specified frequency displayed on the oscilloscope.
3. Set the controls of the function generator to obtain digital logic-level pulses of specified amplitude, frequency, and duty cycle.

EQUIPMENT

1 Triggered-sweep laboratory oscilloscope (dual-trace preferred)
2 Probes for oscilloscope
1 Operator's manual for the oscilloscope
1 Laboratory function generator (preferably with sine, square-wave, and sawtooth functions, a range of direct current to 1 MHz, and offset capability)

MATERIALS

If only a sine wave generator is available, also obtain the following materials:

1 5-V zener diode
1 1-kΩ resistor

PROCEDURE

MODULE 1 Oscilloscope familiarization. Refer to Hall, pages 6–14, and the operator's manual for the oscilloscope for detailed discussion and descriptions of the controls and their uses.

1. For the first-time user, it is helpful to locate the main sections of the instrument and define their functions.
   a. The CRT section.
      (1) This section includes the screen with its grid (graticule) of horizontal and vertical measuring lines; power ON/OFF switch; intensity or brightness control; focus; and perhaps astigmatism, beam finder, position, and trace rotation controls.
      (2) The CRT section creates the visual display by capturing and displaying the signal over and over, in "windows" of time, beginning at some trigger point on the signal being displayed.
   b. The horizontal time base or frequency section.
      (1) This section has a frequency or time selector and may include a horizontal position control. If the oscilloscope has a dual time base, this section also contains delay and intensity controls.
      (2) The horizontal section determines how much time each horizontal division in the CRT display represents.
   c. The triggering functions section.

(1) The triggering section contains source, mode, slope, and level controls.

(2) Triggering determines when each time window begins.

d. The vertical section.

(1) The vertical section contains voltage amplification, vertical position, and coupling selectors, as well as the signal input connector where the probe(s) can be attached. If the oscilloscope is a dual-trace type, this section also contains channel and mode selectors.

(2) The vertical section controls the amplitude of the signal and determines how many volts are represented by each vertical division (V/div) on the CRT display.

2. Turning on the oscilloscope and obtaining a stable trace.

a. Turn on the power switch.

b. Turn up the brightness control.

c. Adjust the horizontal and vertical position controls to the centers of their ranges.

d. Set the triggering controls to internal source, automatic mode. If there are several sweep modes (delayed, delayed triggered, and so on), select the main sweep.

e. Set V/div to 1 V/div (or a similar range).

f. Set time/div to a 1-ms or (1-kHz) range.

g. Set the input coupling to ground.

h. If you do not have a visible trace at this point and your oscilloscope has a beam finder, press it to locate the beam. Use vertical and horizontal position controls to center the display.

i. Reduce brightness until the trace is visible but not brilliant. Adjust the focus (and astigmatism) control for a clear display. A lower brightness gives a finer trace. If it is available and necessary, adjust the trace rotation to make the trace parallel to the horizontal axis.

j. Switch the input coupling to ac. Adjust the trigger level or trigger stability controls as necessary to obtain stable display.

3. This is a 60-Hz experiment for first-time oscilloscope users (adapted from *Basic Oscilloscope Operation* by Tektronix):

a. Obtain a free-running trace centered on CRT as in section 2.

b. Attach a probe to the vertical input (X input, channel 1 input, and so on).

c. Set the input coupling to ac.

d. Make sure both the frequency (s/div) and amplification (V/div) controls are in their calibrated positions.

e. Touch the probe tip to your finger, and adjust the amplification control until you obtain a signal that vertically fills most of the screen. You are acting as an antenna and picking up 60-Hz radiation from ac power lines.

f. To obtain a steady display, use normal triggering, set for a positive slope, and adjust the triggering controls until the signal is steady. If the signal will not stabilize on normal triggering and if your oscilloscope has line triggering (60-Hz ac), then switch to line triggering and adjust the triggering controls for a steady signal.

g. Increase the s/div (time, frequency, horizontal), and you should see more waves. Decrease the s/div until you have about two waves on the screen. You will learn how to measure frequency and voltage in Module 2, after you have learned how to operate the function generator to provide a more stable waveform.

h. Experiment with turning the time/div and V/div knobs out of calibration; then return them to calibration.

i. Adjust the horizontal position control until the left end of trace is at the left vertical grid line. Switch to a negative slope; then vary the triggering level and note the effect on where the wave starts.

4. Probes and probe compensation.

a. Refer to your manual for probe information, and read the discussion of probes in Hall, Chapter 1, page 8.

b. Attach a probe to the vertical input or channel on which it is to be used.

c. Connect the probe tip to the calibrator output of the oscilloscope.

d. Set the V/div (vertical) and time/div (horizontal) controls to get one or two cycles of the calibrator waveform to fill most of the screen.

e. Depending on the type of probe, adjust the trimmer capacitor screw, or loosen and turn the probe barrel, then tighten, to obtain the best square corners on the calibrator waveform.

f. Check the amplitude accuracy of the probe and vertical amplifier, making sure the V/div control is in a calibrated position. Consult the manual for any necessary adjustment here.

5. Dual-trace operations.

a. When you wish to display two signals, you will be using both input channels. So you should attach a probe to each channel and verify the probe compensation and amplitude accuracy for each channel, as in section 4.

b. Turn on both channels, and identify or choose which channel or signal you wish to reference to trigger on.

c. Choose alternate- or chopped-sweep mode as follows:

(1) Refer to the manual for a description of alternate- or chopped-sweep mode controls. Refer to Hall, Chapter 1, page 7, for additional discussion of alternate- and chopped-sweep modes.

(2) For higher frequencies (above 1 kHz), use the alternate-sweep mode.

(3) For lower frequencies (below 1 kHz), choose the chopped-sweep mode.

6. Other special features and operations.

a. Alternating- or direct-current coupling [see your manual and Hall, pages 7–8, for a discussion].

(1) Direct-current coupling allows all input voltage to enter the oscilloscope and be amplified and displayed. On dc coupling, the oscilloscope can be used as a crude voltmeter.

(2) Alternating-current coupling blocks the dc component of a voltage input and only displays and amplifies the varying, or ac, component. Alternating-current coupling is useful when you are looking for noise spikes and ripple voltages.

b. Trigger controls. [Refer to your manual and to Hall, pages 9–10, for a discussion of trigger control details.]

c. *x-y* mode. This mode is used and discussed in Experiment 2. [Refer to your manual and to Hall, page 12, for additional details.]

d. Dual time base. [Refer to your manual and see the discussion in Hall, pages 11–12.]

MODULE 2 Function generator familiarization [see Hall, Chapter 1, page 15].

Do those things in section 1 below. Then do either sections 2 and 3 or section 4, depending on the following: If you have a function generator with square-wave function and offset capability, follow the procedure in sections 2 and 3. If you have a signal generator that produces only sine waves of variable frequency and amplitude, follow only the procedure in section 4.

1. Obtaining a sine wave output from a function generator, displaying the waveform on an oscilloscope, and measuring the waveform's frequency and voltage amplitude, using the oscilloscope.

a. Read the operator's manual for the specific function generator to locate and identify the controls.
(1) Set the frequency range and multiplier controls of the function generator for a 1-kHz signal.
(2) If your function generator has a function selector, set the function selector for sine wave.
(3) If your function generator has an offset control, turn it off, set it to zero, or switch to sine wave functions that are not affected by the offset.
(4) Set the variable-voltage control to minimum, and turn off any voltage attenuator or multipliers.
(5) Attach an output cable to the generator output.

b. Set up the oscilloscope for a stable display on channel 1.
(1) Set the trace across the middle of the CRT screen.
(2) Set for ac coupling.
(3) Set for 1 ms/div (1-kHz horizontal range).
(4) Set for 1-V/div vertical range.
(5) Connect oscilloscope probe to the output of the function generator. Make sure the oscilloscope ground is attached to the function generator ground as required.

c. Turn on the function generator.
(1) Increase the voltage of the generator until the waveform fills more than half the screen vertically.
(2) Adjust the triggering of the oscilloscope to obtain a stable display.

(3) Note that the trace is centered on the horizontal line you set across the middle of the screen (0 V).

d. To measure the frequency:
(1) Adjust the time/div control (frequency, horizontal) until you have about two complete waveforms (cycles) on the screen.
(2) Set the coupling switch to GND, and adjust the trace so that the line is set exactly on the middle *horizontal* (measuring) graticule line of the screen.
(3) Return the coupling switch to ac. Adjust the display, using the *horizontal* position control until the first *zero* crossing of the left wave is at the first *vertical* grid line from the left.
(4) Count the number of large divisions (and any additional fractions of a division) to the next zero crossing on the waveform which is the same point for the next cycle. This gives the number of time divisions for one complete cycle (see Fig. 1-1). For example, one complete cycle is between *A* and *B*, or between *C* and *D*, as shown in Fig. 1-1.
(5) Multiply the count (number of divisions) by the setting of the time/div control. This gives the time period *T* of the waveform (the number of divisions times seconds per division).
(6) Obtain the frequency from $F = 1/T$.

e. To measure the voltage, use the vertical position control to move the wave until a bottom peak (trough) rests on a major horizontal line.
(1) Count the number of divisions to top peak.
(2) Multiply the number of divisions by the V/div setting to obtain the peak-to-peak voltage.
(3) The amplitude, or peak, voltage is half the peak-to-peak voltage for a sine wave.

2. Obtaining a square-wave output of specific frequency and amplitude, and displaying it on the oscilloscope.
a. Set up the function generator.
(1) Set the frequency range and multiplier controls of the function generator for a 1-kHz signal.
(2) Set the function selector for *square wave*.
(3) Set the dc offset to zero (or OFF).
(4) Set the variable voltage to minimum, and turn off any voltage attenuator or multipliers.

b. Set up the oscilloscope for stable display.
(1) Set for dc coupling.
(2) Set for 1-ms/div (1-kHz) horizontal range, and

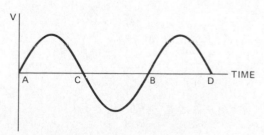

Fig. 1-1 Sine wave cycles.

make sure the knob is in the calibrated position.

    (3) Set for 1-V/div vertical range, and make sure the knob is in the calibrated position.

    (4) Connect the oscilloscope probe to the output from the generator.

c. Turn on the function generator.

    (1) Increase the voltage to obtain a stable trace of 5 V peak to peak, as measured on the oscilloscope.

    (2) Set the coupling switch to GND to note the position of 0 V. Then switch back to dc coupling. Note that the waveform is *centered* on 0 V, from +2.5 to −2.5 V.

    (3) Adjust the variable-frequency control of the generator as necessary until the oscilloscope measures a 1-kHz square wave as closely as possible.

3. Obtaining digital logic-level pulses of specific amplitude and frequency (and duty cycle, if available on the function generator).

a. Many of the digital-logic families require pulses that go from 0 to about 4 or 5 V. *You must remember to check and set these signal levels each time you need to apply a signal to a logic circuit.*

    (1) Set the function generator for a square wave of 1 kHz.

    (2) Set the oscilloscope for 1 V/div.

    (3) Adjust the amplitude control of the generator to produce a 5-V peak-to-peak square wave, as measured on the oscilloscope.

    (4) Switch the oscilloscope to GND, and use the vertical position control to set the trace on the bottom horizontal graticule line of the screen. (Leave this control set at this position; this establishes the bottom graticule line as 0 V dc reference.)

    (5) Switch the oscilloscope to dc coupling.

    (6) Now turn on the offset control on the function generator, and adjust it until the bottom of the square wave rests on the bottom graticule. The top of the waveform should be five divisions above the bottom graticule line. (*Note:* If you switch the coupling to ground, the horizontal trace should still be resting on the bottom graticule line as 0 V reference.)

b. If your generator has variable-symmetry capability, select this function and adjust the variable-symmetry control to obtain a 1-kHz pulse with a 20 percent duty cycle. (The percentage of duty

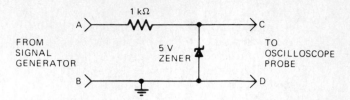

Fig. 1-2 A zener circuit produces TTL-level pulses from a sine wave signal source.

cycle equals the time that the pulse is high W divided by the total time of a complete cycle T, times 100, or $W/T \times 100$.)

c. *Optional:* Experiment with the sine and sawtooth functions and the effect of offset and variable-symmetry controls on these waveforms.

4. Obtaining a digital logic-level square wave from a sine wave signal generator.

a. Read the operator's manual and identify the controls on the signal generator.

    (1) Set the frequency range and multiplier controls for 1 kHz.

    (2) Set the variable-voltage control to minimum.

    (3) Attach an output cable to the generator.

b. Set up the oscilloscope for a stable display.

    (1) Set on dc coupling.

    (2) Set for 1-ms/div (1-kHz) horizontal range.

    (3) Set for 5-V/div vertical range.

    (4) Attach the oscilloscope probe to the generator's output cable.

c. Turn on the signal generator.

    (1) Increase the voltage of the generator to obtain a stable sine wave on the oscilloscope with 10-V peak (20 V peak to peak).

    (2) Leave the generator controls set, and remove the oscilloscope probe from the generator output.

d. Build the circuit shown in Fig. 1-2.

    (1) Attach the circuit to the signal generator at *A* and *B*.

    (2) Attach the oscilloscope to the circuit at *C* and *D*.

    (3) Observe, measure, and draw the waveform displayed on the oscilloscope (set at 1 V/div).

    (4) Some digital-logic families require pulses that go from 0 to about 3 to 5 V. Use the zener circuit of Fig. 1-2 to produce pulses with these levels. *Remember to verify the waveform levels before you apply them to any circuit.*

LOGIC GATES AND TYPICAL TTL INPUT AND OUTPUT CHARACTERISTICS

REFERENCES

Hall: pages 19–27.

7400, 7402 TTL data sheets (see appendix).

OBJECTIVES

At the conclusion of this laboratory exercise, you should be able to:

1. Use a data sheet to determine the pin designations, supply voltages, and specifications for a standard 7400 TTL integrated circuit.
2. Use a data sheet to correctly draw and build a circuit using a standard 7400 TTL IC.
3. Build and use a simple LED logic probe circuit.
4. Demonstrate or verify the truth table for a two-input NAND gate.
5. Use a data sheet to correctly wire a TTL 7402 IC and to predict and verify its truth table.
6. Measure typical output voltage levels and input current requirements for a standard TTL gate.
7. Use a data sheet to determine the fan-out, noise margin, and output current specifications for a standard TTL gate.
8. Measure the typical output low voltage level under a simulated maximum load condition.
9. Plot a static transfer curve for a TTL NAND gate wired as an inverter.
10. Use the x-y mode of an oscilloscope to obtain a dynamic transfer curve for a TTL inverter.
11. Use a transfer curve to obtain useful data regarding the threshold voltage, $V_{IH.MIN}$, $V_{IL.MAX}$, and noise margins for a standard TTL gate.
12. Troubleshoot an IC circuit containing simple logic gates.

EQUIPMENT

1 5-V power supply
1 dc voltmeter
1 dc milliammeter or microammeter
1 Oscilloscope with x-y mode capability
1 Sine (square or sawtooth) wave function generator with 10-V peak

MATERIALS

1 7400 TTL IC quad two-input NAND gate
1 7402 TTL IC quad two-input NOR gate
1 7404 TTL IC hex inverter (optional)
1 2N3904 transistor
1 LED
1 5-V zener diode (optional)
1 1N4148 diode (optional)
1 500-Ω potentiometer
1 220-Ω resistor
1 390-Ω resistor
1 1-kΩ resistor (optional)
1 10-kΩ resistor
1 Solderless prototyping board (AP, Global Specialties, or equivalent)
Assorted 22- to 24-gage solid-core, insulated, color-coded wire

PROCEDURE

MODULE 1 In this module you use a data sheet to draw and build a circuit for a TTL IC and to establish its proper operating conditions.

1. Read the TTL data sheet pages for a 7400 quad two-input NAND gate. Find and record the following information:

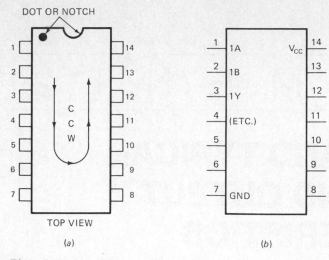

TOP VIEW

(a)   (b)

Fig. 2-1 *(a)* **Pin numbering on ICs, top view.** *(b)* **Standard schematic notation for drawing and labeling ICs.**

    a. The logic diagram of the device, with pin numbers. (Note that pin 1 may be identified to the left of a notch in the top of the package, as in Fig. 2-1*a*, or by a dot next to pin 1 when there is a notch at both ends. The numbers increase counterclockwise around the device when it is viewed from the top. An IC may have any number of pins between 4 and 64.)
    b. The recommended operating supply voltage V_{CC}.
    c. The minimum input high voltage V_{IH} and the maximum input low voltage V_{IL}.
    d. The typical output high voltage V_{OH} and the typical output low voltage V_{OL}.
    e. The input high and input low currents I_{IH} and I_{IL}, respectively.
    f. The maximum output high current I_{OH} and the output low current I_{OL}
2. Draw a circuit diagram as follows:
    a. Show V_{CC} and ground connected to the proper pins.
    b. Label all pin numbers and pin function names. For example, 1A, 1B, 1Y are the labels for pins 1, 2, and 3 to identify *A* and *B* as inputs and *Y* as output for gate 1 inside the device. Standard schematic drawing notation usually shows the pin *numbers* written *externally* next to the line that represents the pin and the pin *function* name written *internally* next to the pin, as shown in Fig. 2-1*b*.
3. Build the circuit. Use standard color-coded wiring, for example, red is V_{CC} and black is ground. Before applying power to the circuit, you must do the following:
    a. Check the wiring against the schematic diagram pin by pin, at least twice. Although this first circuit is very simple, you should develop the habit of checking the wiring before applying power from the very *first* circuit, because wiring errors are the *most* common source of circuit failure.
    b. Verify that the power-supply output voltage for V_{CC} is at the correct level *before* connecting it to the circuit.

4. Apply the ground and supply voltages to the circuit. Verify that V_{CC} and ground voltages are correct as measured at the proper pins of the IC.
5. Initial troubleshooting tips:
    a. If a circuit fails to function correctly or an IC gets very hot or starts smoking or popping, turn off all signals and power immediately (since no smoking is permitted in the laboratory).
    b. If an IC or any other component smokes, it should be removed and replaced, for quite likely it has been damaged in some way.
    c. Before reapplying power, recheck the wiring and IC number—make sure you have used the correct pin diagram for your IC number and that you used the prototyping board correctly.
    d. Detach the supply from the circuit and recheck V_{CC} and ground at the supply, before you reapply power to the circuit.
    e. Apply power to the circuit, and check whether V_{CC} and ground are getting to the board and to the proper IC pins. If power or ground is not getting to the circuit or the pins, check the *continuity* of the wires and prototyping board. Check for short-circuits between pins and in wiring.
    f. A common symptom is that V_{CC} appears on all pins of a device. Often this is due to an incorrect or faulty *ground* connection.

MODULE 2 In this module you verify the truth tables for some common logic gates.
    Note: Described here are two common ways for drawing schematics for logic circuits.

    Method 1. Draw each IC as a box with all pins numbered and labeled. Show all wiring connections between appropriate pins, and account for all pins. Unused pins are often labeled NC, meaning "not connected." See Fig. 2-2*a*.

    Method 2. Draw the logic gate *symbol*, and label the pin number on the gate. If there are several gates inside an IC package, identify each one by a number. V_{CC} and ground connections for a specific IC are shown as notes in a corner of the schematic. See Fig. 2-2*b*.

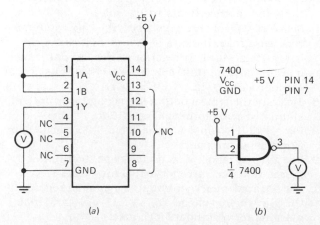

(a)   (b)

Fig. 2-2 *(a)* **Drawing logic circuit schematics with IC symbols.** *(b)* **Drawing logic circuit schematics with gate symbols.**

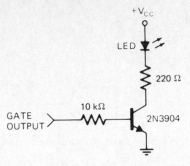

Fig. 2-3 A simple LED logic probe.

1. Choose one of the four NAND gates in the IC package as a test gate.

   a. Draw the truth table for a two-input NAND gate.

   b. A simple LED logic probe circuit, as shown in Fig. 2-3, can be used to monitor the output state of common logic gates. Determine whether the LED lights when the gate output is high or low.

   c. Draw a circuit diagram showing the LED circuit connected to the output of the NAND gate you will be testing. Label pin numbers and functions as described above.

   d. Build the circuit as drawn.

   e. To verify the truth table for your test NAND gate:
      (1) Apply each input combination by connecting the inputs to V_{CC} for high or to ground for low.
      (2) Observe and record the state of the LED probe at the output for each input combination.

   f. Troubleshooting tips.
      (1) If the circuit initially fails to function or if the IC or any component gets hot or smokes, *disconnect* all signals to the *gate* inputs and follow the procedure outlined in Module 1, steps 5a to 5f above.
      (2) When the power and ground are correct and verified at the IC pins, check that the signal voltages you wish to apply are the correct type and level.
      (3) With V_{CC} and ground applied to the circuit, reconnect the signals to the circuit and verify that the correct signals are reaching the correct IC pins.
      (4) If the inputs are correct but the output fails to verify, disconnect the LED probe and use a DVM to check whether the output voltage is correct. An output high should be at least 2.4 V, but no more than V_{CC}. An output low should be no greater than 0.4 V and no less than the ground. If inputs are correct and output are incorrect, then try using another gate in the package, for the test gate may be damaged.
      (5) When or if gate outputs are correct, retry the LED probe after verifying its wiring. Possible errors in the LED probe are a backward LED, transistor leads that are identified or wired incorrectly, and wrong-value resistors. Use a DVM to check voltages around the probe. If the gate output is high, the emitter should be at ground, the base at about 0.6 V, the collector at about 0.2 V, and the cathode of the LED at about 3.6 V. If the gate output is low, the emitter should be 0 V, the base should be about 0 V, and the collector should be at V_{CC}.

2. A NAND gate can be wired to function as an inverter.

   a. Examine the NAND gate truth table.
      (1) Note that whenever one input is held low, the output is high no matter what state the other input is in. (The low input disables the effect of the other input and makes the output ON.)
      (2) However, whenever one input is held high, the output is the opposite, or the inverse, or complement of the other input. Therefore, by tying one input of a NAND gate high and using the other input for your signal input, you convert the gate to an *inverter*.
      (3) If you wish to convert a NAND gate with more than two inputs to an inverter, tie all but one input high and use the remaining input for your signal.

   b. Draw the truth table for an inverter.

   c. Draw the circuit for your NAND gate wired as an inverter.
      (1) Label your signal input as a test input.
      (2) Add the LED logic probe to the output.

   d. Build the circuit and verify the truth table.

   e. *Optional:* Obtain a 7404 IC. Look up its data sheet to determine its logic diagram and pin numbers. Draw a circuit to test and verify the truth table for one of the gates in the package.

3. Look up the data sheet for a 7402 IC to determine the logic diagram of the device and the pin numbers.

   a. Draw a pin diagram for the device. Use this schematic to indicate the proper wiring connections for building and testing the circuit as described in the following steps.

   b. Connect V_{CC} and ground to the 7402 IC.

   c. Predict the truth table for the 7402 logic gates.

   d. Use the LED logic probe to verify the truth table for one of the gates in the package. Record your results.

MODULE 3 In this module you measure *static* characteristics for a standard TTL gate. (*Static* refers to fixed voltages applied as signals to gate input rather than pulse, or time-variable, waveforms.)

1. Measuring typical input and output voltages.

   a. Using the *7400* NAND gate IC, draw and label a circuit diagram that meets the following requirements.
      (1) Connect V_{CC} and ground to the proper pins of the 7400. Specify V_{CC}.
      (2) Connect one input of one of the four NAND gates in the package to V_{CC} (high). Remember, this converts it to a simple inverter.
      (3) Connect one side of a 500-Ω potentiometer to ground and the other side to V_{CC}. Connect the wiper arm of the potentiometer to the open (test) input of the same NAND gate inverter.

   b. Build the circuit and double-check the wiring.

   c. Apply power to the circuit and verify V_{CC} and ground at the IC.

   d. Setting V_{IL}: With power applied to the circuit, ad-

LOGIC GATES AND TYPICAL TTL INPUT AND OUTPUT CHARACTERISTICS

just the potentiometer to set the test input voltage of the NAND gate inverter as near to 0.4 V as possible.

   e. Measuring V_{OH}: Measure and record the output voltage of the gate. Since a V_{IN} of 0.4 V is a logic low and the device is acting as an inverter, the output should be a typical output high of 3 to 5 V.
   f. Setting V_{IH}: Adjust the potentiometer to set the test input voltage of the NAND gate inverter as near to 2.4 V as possible.
   g. Measuring V_{OL}: Measure and record the output voltage of the gate. Since a V_{IN} of 2.4 V is a logic high and the device is acting as an inverter, the output should provide a typical output low of 0 to 0.4 V.

2. Measuring typical input currents:

   a. I_{IH}: Determine how much current is typically required to produce an input high by adding a milliammeter in series with the wiper arm of the 500-Ω potentiometer. (Observe proper polarity for meters that do not have automatic polarity.) Set the *gate* input voltage to 2.4 V with the potentiometer. The meter should show the current required to pull the input high. Record this value.
   b. I_{IL}: Again use the milliammeter in series with the wiper arm of the 500-Ω potentiometer (note the proper meter polarity as required). Adjust the potentiometer to set the gate input voltage to 0.4 V. The milliammeter should now indicate the current required to pull the input to a low state. Record and compare this value with that required to produce a high.
   c. *Optional:* Using a diagram of the transistors inside the device, explain the large difference in currents between I_{IL} and I_{IH}.

3. Maximum sink and source currents:

   a. I_{OH}: Refer to the data sheet to determine how much current the output must source to pull a load of 10 TTL inputs to a high state.
   b. I_{OL}: Refer to the data sheet to find the maximum current the output must sink to pull 10 TTL inputs to a low state.

4. To determine fan-out:

   a. Manufacturers specify that each TTL gate will drive 10 gate inputs (in the same TTL family). This is called a *fan-out* of 10.
   b. Fan-out is equal to either I_{OL}/I_{IL} or I_{OH}/I_{IH}, whichever is lower.
   c. Locate the fan-out parameter in the data sheet, and/or use the appropriate values from the data sheet to calculate fan-out as described.

5. To determine *noise margin:*

   a. Measure $V_{OL.MAX}$. For the output low condition, which is the main one to worry about because it requires the greatest current, a load of 10 gate inputs can be simulated with a 390-Ω resistor and diode in series to V_{CC}, as shown in Fig. 2-4. Add this to the output as shown, set the test input to high, and measure the output low voltage. Typically this is about 0.2 V.
   b. Manufacturers usually specify that $V_{OL.MAX}$ will be less than 0.4 V with a full load of 10 gates over the

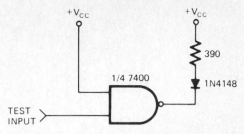

Fig. 2-4 A NAND gate with a simulated load of 10 gate inputs.

full temperature range. Compare this with the requirements for an input low $(V_{IL.MAX})$. This 400-mV difference is called a *noise margin.* Since an output is guaranteed to be less than 0.4 V and an input can be anything less than 0.8 V, this gives an additional 0.4 V of insurance that noise pulses on connecting wires will not change the output state of the gate.
   c. Refer to the data sheet to find the guaranteed $V_{OH.MIN}$. Compare this with the requirement for the minimum input high voltage $V_{IH.MIN}$. How much noise margin is there between these?

MODULE 4   Transfer curve.

1. Plotting a transfer curve from static measurements.
   a. Remove the resistor and diode load from the test gate output.
   b. Remove the milliammeter, and reconnect the wiper arm of the potentiometer directly to the test input of the NAND gate inverter.
   c. Adjust the potentiometer to set the test input voltage of the NAND gate as near to 0 V as possible.
   d. Measure and record V_{OUT}.
   e. Vary the potentiometer to increase V_{IN} in steps of 0.2 V up to 4 V, and record V_{OUT} for each step.
   f. Plot a graph of V_{OUT} versus V_{IN}. This graph is called the *transfer curve* for the device. It shows the effect of V_{IN} on the output voltage.
   g. At about what input voltage does the output change most steeply from high to low? This voltage is referred to as the *threshold voltage.* Label this on your graph.

2. Plotting a dynamic transfer curve, using the *x-y* mode of the oscilloscope and the signal generator.
   a. Figure 2-5 shows how to attach the NAND gate inverter to an oscilloscope to use the *x-y* mode to display the transfer curve of the gate. [Refer to Hall, page 12, for a detailed discussion of this circuit.] A dual-channel or dual-trace oscilloscope may use channel 2 as the horizontal input when the oscilloscope is set in the *x-y* mode.

CAUTION

1. Always remember to offset any signal that is to be applied to a logic gate, so that it does not exceed the nominal input low and input high voltages for that

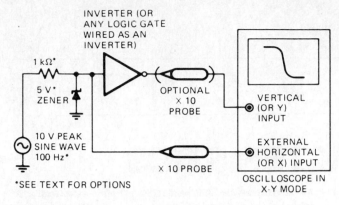

Fig. 2-5 An oscilloscope set up in the *x-y* mode to show the transfer function of a logic gate.

gate. A rule of thumb is that the signal should not exceed the nominal power-supply voltages, for example, V_{CC} as maximum input high and ground as minimum input low for a TTL gate input signal.

2. Always make sure the dc supply voltages are applied to a logic gate IC before or at the same time as the signal is applied to the gate input. Never apply a signal before applying the dc supply voltage, and never remove the dc supply voltage while a signal is being applied to any gate input.

---

b. Setting and applying a signal. Choose and perform *either* step 1 *or* step 2 below according to the type of function generator you are using. Use your oscilloscope's channel 1, X, or horizontal input to set up and verify the signal source (pulse or ramp) with legal voltage levels *before* you apply the signal to the gate input.

(1) If you do not have a function generator with sawtooth and offset capability, build the circuit as shown, using a standard signal generator set to apply a 10-V-peak 100-Hz sine wave. The 5-V zener and 1-kΩ resistor are used to limit, offset, and shape the signal into 0- to 5-V approximate square-wave pulses for the test input of the NAND gate inverter.

(2) If you have a function generator with sawtooth and offset capability, you may omit the 1-kΩ resistor and 5-V zener diode and use the offset and amplitude controls to set a sawtooth signal which runs from 0 to 5 V (as measured by the oscilloscope on dc coupling) rather than

the 10-V-peak sine wave. Apply this sawtooth waveform directly to the test input of the gate.

c. After applying the signal to the test gate input:

(1) Use the channel 1 oscilloscope probe to verify that the input signal is still the correct voltage pulse or ramp.

(2) Next turn on the channel 2 oscilloscope probe at the gate output to observe the output waveform, which should be an approximate rectangular pulse waveform of less than 50 percent duty cycle.

(3) Finally, switch the oscilloscope to *x-y* mode to observe the V_{OUT}/V_{IN} transfer curve.

d. When you have obtained a reasonable display of the transfer curve on the oscilloscope, draw a graph of the display and compare it with the transfer curve you plotted from static measurements. (You must understand how to obtain a transfer curve on the oscilloscope and how to interpret and record the displayed curve graphically, because you will use this method for other devices.)

3. Analyzing the transfer curve graph.

a. First observe the graph. As V_{IN} increases from 0 V, at what V_{IN} does the output voltage start to change from high to low? This voltage could be called $V_{IL.MAX}$. Label this point on your graph. With the data sheet specification of $V_{IL.MAX} = 0.8$ V, the manufacturer tells you that any input voltage of less than 0.8 V will be recognized by the device as a legal logic low.

b. On the graph, as V_{IN} increases beyond $V_{IL.MAX}$, at what voltage does the output seem to change most steeply from high to low? This voltage could be called the *threshold voltage.* Label this point on your graph. With any input voltage greater than $V_{IL.MAX}$, a noise pulse on the input might more easily reach this threshold voltage and switch the output temporarily to a low.

c. On the graph, as V_{IN} increases beyond the threshold voltage, at about what voltage does V_{OUT} reach a solid low? This voltage could be called $V_{IH.MIN}$. Label this point on your graph. The $V_{IH.MIN}$ specification of 2.0 V on the data sheet indicates that an input voltage greater than 2.0 V will be recognized as a logic high. You can see from the graph that the output does not really change states until V_{IN} drops to about 1.4 V at room temperature. The specification of 2.0 V for $V_{IH.MIN}$ guarantees recognition by any 7400 family gate over the full temperature range.

E X P E R I M E N T 3

ECL CHARACTERISTICS

REFERENCES

Hall: pages 31–33.
ECL data sheet for MC10102 (see appendix).

OBJECTIVES

At the conclusion of this laboratory exercise, you should be able to:

1. Measure typical output high and output low voltages for ECL gates.
2. Measure typical input low and input high currents for an ECL gate.
3. Demonstrate the V_{OUT} versus V_{IN} transfer curves of ECL OR and NOR gates.
4. Read and interpret the data sheet parameters for an ECL gate.
5. Show the need for terminating transmission lines.

EQUIPMENT

1 Power supply adjustable to −5.2 V
1 dc voltmeter
1 dc microammeter or milliammeter
1 Sine wave or square-wave function generator
1 Oscilloscope with x-y mode capability and 10-MHz bandwidth

MATERIALS

1 MC10102 quad two-input ECL OR/NOR gate
1 3.3-V zener diode
1 10-kΩ potentiometer
1 82-Ω resistor
1 130-Ω resistor
2 510-Ω resistors
1 1-kΩ resistor
10 feet of RG-58A/U 50-Ω coaxial cable or equivalent

PROCEDURE

MODULE 1 Using a data sheet to draw and build a circuit to test an ECL integrated circuit.

1. Carefully read the reference material in Hall, and the MC10102 data sheet in the appendix of this manual.
   a. Record the device's logic diagram and pin-outs. Note the two V_{CC} pins V_{CC1} and V_{CC2}. Pin V_{CC2} supplies the internal differential switches, and pin V_{CC1} supplies the emitter-follower output transistors. The separate V_{CC} inputs reduce cross-talk among outputs and the internal circuits. The best operating V_{EE} supply voltage for ECL is −5.2 V ± 10 percent with respect to V_{CC}. Most ECL systems use V_{CC} = ground and V_{EE} = −5.2 V.
   b. Find and record $V_{IL.MIN}$ and $V_{IH.MAX}$ for 25°C.
   c. Find and record $V_{OH.MIN}$ and $V_{OL.MAX}$ for 25°C.
   d. Find and record $I_{inL.MIN}$ and $I_{inH.MAX}$. (The input currents for ECL are specified at $V_{IL.MIN}$ and $V_{IH.MAX}$.)
   e. Find and record the following worst-case −30 to +85°C parameters for the MC10102 ECL OR/NOR gate.
      (1) Risetime (note that the data sheet gives 20 to 80 percent).
      (2) Falltime.
      (3) Propagation delay.
2. Draw the circuit diagram as follows:
   a. Connect V_{CC} to ground and V_{EE} to −5.2 V.
   b. Note that the 50-kΩ internal pull-down resistors will keep each input at a logic low if they are left open, so leave the inputs open.
   c. Connect the 510-Ω emitter pull-down resistors from the outputs of an OR/NOR gate in the MC10102 to −5.2 V.
3. Build the circuit as drawn.
   a. Verify the power-supply voltages before you apply them to the circuit.

b. Apply power to the circuit, and verify the supply voltages V_{CC} and V_{EE} at the proper pins of the IC.

MODULE 2 Demonstrating static characteristics.

1. Output voltages.
   a. With each input open (low), predict the output logic levels you would expect to find at the NOR output and at the OR output.
   b. Measure and record V_{IN} for each input.
   c. To get a rough idea of typical values of V_{OH} and V_{OL}, measure and record the voltages found on the NOR and OR outputs.
   d. To see the effect of leaving an ECL output totally open, remove the emitter pull-down resistor from the NOR output.
      (1) Measure and record the output voltage again.
      (2) Explain why this voltage is different from your previously measured value.
2. Input currents.
   a. Connect the ends of a 10-kΩ potentiometer from V_{CC} to V_{EE}.
   b. Connect the wiper of the potentiometer to one input of the OR/NOR gate of the MC10102. Insert a current meter in series with this input for measuring the input current.
   c. Adjust the input voltage to $V_{IH.MAX}$.
   d. Measure and record the input high current I_{inH}.
   e. Adjust the potentiometer to give a voltage of $V_{IL.MIN}$.
   f. Measure and record the input low current I_{inL}.
   g. Note that the I_{inH} and I_{inL} are both positive *sink* currents. Why? Why is the input high current greater than the input low current? The potentiometer represents any driving gate which would have to be able to source these input low-level and high-level currents to this test gate input.

MODULE 3 Examining transfer curves for ECL.
The V_{OUT} versus V_{IN} transfer curves for ECL can be found by using a signal generator and the x-y mode of an oscilloscope, just as you did for the TTL gate in Experiment 2, Module 4, but with the following modifications:

1. Inverting transfer curve.
   a. If you have a function generator with sawtooth (ramp) and offset capability, set the generator for a ramp that runs from −2 to −0.5 V. If you do not have a ramp output signal generator with offset capability, build the zener circuit shown in Fig. 3-1 to produce an input sweep voltage.
   b. Connect the output of the ramp generator or the zener circuit to one of the inputs of the OR/NOR gate in the MC10102.
   c. Connect the x (horizontal) input of the oscilloscope (set in x-y mode) to the input signal and the y (vertical) input of the oscilloscope to the NOR output.
   d. Observe and sketch the transfer curve.
   e. What value of V_{IN} is at the center of the V_{OUT} change from high to low?
2. Noninverting transfer curve.
   a. Move the vertical input of the oscilloscope from the

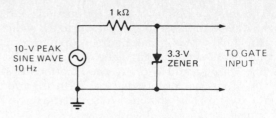

Fig. 3-1 A zener circuit to produce the V_{IN} sweep signal for ECL from a sine wave signal source.

NOR output to the OR output. The oscilloscope should show the noninverting transfer curve.
   b. Sketch the curve on the same graph and axis that you used for the NOR transfer curve. The result should look like Fig. 3-2.
   c. Figure 3-2 and your transfer curves show graphically the meaning of the voltage parameters given on the data sheet. Use your transfer graph to determine the value of the switching threshold voltage.

MODULE 4 Explanations of data sheet parameters.
At first glance, the ECL data sheets seem confusing because of the number of voltage parameters given. Taking them one at a time can clarify matters.

1. Voltage parameters.
   a. The $V_{IH.MAX}$ of −0.810 V at 25°C means that at an input voltage any more positive than this, the manufacturer will not guarantee the output voltage of the device to be in the proper range for the input of a following device.
   b. A $V_{IL.MIN}$ of −1.850 V indicates the most negative input low voltage for proper output levels to a following gate.

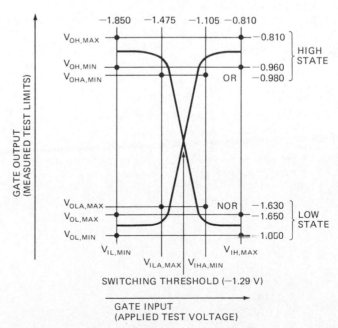

Fig. 3-2 ECL OR and NOR transfer curves. *(Courtesy of Motorola Incorporated.)*

c. The $V_{IHA.MIN}$ and $V_{ILA.MAX}$ specifications indicate how close an input voltage can get to the switching threshold without making the output at a voltage not legal for a following gate.

d. The $V_{OHA.MIN}$ and $V_{OLA.MAX}$ specifications indicate the worst-case output voltages with the input at the worst-case voltages nearest the switching threshold ($V_{IHA.MIN}$ and $V_{ILA.MAX}$).

2. Noise margins.

    a. The noise margin for the low state is defined as $V_{ILA.MAX} - V_{OLA.MAX}$. To compute the low-level noise margin for the MC10102 gate, use the data sheet values for 25°C.

    b. The noise margin for the high state is defined as $V_{OHA.MIN} - V_{IHA.MIN}$. Compute this noise margin for the MC10102 gate at 25°C.

    c. Compare the ECL noise margins with those for TTL. The ECL is designed with lower noise margins than the TTL because its lower output impedance makes it less susceptible to noise.

MODULE 5 Transmission lines.

1. To transmit signals from an ECL gate output to an ECL gate input that is more than a few inches away, transmission lines must be used. Refer to Hall, pages 45–48, for a discussion of transmission lines.

2. To demonstrate the need for terminating these transmission lines:

    a. Connect a 10-ft length of RG-58A/U or other 50-Ω coaxial cable to the output of an MC10102 NOR gate.

    b. Leave the 510-Ω pull-down resistor in place on the output of the gate.

    c. Apply 100-kHz to 1-MHz ECL-level pulses to the input of the gate. If a signal generator with offset capability is not available, the output of the zener circuit used for the transfer curve will work.

    d. Observe and sketch the pulse waveforms at the output of the gate and at the end of the 50-Ω cable.

        (1) What problem does this waveform show?

        (2) How can it be solved?

3. Terminated transmission lines.

    a. As described in Hall, pages 32–33, one way of terminating a 50-Ω ECL transmission line is with an 82-Ω resistor to ground and a 130-Ω resistor to −5.2 V. Show that this scheme is equivalent to 50 Ω to −2 V.

    b. Connect this termination (82 Ω to ground and 130 Ω to −5.2 V) on the end of the coaxial transmission line.

    c. Observe and sketch the waveforms at the end of the transmission line and at the output of the gate.

    d. Compare these terminated-line waveforms with the waveforms for no termination. Why did the termination affect both the waveform at the output of the gate and the waveform at the end of the transmission line?

CMOS LOGIC 4000 SERIES CHARACTERISTICS

REFERENCES

Hall: pages 34–40.

CD4001 CMOS IC data sheet (see appendix).

OBJECTIVES

At the conclusion of this laboratory exercise, you should be able to do the following for a 4000 series CMOS logic gate:

1. Use a data sheet to draw and construct a test circuit, observing special MOS handling precautions.
2. Measure typical output voltage levels.
3. Measure the current required to produce an input low and an input high.
4. Determine the output sink and source currents.
5. Observe the input-output transfer curve at $V_{DD} = 5$ V, using the x-y mode of an oscilloscope.
6. Determine the relationship between input frequency and power dissipation.
7. Demonstrate the need for bypass capacitors between V_{DD} and ground near logic circuits.
8. Measure T_{PLH} and T_{PHL} (propagation delay times) and output risetime and falltime.

EQUIPMENT

1 Variable dc power supply, 0 to 10 V
1 dc voltmeter
1 dc microammeter or milliammeter
1 Oscilloscope with x-y mode capability
1 Sine (square or sawtooth) wave function generator of 1-MHz capability

MATERIALS

1 CD4001 (or equivalent) CMOS IC
1 10-kΩ potentiometer
1 50-pF capacitor
1 0.1-µF capacitor
1 1-kΩ resistor
1 5-V zener diode
1 10-V zener diode
1 Solderless prototyping board
Assorted 22- to 24-gage solid-core, insulated, color-coded wire

PROCEDURE

MODULE 1 Using a data sheet to draw and build a circuit utilizing a CMOS IC, and establish proper signal conditions while observing special MOS handling precautions.

1. Read the MOS and CMOS handling precautions in the text before you attempt this experiment. Some of these precautions are reemphasized here.
   a. When working with MOS or CMOS, *always apply dc supply power to the circuit before applying the signal to the input.*
   b. Always remove the signal source from the gate input before turning off the dc supply voltage.
   c. For MOS families, *inputs should never be left open.*
   d. *Always set input signals so that they do not exceed the minimum V_{IL} or maximum V_{IH}.* For the CMOS device in this experiment, $V_{IL} = V_{SS}$ (or ground) and $V_{IH} = V_{DD}$ (which is 5 V for this experiment).
2. Read carefully the data sheet for the CMOS device you are using, and record the following information:
   a. The device's logic diagram and pin-outs.
   b. The recommended operating supply voltages.
   c. The input logic low and logic high voltages.
   d. The output logic low and logic high voltages.
   e. The input low and input high currents.
   f. The output low sink current and output high source current.

3. Draw a circuit diagram as follows:
  a. Connect V_{DD} and ground to the proper pins.
  b. For three of the gates in the package, connect both inputs to ground. (Unused CMOS inputs should never be left open.)
  c. The remaining gate is your test gate. You need to wire this gate to function as a simple inverter for your measurements.
    (1) Use the truth table for this gate to decide whether you should connect the unused input to V_{DD} (high) or to ground (low) so that the test input and output will act as an inverter.
    (2) Indicate the correct connection for the unused input on your circuit diagram. Connect the *test* input of the gate to ground on your diagram for your initial measurements so that it is not open.
4. Build the circuit. Before you apply the input signals, you must do the following:
  a. Set the power supply to 5 V.
  b. Connect the power to the circuit.
  c. Verify that the device has proper voltages at its power-supply pins.
5. *Troubleshooting tips.* Refer to Experiment 2, Module 1, section 5, for initial troubleshooting steps.

MODULE 2
Verifying static input and output characteristics for a standard CMOS gate operating as an inverter. If the gate fails to operate correctly, use the troubleshooting techniques described in Experiment 2, Modules 1 and 2, but remember to use CMOS-specified legal levels for verification and reference.

1. Typical CMOS input and output voltages.
  a. With the test input of the gate connected to ground (V_{IL}), measure the output voltage of the gate, V_{OH}.
  b. Connect the test input to V_{DD} to set it to V_{IH}. Measure and record the output voltage of the gate, V_{OL}.
  c. Compare these CMOS output levels to the corresponding typical TTL output levels.
2. Input currents.
  a. Use a microammeter to measure the current required to produce an input high, I_{IH}.
  b. Measure the current required to produce an input low, I_{IL}.
  c. Compare these values to those for a TTL gate.
3. *Fan-out.* Use the measured values, I_{IL} and I_{IH}, to determine the theoretical dc fan-out of a CMOS gate.
4. To find the output current sink capability with a V_{DD} of 5 V:
  a. Connect a 10-kΩ potentiometer set to maximum resistance from V_{DD} to a gate output, as shown in Fig. 4-1.

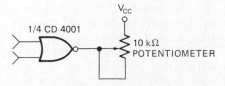

Fig. 4-1 A potentiometer connected to measure the output current sink capability of a logic gate.

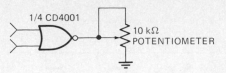

Fig. 4-2 A potentiometer connected to measure the output current source capability of a logic gate.

  b. Connect the test input of the gate high so the output will be low.
  c. Adjust the potentiometer until the gate output voltage reaches 0.4 V.
  d. Remove the potentiometer and measure the resistance.
  e. Use this resistance and the 4.6-V drop across it to determine the current.
  f. Will this output drive a standard TTL input low?
5. To find the output high source current with a 5-V supply:
  a. Connect the potentiometer from the gate output to ground, as shown in Fig. 4-2.
  b. Change the test input to low.
  c. Adjust the potentiometer until the output voltage drops to 2.4 V.
  d. Remove the potentiometer and measure its resistance.
  e. Use this resistance to calculate the output high source current.
  f. Will this output source enough current to pull a standard TTL input high?

MODULE 3
CMOS transfer curves.

1. To obtain the CMOS transfer curve for a 5-V supply voltage, keep the test gate wired as an inverter.
2. Use your oscilloscope in the x-y mode. The diagram and method for performing this measurement are described in Experiment 2, Module 4. As for the TTL gate, you may use either the 10-V-peak sine wave, 5-V zener, and 1-kΩ resistor or the 0- to 5-V sawtooth without the zener and resistor. Observe the standard precautions of presetting the sawtooth offset and applying V_{DD} before or at the same time as applying the signal to the gate.
3. Draw a graph of the transfer curve from the display.
4. Analyze the CMOS transfer curve to determine $V_{IL.MAX}$, the threshold voltage, and $V_{IH.MIN}$.
5. Refer to the data sheet for the noise margins specified for this gate. Use your transfer curve to explain why noise margins are much larger for CMOS than for TTL using the same supply voltage.

MODULE 4
Power dissipation versus frequency for a CMOS test gate operating as an *inverter*.

1. Remove all signals, turn off the V_{DD} supply, but leave the test gate wired as an inverter.
2. Connect a microammeter in series between the V_{DD} supply and the V_{DD} pin of the CMOS 4001 device.
3. Connect a 0.1-μF bypass capacitor from V_{DD} to ground, as close to the device as possible.
4. Connect a 50-pF capacitor from the gate output to ground. This is equivalent to a load of 10 CMOS gate inputs.

5. Set the V_{DD} supply at 5 V, and apply power to the IC.

6. Connect a signal generator, with its output set for a 0- to 5-V *square wave*, to the test input of the test gate.

7. Make a table showing the measured current and calculated power dissipation for frequencies of 100 Hz, 1 kHz, 10 kHz, 100 kHz, and 1 MHz.

8. Examine the table of power dissipation. What happens to the power dissipation as the frequency goes up? Give two reasons.

9. Remove the 50-pF load capacitance, and note the effect on the supply current with a 1-MHz input signal on the gate.

MODULE 5   Need for bypass capacitor.

1. Keep the test gate wired as an inverter, with a 50-pF capacitor load on the gate output and a 0.1-μF bypass capacitor between V_{DD} and ground as close to the IC as possible.

2. Connect an oscilloscope probe to the V_{DD} supply line next to the IC.

3. Apply a 1-MHz square-wave signal to the test input of the gate.

4. Select the ac input coupling for the oscilloscope, and observe the V_{DD} voltage trace.

5. While continuing to monitor V_{DD} with the oscilloscope, remove the 0.1-μF bypass capacitor and observe the waveform produced on V_{DD} by the 1-MHz input to the gate.

6. To verify the source of this unwanted waveform on V_{DD}, a dual-trace oscilloscope can be used to display the signal input to the gate on one channel while the V_{DD} trace is displayed on the other channel.

7. Measure the peak-to-peak voltage of the largest spike of the undesirable (noisy) waveform.

8. Using drawings of the various waveforms observed during this procedure, explain why bypass capacitors are required between V_{DD} and ground on digital-logic circuits.

MODULE 6   Propagation delay and transition times.

1. Keep the test gate wired as an inverter, connect the 0.1-μF bypass capacitor between V_{DD} and ground, and maintain the 50-pF load capacitor on the CMOS IC logic gate output.

2. Apply power to V_{DD} and then a 1-MHz square-wave signal to the test input of the gate.

3. Use a dual-trace oscilloscope to display the input and output waveforms, and measure the propagation delay times T_{PLH} and T_{PHL}.

   a. Draw and label a diagram of the waveforms to illustrate how these measurements are made.

   b. Compare these values to the data sheet values. Note that the data sheet values are for an effective load of only three gate inputs. The 50-pF capacitor you used is equivalent to about 10 gate inputs.

4. Use the oscilloscope to measure the *output* low-to-high transition time T_{TLH} and high-to-low transition time T_{THL}.

5. Draw and label the waveform diagram to illustrate how these transition times are measured.

SIMPLE COMBINATIONAL LOGIC CIRCUITS AND DE MORGAN'S THEOREM

REFERENCE

Hall: pages 54–58.

OBJECTIVES

At the conclusion of this laboratory exercise, you should be able to:

1. Predict and verify the truth tables for combinational digital-logic circuits.
2. Build and trace input and output logic voltage levels of combinational digital-logic circuits.
3. Verify De Morgan's theorem by:
   a. Building an OR function circuit using a NAND gate and inverters.
   b. Building an AND function circuit using a NOR gate and inverters.

EQUIPMENT

   1 5-V power supply
   1 Voltmeter, oscilloscope, or logic probe to measure logic voltage levels

MATERIALS

   1 7400 quad two-input NAND gate
   1 7402 quad two-input NOR gate
   1 LED (optional)
   1 2N3904 transistor (optional)
   1 180-Ω resistor (optional)
   1 10-Ω resistor (optional)

PROCEDURE

MODULE 1   Simple combinational logic circuits.

1. Analyzing a combinational logic circuit that fulfills a particular boolean expression.

a. Examine and analyze the circuit shown in Fig. 5-1.
   (1) How many possible input combinations are there for the three inputs?
   (2) Predict the output logic state for each of these inputs, and write your predictions as a truth table.
b. Build the circuit with color-coded wiring, and check it carefully before applying power.
c. Apply power and check the output state (logic voltage level) for each input combination using a voltmeter, an oscilloscope, a commercial logic probe, or the single-transistor LED logic probe that you built and used in Experiment 2.
d. Compare your measured results with your predictions. If the output is not as predicted:
   (1) Check that your predictions are correct. Did you trace the 1s and 0s through correctly?
   (2) Recheck the wiring pin by pin.
   (3) Check that you applied the correct inputs.
   (4) Check that the signals applied are actually getting to the pins of the device.
   (5) Check that the signal on the output pin of one gate is actually getting to the input pin of the gate that it is driving. Sometimes connecting wires do not make contact or may be broken (open).
   (6) Check that an output low or high is actually a

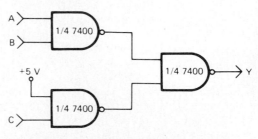

Fig. 5-1 A combinational NAND gate logic circuit that fulfills a particular boolean expression.

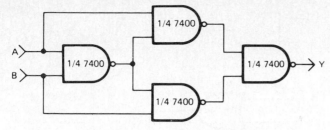

Fig. 5-2 A combinational NAND gate logic circuit that performs the logic function of a single gate of another type.

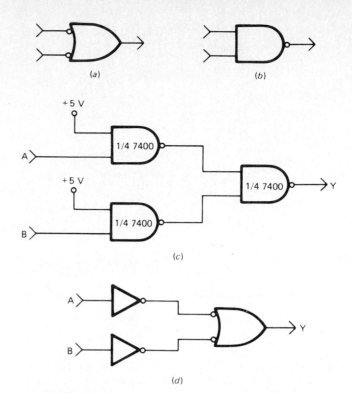

Fig. 5-3 *(a)* De Morgan's theorem: Alternative symbol for NAND gate. *(b)* Standard NAND gate symbol. *(c)* A combinational NAND gate logic circuit. *(d)* Circuit of part *c* redrawn with inverted input OR representation for NAND gate.

legal low or high voltage. (a) If an output voltage is too close to the threshold, the input of a following gate may treat it as the wrong logic level. (b) If you find an illegal output, disconnect the output from the gate input it is driving and recheck the output. (c) If disconnecting the load permits the output to go to a legal level, then the loading gate may be faulty or wired incorrectly. (d) If the output is still incorrect after it is unloaded, the gate itself may be faulty.

e. Write the boolean expression for output *Y* in terms of inputs *A*, *B*, and *C*.

2. Analyzing a combinational logic circuit that performs the logic function of a single gate of another type.

a. Repeat steps A to D from section 1 to analyze the circuit shown in Fig. 5-2.

b. Write the boolean expression for output *Y* in terms of inputs *A* and *B*.

c. The logic function represented by this circuit is often shown by a single-gate symbol. Show this symbol and give its name.

MODULE 2 De Morgan's theorem, Part 1.

1. Many circuit schematics represent a two-input NAND gate with the symbol shown in Fig. 5-3*a* rather than the familiar symbol shown in Fig. 5-3*b*. This is done to make a circuit easier to analyze. To demonstrate how the inverted-input OR representation of the NAND function can be useful in simplifying the tracing of the logic levels through a circuit, proceed as follows:

a. Predict the truth table for the circuit shown in Fig. 5-3*c*.

b. Build the circuit of Fig. 5-3*c*.

c. Apply power and verify the truth table.

d. What simple logic gate function does this truth table represent?

e. *Discussion:* Stated in words, this result means that a NAND gate with its inputs inverted performs an OR function. Using the symbol in Fig. 5-3*a* for the NAND gate makes this easy to see. If the circuit of Fig. 5-3*c* is redrawn as in Fig. 5-3*d*, then you can see that the inverting bubbles on the outputs of the inverters are canceled by the inverting bubbles on the inputs of the inverted-input OR symbol. Mentally removing all these bubbles, you can see directly from the diagram that the output expression is $Y = A + B$. In boolean al-

gebra, this is represented by

$$Y = \overline{\overline{A} \cdot \overline{B}} = A + B$$

(Splitting the top bar changes the sign between *A* and *B* to plus. Double bars over any variable cancel.) This demonstrates that the OR function can be produced by using only inverters and a NAND gate. A NOR function is produced by adding another inverter to the output.

f. Redraw the circuit of Fig. 5-1, using the inverted OR representation of the NAND gate(s) which would simplify tracing the logic. Can you now determine the output expression from the diagram directly?

2. *Optional:* To demonstrate that the two symbols shown in Fig. 5-3*a* and *b* are equivalent, proceed as follows:

a. Recall from Experiment 4 that a two-input NOR gate with one input tied low functions as an inverter.

(1) Use this fact to predict the truth table for the circuit of Fig. 5-4*a*.

(2) Build the circuit of Fig. 5-4*a*.

(3) Apply power and verify the truth table.

(4) Name the logic function produced by this circuit.

b. Predict the truth table for the circuit of Fig. 5-4*b*.

(1) Build the circuit of Fig. 5-4*b*.

(2) Apply power and verify the truth table.

(3) Name the logic function produced by this circuit.

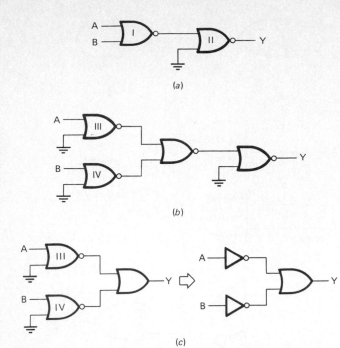

Fig. 5-4 *(a)* Converting a NOR gate to an OR gate. *(b)* Logic circuit using only NOR gates. *(c)* Reducing the all-NOR circuit to a simpler equivalent circuit.

c. *Discussion:* In step 1, you demonstrated that the OR function can be produced by adding an inverter made from a NOR gate to the output of a NOR gate. Since gates I and II of Fig. 5-4*b* produce the logical OR function, note that these two gates are replaced by an OR symbol in the first part of Fig. 5-4*c*.

Also, since gates III and IV in Fig. 5-4*b* are merely inverters, they are replaced by the inverter symbol in the second part of Fig. 5-4*c*. This circuit represents an OR gate with inverted inputs. A simpler way of showing an OR gate with inverted inputs is the symbol of Fig. 5-3*a*. Your truth table for the circuit of Fig. 5-4*b* should have provided the NAND logic function, represented by the symbol of Fig. 5-3*b*. Therefore, you have shown that an OR gate with inverted inputs is equivalent in function to a NAND gate. Also this section has provided a further chance to show how several different logic functions can be produced by using just one type of logic gate.

MODULE 3 De Morgan's theorem. Part 2.

1. A NOR gate is often represented as shown in Fig. 5-5*a* rather than with the familiar symbol shown in

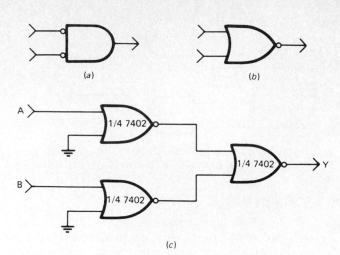

Fig. 5-5 *(a)* Alternative symbol used for NOR gate. *(b)* Standard NOR gate symbol. *(c)* NOR gate logic circuit.

Fig. 5-5*b*. Again, this is done to make a circuit easier to analyze. To show this:

a. Predict the truth table for the circuit in Fig. 5-5*c*.
b. Build the circuit of Fig. 5-5*c*.
c. Verify the truth table for the circuit.
d. What simple logic gate function does this truth table represent? In other words, what logic function is performed by a NOR gate with inverted inputs?
e. Write the boolean equation that summarizes this circuit.
f. Redraw Fig. 5-5*c*, using the inverted-input AND symbol.
g. *Discussion:* Here, again, the inverting bubbles on the outputs of the inverters are canceled by the bubbles on the inputs of the inverted-input AND gate. You can read directly from the diagram that the output expression is $A \cdot B = Y$. This demonstrates that an AND function can be produced by using only a NOR gate and inverters.
h. Show how you would modify the redrawn circuit of Fig. 5-5*c* to produce a NAND function.
2. *Optional:* To demonstrate that the two symbols in Fig. 5-5*a* and *b* are equivalent, devise a procedure similar to that described in Module 2, section 2, but use NAND gates instead of NOR gates.
3. Summarize De Morgan's theorem.
a. Draw a chart to illustrate De Morgan's theorem.
b. State the advantages for using De Morgan's theorem.

SIMPLIFYING AND SYNTHESIZING COMBINATIONAL LOGIC CIRCUITS

REFERENCES

Hall: pages 62–68.

Data sheet for 7410 and 7420 TTL ICs (see appendix).

OBJECTIVES

At the conclusion of this laboratory exercise, you should be able to:

1. Develop a truth table for a stated problem.
2. Write the boolean expression for the truth table.
3. Produce a simplified boolean expression, using a Karnaugh map.
4. Gain further practice building, testing, and debugging TTL digital-logic circuits.

EQUIPMENT

1 5-V power supply
1 Voltmeter, oscilloscope, or logic probe to measure logic levels

MATERIALS

2 7410 TTL ICs (1 is optional)
1 7420 TTL IC
1 2N3904 transistor
1 LED
1 10-kΩ resistor
1 220-Ω resistor
1 7404 TTL IC (optional)
1 74151 multiplexer (optional)

PROCEDURE

STATEMENT OF PROBLEM The city council of a small city consists of four members who must vote on various issues. They would like to have a circuit that lights an LED when a majority (three out of four) vote yes on an issue. They would like another LED to light when there is a tie vote, to let the mayor know she or he will have to vote to break the tie. Each member of the council has a switch that represents a yes vote as a high.

MODULE 1 Majority-vote circuit.

1. Truth table.
   a. Construct a truth table for the first part of the stated problem which shows the desired logic outputs for *majority* for each possible vote combination.
   b. Without attempting to simplify it, write the boolean expression for majority directly from the truth table.
      (1) How many terms does the result contain?
      (2) How many variables are in each term?
2. Karnaugh map.
   a. Draw a Karnaugh map for the majority function.
   b. Extract the simplified boolean expression from the Karnaugh map.
      (1) How many terms does this expression contain?
      (2) How many variables are there in each term?
3. Circuit diagram.
   a. Draw a circuit diagram that satisfies the simplified boolean expression.
   b. Analyze the data sheets for the commonly available and suitable standard TTL parts specified in your list of materials. (Data sheets are in the appendix.)
   c. Modify your circuit schematic to utilize these parts, and include pin numbers and part numbers.
4. Building and testing of the circuit.
   a. Carefully build the circuit. Color-coded wiring is suggested. Double-check your wiring against the circuit diagram. Make sure each pin on each IC is accounted for.

b. Use one or more of the following methods to observe and verify the output for each of the 16 input possibilities.

   (1) If no other options are available, wire each input combination and check for the correct output, using either a voltmeter or the transistor-driven LED circuit of Experiment 2, Fig. 2-3, on the output, which indicates a majority vote when lighted. If circuit shows an error, locate and fix the problem. Then repeat the complete test.

   (2) A fast way to check all these possibilities is with a microcomputer-based tester. This is how integrated circuits and printed-circuit boards are often tested in industry. Find out the specific procedure from your instructor if a microcomputer tester is available.

   (3) Another way to speed up the testing of this circuit is to use a binary-coded thumbwheel switch, if available, to set your input combinations, observing the output with a voltmeter or the LED logic probe circuit of Experiment 2, Fig. 2-3.

MODULE 2   Tie-vote circuit.

1. When you get the majority circuit working, add another output column to your original truth table that shows the tie-vote output for each input combination.

   a. Write the boolean expression for the tie vote.

   b. Draw a Karnaugh map for the tie vote.

   c. Are there any squares in the Karnaugh map that can be grouped to simplify the boolean expression?

2. Draw a schematic for a circuit to implement the boolean expression for the tie vote, using standard TTL parts. How many IC packages are required?

3. *Optional:* Read the section on multiplexers in Hall, pages 68–73, to understand how this function can be implemented with a single-IC package plus inverters.

   a. Draw a schematic, using a 74151 eight-input multiplexer to produce the expression for a tie vote.

   b. Build and test the multiplexer tie-vote circuit to verify the correct output for each input combination.

A SIMPLE DIGITAL SYSTEM: AN EIGHT-CHANNEL OSCILLOSCOPE MULTIPLEXER

REFERENCE

Hall: pages 70–71.

OBJECTIVES

At the conclusion of this laboratory exercise, you should be able to:

1. Given the schematic for a simple digital system, prepare a list of materials.
2. Plan a logical parts layout for the construction of a simple digital system.
3. Systematically build and debug a simple digital system.
   a. Predict and observe the output frequency of a 555 timer used as a pulse source.
   b. Observe and verify the QA, QB, and QC output pulse frequencies and binary count sequence of a 7493 counter which uses the 555 pulses as its input clock.
   c. Demonstrate the operation of a CMOS 4051 eight-input analog multiplexer.
   d. Demonstrate the operation of a 74S151 eight-input digital multiplexer.
   e. Examine chopped- and alternate-mode operation of a complete eight-input oscilloscope multiplexer.

EQUIPMENT

1 Oscilloscope
1 5-V power supply

MATERIALS

Refer to the Procedure section and Fig. 7-1.

PROCEDURE

SYSTEM OVERVIEW Figure 7-1 is the schematic of a simple digital system that will enable a standard, single-channel oscilloscope to display simultaneously up to eight channels of digital data input to the circuit. The circuit consists of a 74S151 eight-input digital multiplexer to multiplex the digital data to the oscilloscope, as well as a CD4051 eight-input analog multiplexer to add voltage steps to separate the traces on the screen. The 555 timer is wired to produce the clock pulses for the 7493 binary counter, which then repeatedly outputs the eight select address inputs to the multiplexers.

Whenever possible, a circuit such as this should be built one section at a time after the general overall layout of the complete circuit is planned. A section is built and tested and then debugged, if necessary. When a section works correctly, it is connected to the previously built and tested sections. Then the combined circuit is tested.

MODULE 1 Planning the circuit.

1. **Parts list.** Examine the schematic of the eight-input oscilloscope multiplexer in Fig. 7-1, and make a list of the parts required to build it. Simple jumper wires can be used for S1, S2, and S3.
2. **Layout.** Plan an orderly layout of the major ICs on your prototyping board, leaving room for transistors and resistors. Try to arrange the ICs so that the signal flows in a logical sequence from one IC to the next, to minimize the number of long wires that have to run from one end of the prototyping board to the other. For example, do not put the 555 timer at one end of the board and the 7493 binary counter at the other end.

MODULE 2 The 555 timer section—a pulse source (clock).

1. Carefully build the 555 timer part of the circuit.
2. Using the formula

$$f = \frac{1}{T} = \frac{1.44}{(RA + 2RB)C}$$

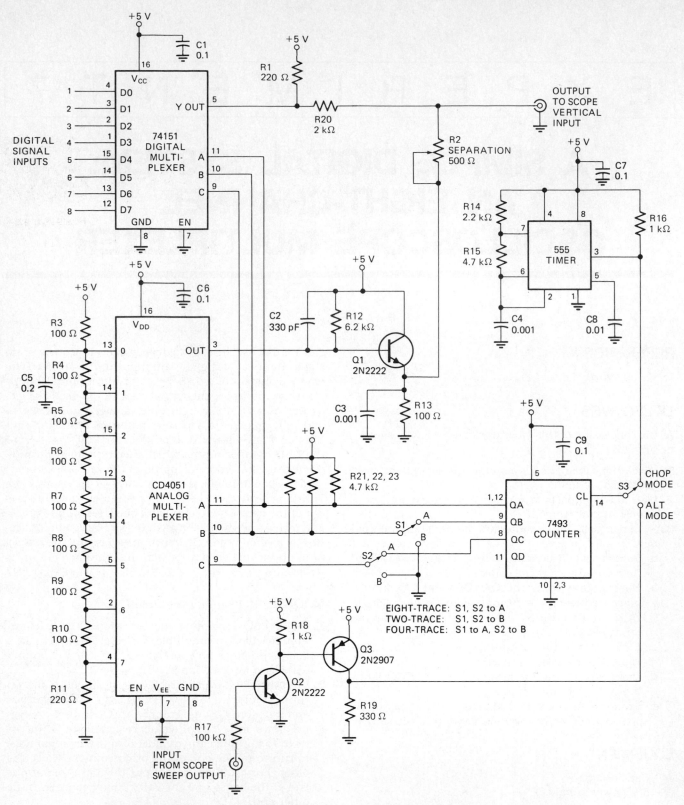

Fig. 7-1 A multiplexer circuit displays eight digital input signals on an oscilloscope. This circuit was modified from one found in the October 14, 1976 issue (vol. 49) of *Electronics* magazine, published by McGraw-Hill.

where RA = $R14$, RB = $R15$, and $C = C4$, calculate the expected output frequency of the circuit.

3. When you have checked the wiring on the 555 at least twice, apply power.
   a. Check the timer output with an oscilloscope. If there is no output or the output is not correct, turn off the power and recheck the circuit, pin by pin. If you find no wiring error, turn on the power again and check the signals and voltage levels on each pin with an oscilloscope to try to locate the problem.
   b. When the timer output is correct, draw the output waveform and record its frequency. Since capacitors usually have a wide tolerance, the actual output duty cycle and frequency may be off by as much as the capacitor tolerance.

MODULE 3 The 7493 section—an address selector.

1. When the 555 timer works correctly, wire the 7493 section.
   a. Connect the output of the 555 to the 7493 clock input at pin 14. Do *not* add the alternate-mode circuitry at this point.
   b. Pin 12 of the 7493 should be jumpered to pin 1.
   c. Pins 2, 3, and 10 of the 7493 should be grounded.
   d. QD is an output and should be left open.
   e. Consult the 7493 data sheet to see what should be done with the pins not shown on the schematic. Remember, each pin should be accounted for.
2. After checking the wiring on this section, turn on the power again.
   a. The QA output should show a train of pulses at one-half the input clock frequency; QB, a train of pulses at one-quarter the input frequency; and QC, a train of pulses at one-eighth the input frequency. Use a dual-trace oscilloscope or frequency counter to check this.
   b. The A, B, and C outputs of the 7493 step through the 3-bit binary count from 0 to 7 over and over. Draw the QA, QB, and QC output waveforms to illustrate this pattern. This binary count sequence contains the addresses for the multiplexers.

MODULE 4 The CD4051 section—an analog multiplexer.

1. When the 7493 section checks out, add the 4051 circuitry. The 4051 is a CMOS analog multiplexer, so *observe all MOS handling precautions.*
   a. The voltage-divider chain on the inputs of the 4051 produces voltage steps between 0 and 5 V. Calculate the approximate voltages you would expect to measure on each of the 0 to 7 inputs connected to this divider.
   b. With $S1$ connected to QB and $S2$ connected to QC, the 4051, when powered up, should show a stepped sawtooth waveform on its output.
      (1) How many steps should each sawtooth show?
      (2) What symptom would you expect to see if the inputs to the multiplexer select inputs A and C were accidentally interchanged?

2. Apply power.
   a. Verify the divider voltages on the 4051 inputs.
   b. Verify the correct output for the 4051.
   c. Draw the output waveform.
   d. Test your prediction of interchanged A and C inputs.
3. Adding the buffer.
   a. Make sure to return the A and C select inputs to the correct pins on the 4051.
   b. Add the 2N2222 emitter-follower buffer circuitry to the 4051 output.
      (1) What signal do you expect to see on the emitter of $Q1$?
      (2) Verify this output.

MODULE 5 The 74S151 digital multiplexer section.

1. Build the 74S151 digital multiplexer section, leaving the Y output, pin 5, open.
   a. Connect inputs D0, D2, D4, and D6 to ground.
   b. Connect inputs D1, D3, D5, and D7, to V_{CC}.
2. Apply power.
   a. As the counter steps the select inputs of the 74S151 through the binary count sequence, what output pattern do you expect to see on the Y output?
   b. Verify and draw the output waveform.

MODULE 6 Test the complete circuit or system in chopped mode.

1. Adding the chopped-mode circuitry.
   a. If the expected square-wave pattern appears on the Y output of the 74S151, depower the circuit and remove the ground and V_{CC} connections from inputs D0 to D7 of the 74S151.
   b. Add $R1$, $R2$, and $R20$ to the circuit. Now the circuit is ready to test as a whole.
   c. Connect the circuit output to the vertical input of the oscilloscope.
2. Apply power.
   a. Connect a 100-Hz TTL-level square-wave signal to all eight inputs of the 74S151.
   b. By adjusting the vertical V/div, the time base, and the trigger control on the oscilloscope, you should get eight parallel traces on the screen.
   c. Adjust the 500-Ω potentiometer, $R2$, on the $Q1$ emitter for best trace separation.
   d. If stable triggering is difficult, connect an oscilloscope probe from the input signal to the external trigger input of the oscilloscope.
   e. Draw the output display.
3. When you have a stable display of the eight channels, try connecting the input signal to just one input at a time, to ensure that the input channels are being displayed in the correct order. Unused inputs may be left open.
   a. When you have verified the proper order, draw a representative waveform diagram of the oscilloscope display.
   b. Predict what might cause the signals to be displayed out of order. Test your prediction(s).

4. Varying the number of channels.

    a. Connect switch S2 to ground *(B)* but leave S1 connected to A. Record what happens to the output.

    b. Connect both S1 and S2 to ground *(B)*, and note what this does to the output.

5. Summarizing the chopped-mode multiplexer.

    a. Describe the operation of the multiplexer circuit, using the 555 as a clock for chopped mode.

    b. Why can this circuit operating in the chopped mode not be used to observe high-frequency signals?

MODULE 7 Optional: Multiplexer system in alternate mode. (Do this module only if your oscilloscope has a sweep output.)

1. Adding the alternate mode.

    a. While the chopped mode operating off the 555 timer clock is more effective for displaying several lower-frequency signals at the same time, there is a need for a clock source to multiplex and display several higher-frequency signals above about 1 kHz. The simplest way to do this is to use the higher sweep frequencies of the oscilloscope as the counter clock. Then one sweep will select and display the complete trace and voltage level for one input channel signal, and the next sweep will select and display the complete trace and voltage level for the next input channel signal, and so on through all the channel inputs. Then the sequence will repeat. This is referred to as *alternate mode*.

    b. Add the Q2 and Q3 circuitry for alternate mode.

    c. Connect the oscilloscope sweep output to the Q2 base input through R17.

    d. Connect S3 to the alternate-mode position.

    e. Connect S1 and S2 each to their A positions for eight-trace operation.

2. Apply power to the circuit.

    a. Connect a 10-kHz TTL-level signal to all eight inputs of the 74S151.

    b. Adjust the sweep frequency, triggering, R2, and so on for stable operation.

    c. Draw the output display.

3. Explore the effects of:

    a. Different frequency signals.

    b. Applying one input at a time.

    c. Setting S1 and S2 for different numbers of traces.

4. Summarize the alternate-mode operation of the multiplexer circuit.

ENCODERS, DECODERS, AND SEVEN-SEGMENT DISPLAYS

REFERENCES

Hall: pages 74–86.

7447 data sheet (in appendix).

74148 data sheet (in appendix).

Seven-segment display data sheet (example in appendix).

OBJECTIVES

At the conclusion of this laboratory exercise, you should be able to:

1. Determine the proper circuit connections for a seven-segment common-anode LED display.
2. Use a data sheet to determine the proper circuit connections for a 7447 BCD-to-seven-segment decoder.
3. Demonstrate a practical application of a 74148 as a keyboard encoder.

EQUIPMENT

1 5-V power supply
1 Calculator-type key pad with interface connector

MATERIALS

1 Seven-segment common-anode LED display and data sheet
1 7447 BCD-to-seven-segment decoder
1 7400 quad two-input NAND gate IC
2 74148 eight-line to three-line priority encoders
7 150-Ω, 0.25-W resistors

PROCEDURE

SYSTEM OVERVIEW Examine the partially completed schematic provided for a keyboard encoder and display in Fig. 8-1. In this circuit, a key pressed on a key pad (such as that used on calculators) provides a low signal to an input of one of the 74148 eight-input priority encoder ICs. The outputs from the two 74148s are combined by some NAND gates to produce the BCD code for the number of the key pressed. The BCD code is applied to the inputs of a 7447 BCD-to-seven-segment decoder. This decoder drives a common-anode seven-segment LED display which lights up with the decimal number of the key pressed.

As described in Experiment 7, when you are building a more complex circuit or small digital system, it is often more effective to plan the overall layout and then build and test the circuit one section at a time. In this experiment, prior to planning the layout, you will gain additional experience both in determining the proper wiring for the 7447 decoder and seven-segment display from their data sheets and in calculating the values for the current-limiting resistors needed for proper operation of the display.

MODULE 1 Decoder and display section.

1. Planning the 7447 BCD-to-seven-segment decoder wiring.
   a. Analyze the data sheets for a 7447 BCD-to-seven-segment decoder.
      (1) Is it intended to directly drive a common-anode or a common-cathode display?
      (2) What is the maximum current each segment output can sink?
   b. An important process in wiring any circuit is to make certain that every pin on each device is accounted for. In other words, each *input* pin must be tied high, tied low, or connected to some signal. Unused *outputs* can usually be left open.
      (1) Use the 7447 data sheet pin diagram to find the V_{CC} and ground pins, the segment output pins, and the data input pins.
      (2) Start your schematic diagram, showing the

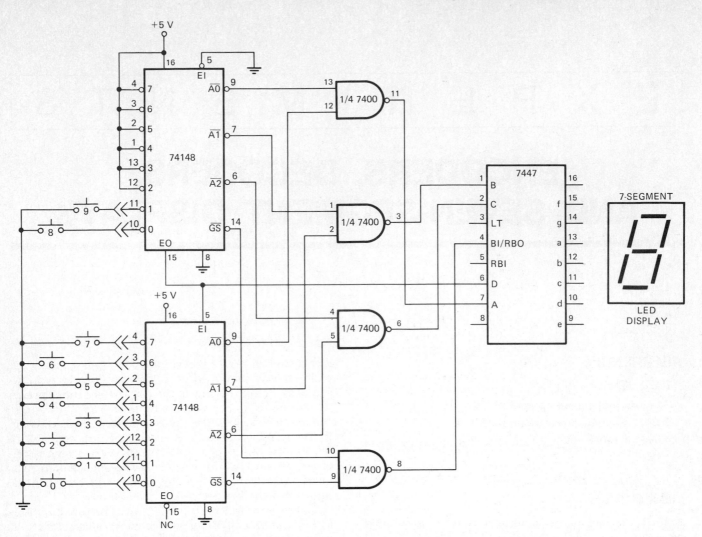

Fig. 8-1 A partially completed schematic for a keyboard encoder and display circuit.

7447, and mark these pins on your circuit diagram.

(3) Use the function table and notes in the data sheet to determine the effect of each of the three remaining pins: lamp test $\overline{LT}$, blanking input/ripple blanking output $\overline{BI}/\overline{RBO}$, and ripple blanking input $\overline{RBI}$. Decide whether each should be tied high or tied low so that the proper segments will be lighted for any BCD code.

(4) Indicate these connections for $\overline{LT}$, $\overline{BI}$, and $\overline{RBI}$ on your schematic drawing.

2. Adding the single-digit, seven-segment common-anode LED display to your drawing.

a. Analyze the data sheet for the seven-segment display to determine the pin connections.

b. Add the seven-segment display to your schematic drawing. Connect all anodes of the display to V_{CC}.

c. Since LEDs are current-operated devices, a resistor must be selected to limit the maximum current of each segment to the typical operating ratings for the device. Calculate the values for these current-limiting resistors, using

$$R = \frac{V_{CC} - V_F - V_{O(ON)}}{I_F}$$

where typical values of I_F and V_F will suffice for the desired current and forward voltage drop, respectively, of the display LED. The typical on-state output voltage of the 7447 output transistors that will drive the display is $V_{O(ON)}$, and it is specified in the electrical characteristics section of the 7447 data sheet.

d. Once you have calculated the values of the current limiting resistors, draw on your schematic diagram the proper connections from the segment output pins of the 7447 to the corresponding seven-segment display input pins, being sure to include a current-limiting resistor in series with each segment.

3. Building and testing the decoder and display section.

a. After planning an overall layout for the complete system, wire the seven-segment display, resistors, and 7447.

(1) Make sure both (all) anodes of the display are connected to 5 V.

(2) Make sure each segment has its current-limiting resistor in series with it.

(3) The data inputs of the 7447 may be temporarily left open.

b. Power up the circuit, and verify V_{CC} at the proper pins.

c. The display can be tested by tying the $\overline{LT}$ input of the 7447 low. As shown by the function table, this should light all segments.

d. If all the segments light, then tie the $\overline{LT}$ high again and try a few BCD input combinations on the four data inputs to make sure the correct digit is displayed.

MODULE 2 Encoder and keyboard section.

1. *Encoder operation.* When the display section works properly, power down and read the data sheets for the 74148.

a. Examine the function table and observe the following regarding the basic inputs and outputs:

(1) Each output code on $\overline{A2}$, $\overline{A1}$, and $\overline{A0}$ is given for the highest-numbered input that has a low on it.

(2) The output code is in *inverted* binary. For example, a low on input 0 with all other inputs high gives outputs $\overline{A2} = H$, $\overline{A1} = H$, and $\overline{A0} = H$. If each of these is inverted, it gives the BCD code for 0—LLL, or 000. For another example, if input 3 has a low on it, then $\overline{A2} = H$, $\overline{A1} = L$, and $\overline{A0} = L$. Inverting each of these gives LHH, or 011, which is the BCD code for 3.

(3) What output code will 74148 outputs show when inputs 3 and 6 are both low? (The term *priority* encoder indicates that only the code for the highest-priority (number) input will be output.)

b. Controlling (enabling) the inputs and outputs.

(1) Determine what logic level must be present on the enable input $\overline{EI}$ in order for the device to function.

(2) What logic level will be present on the enable output $\overline{EO}$ if any input has a logic low on it?

(3) The $\overline{EO}$ is often tied to the $\overline{EI}$ of a lower-order device when two 74148s are cascaded. The circuit for this experiment uses two 74148s connected in this cascade mode.

(4) Some NAND gates are added to produce a 16-input priority encoder. In this circuit, what logic function are the NAND gates performing?

(5) $\overline{GS}$ stands for group signal. What information will the NANDed output of the two $\overline{GS}$'s give?

(6) The NANDed $\overline{GS}$ output is to be connected to the $\overline{BI}$ pin of the 7447. Under what input conditions will the display be blanked?

2. Building and testing the encoder section.

a. When you understand the operation of this encoder section, add the circuitry to your schematic. If desired, 1-kΩ pull-up resistors to V_{CC} may be added to each of the used data inputs D0 to D7 of the 74148 encoders to ensure adequate TTL logic highs on these inputs when no key is pressed.

b. Build the encoder section, and add it to the decoder and display section of your circuit. The 74148 data inputs can be left open initially.

c. Test the circuit by grounding one input at a time, and verify that the correct number appears on the seven-segment display. The display should be blanked unless one input has a low.

3. Adding the keyboard.

a. The key switches shown on the inputs of the 74148s in Fig. 8-1 represent a keyboard such as is used on calculators. Pressing a key short-circuits to ground the encoder input to which that key is connected, placing a low on that input. Since the keyboard is on a separate circuit board, your circuit must interface to it, using, for example, a 16-pin DIP connector and ribbon cable. Your instructor will provide you with the keyboard and a diagram detailing the interface connections.

b. Draw the keyboard portion of the schematic and the interface connection diagram from provided data.

c. Build the interface circuitry necessary to attach the keyboard connector to your circuit board.

d. Connect the keyboard to your circuit.

e. Apply power. Verify that when a key is pressed on the keyboard, the corresponding number appears on the seven-segment display.

f. Try pressing two keys at once, and note the output display.

E X P E R I M E N T 9

LATCHES AND FLIP-FLOPS

REFERENCES

Hall: pages 96–104.

Data sheets (in appendix) for 7475 D latch, 7474 D flip-flop, and 7476 JK flip-flop.

OBJECTIVES

At the conclusion of this laboratory exercise, you should be able to:

1. Build a circuit that can be used to debounce mechanical-switch contacts.
2. Wire and verify the truth tables for several common types of flip-flops and latches:
   a. Simple RS latch.
   b. Gated RS latch.
   c. D latch.
   d. D flip-flop.
   e. JK flip-flop.
   f. T flip-flop.

EQUIPMENT

1 5-V power supply
1 Pulse generator
1 Storage oscilloscope (optional)

MATERIALS

1 7400 quad two-input NAND gate
1 7404 hex inverter
1 7475 D latch
1 7474 D flip-flop
1 7476 JK flip-flop
1 7476 JK flip-flop
2 LEDs
2 2N3904 transistors
2 10-kΩ resistors
2 1-kΩ resistors
2 220-Ω resistors
1 single-pole double-throw toggle switch

PROCEDURE

MODULE 1   Debouncing mechanical switches by using a simple latch circuit.

1. Mechanical-switch contact bounce—observing the need for debouncing.
   a. Read the text reference material in Hall, pages 41–42, on switches and switch debouncing.
   b. Pushbutton or toggle switches often are used to enter data in digital systems. For many of these applications, a major problem of mechanical switches is contact bounce. As shown in Fig. 9-1, contact bounce may cause a series of pulses rather than a single transition to be input to a circuit.
   c. If a frequency counter with a total-counts function (or a storage oscilloscope) is available, you can build the circuit in Fig. 9-1 and demonstrate this

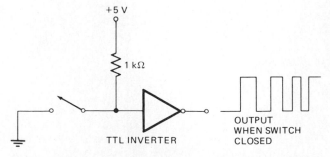

Fig. 9-1 The output of the TTL inverter shows the effect of switch bounce.

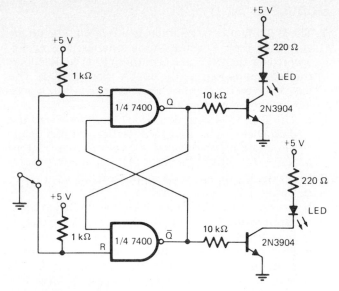

Fig. 9-2 A simple RS latch circuit used as a switch-debounce circuit.

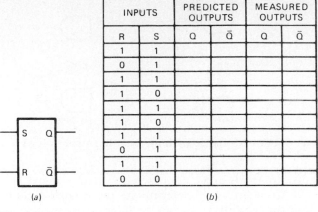

INPUTS		PREDICTED OUTPUTS		MEASURED OUTPUTS	
R	S	Q	$\bar{Q}$	Q	$\bar{Q}$
1	1				
0	1				
1	1				
1	0				
1	1				
1	0				
1	1				
0	1				
1	1				
0	0				

(a)   (b)

Fig. 9-3 (a) A schematic symbol for an RS latch. (b) An example of a truth table (incomplete) for an RS latch shows the input pattern for predicting and measuring outputs.

bouncing. The bouncing usually lasts for several milliseconds.
2. A switch-debounce circuit—the latch.
   a. Figure 9-2 is a circuit that demonstrates the basic principle of a simple latch and can be used to debounce the input from switches. The transistor and LED circuits allow visual monitoring of the output logic states.
   b. Analyze the circuit of Fig. 9-2 as follows:
      (1) Make a chart and record the predicted logic state on each input and output with the switch in the R position.
      (2) Next record the predicted logic state for each input and output when the switch makes contact with the S input.
      (3) Examine your chart. Did the Q output change states from step (1) to step (2)?
   c. Now assume the switch bounces off the S contact but does not bounce back far enough to make contact with the R contact.
      (1) Record the predicted logic levels for each input and output.
      (2) Does the Q output change states when the switch bounces? Why or why not?
   d. Build the circuit of Fig. 9-2 and test it.
      (1) Compare your results with your predictions.
      (2) Note that the Q and $\bar{Q}$ outputs are, by definition, inverses of each other.
      (3) Optional: If a storage oscilloscope is available, observe the Q output as the switch is toggled back and forth.

MODULE 2 The simple RS latch.

1. The circuit of Fig. 9-2 has many other uses besides being a switch debouncer. It is called an RS latch and is often represented with the schematic symbol shown in Fig. 9-3a.
   a. Remove the switch from the circuit of Fig. 9-2.
   b. Make a table similar to Fig. 9-3b, and record the predicted Q and $\bar{Q}$ outputs for the R and S inputs, taken in the order shown in the table.
2. Testing the RS latch.
   a. Apply the inputs in the same sequence shown in your table, and record the outputs observed.
   b. Compare your results with the predictions.
      (1) If the device has a high on the Q output and a low on the $\bar{Q}$ output, the device is said to be in the set condition. What input condition on the S input produces this?
      (2) If the device has a high on the $\bar{Q}$ output and a low on the Q output, it is said to be in the reset condition. What input condition on the R input produces this?
      (3) Does this circuit have active high or active low R and S inputs? How might this be indicated on the schematic symbol?
      (4) What logic levels are present on the device outputs when both inputs are low? Is this state consistent with the definition of Q and $\bar{Q}$ for these outputs? This is often referred to as an illegal, or indeterminate, state.
   c. Summarizing the operation of a simple RS latch circuit.
      (1) When both inputs are at a logic high, the outputs are held or latched in whatever state they were put in by the most recent low on the set input or on the reset input.
      (2) Note that once the circuit is set by a low on the S input, further pulses on the S input have no effect.

MODULE 3 A gated RS latch.

1. An improved version of the RS latch is shown in Fig. 9-4. In this circuit, the effect of the R and S inputs is controlled by a strobe or enable input.
2. Predict the output truth table for the circuit.
3. Build the circuit of Fig. 9-4.
4. Test the gated RS latch as follows:
   a. Apply power and verify your predictions.
   b. Is the enable input active high or active low for allowing data on the S and R inputs to affect the output?

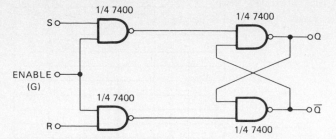

Fig. 9-4 An RS latch with an enable (strobe) input.

c. Are the R and S inputs active high or active low?
d. What are the indeterminate input conditions for this circuit?

MODULE 4 The D latch.

1. The gated RS latch is a useful circuit, but it still has the problem of one set of indeterminate input conditions where S is high and R is high while the enable is high. This problem is solved in the data or D-type latch by putting an inverter between the S and R inputs, as shown in Fig. 9-5. In TTL four of these latches are available in the 7475.
   a. Read the data sheet for the 7475.
   b. Write the truth table for the device.
   c. Is the enable input active high or active low?
2. Build the latch test circuit as follows:
   a. Wire a 7475 to V_{CC} and ground.
   b. Set up a 1-Hz TTL-level signal which will be applied to the D input of one latch when power is applied to the circuit.
   c. Connect one of the LED circuits to monitor this input and the other to monitor the Q output of the latch.
   d. Connect the enable input high.
   e. Unused D and G inputs can be left open for this experiment.
3. Test the D latch as follows:
   a. Apply power.
   b. Apply the 1-Hz signal to the test latch D input.
   c. Observe the relationship between the D input and the Q output. Record your observations.
   d. With the power still on, change the enable input from high to low. What effect does the D input have on the Q output when the enable is low?
   e. Lift the enable input lead from ground; then reconnect it to ground when the D input is high. What state gets latched on the Q output?
   f. Try the same procedure as in step e for a low on the D input.
   g. Summarize the operation of a D latch.

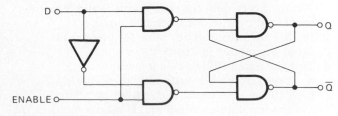

Fig. 9-5 A D latch circuit.

MODULE 5 The D flip-flop.

1. The D flip-flop is very similar to a D latch. The difference is in their clocking characteristics. As you discovered for the 7475, the Q output of a D latch follows the D input as long as the enable input is high. The logic state on the D input when the enable input goes low will be latched on the Q output.
   a. The TTL 7474 contains two D flip-flops. Read the data sheet for it, and see whether you can determine how a D flip-flop is different from a D latch.
   b. Write the truth table for a D flip-flop.
2. Build the D flip-flop test circuit as follows:
   a. Connect V_{CC} and ground to a 7474.
   b. Set up a 1-Hz TTL-level pulse to be applied to the D input of one flip-flop in the device when the circuit is powered up.
   c. Preset and clear on both flip-flops, and the inputs of the unused flip-flop in the package can be left open for this experiment. In actual system circuits, unused input pins should be connected high or low as required for proper operation of that circuit.
   d. Connect one LED indicator to the D input and the other to the Q output.
   e. Connect the clock input low.
3. Test the D flip-flop as follows:
   a. Apply power.
   b. Apply the 1-Hz signal to D input of the test flip-flop.
   c. Observe and record the operation. Does the D input have any effect on the Q output?
   d. With the power on, lift the clock input from ground. This acts as a high input to the clock. What effect does the D input have on the Q output when the clock input is high?
   e. Reconnect the clock input to ground.
      (1) Quickly disconnect the clock input when the D input is low. What state does the Q output show?
      (2) Try the same for the D input high. What state does the output show now?
      (3) At what time does a D flip-flop look at the input data and update its Q output?
   f. Now jumper the reset/clear input to ground.
      (1) What effect does this have on the Q output?
      (2) Can any combination of D and clock inputs change the Q output while this input is low?
      (3) This input is often referred to in data sheets as a *direct*, or an *asynchronous*, *reset* because it overrides all other inputs.
   g. Summarize the operation of a D flip-flop.

MODULE 6 The JK flip-flops.

1. The JK flip-flop is another solution to the problem of a set of indeterminate, or illegal, input conditions. The clock input of JK flip-flops may be positive-edge active, negative-edge active, or level active.
   a. A common TTL JK flip-flop is the 7476. Study the data sheet and truth table for this device.
   b. What will the outputs of a 7476 flip-flop do if both J and K are high when it is clocked?

c. What will the output of the 7476 do if the input state is changed while the clock is high?

2. Wiring the 7476 JK flip-flop in a test circuit.

 a. Use the data sheet to determine the proper connections.

 b. What should be done with the direct preset and clear inputs so that they do not affect the JK input operations?

3. Testing the 7476 JK flip-flop.

 a. Apply power.

 b. Verify the truth table for one of its flip-flops.

 c. To demonstrate "1s catching":

 (1) Apply an input combination that *resets* the Q output to zero; for example, with J low and K high, take the clock high and then low.

 (2) While the clock is low, make J and K both low so that when the clock goes high again, the output will be latched. (Verify the latched low on Q by taking the clock high and then low.)

 (3) Take the clock high again. This time, while the clock is high, take J high and then low, while leaving K low. Now take the clock low. The Q output should change to high, "catching" the 1 that momentarily appeared on the J input while the clock was high.

 d. Summarize the operation of a JK flip-flop.

MODULE 7 The T flip-flop.

1. When you finish verifying the truth table for a 7476 flip-flop, you can use it to build another type of flip-flop circuit.

 a. Connect the J and K inputs high.

 b. Set up a 1-Hz TTL-level pulse to be applied to the clock input when powered up.

 c. Connect one LED indicator circuit to the clock input and the other indicator to the Q output.

2. Apply power and the 1-Hz signal.

 a. Note that the Q output changes for each input clock pulse. This connection is often called a *toggle*, or T, flip-flop circuit.

 b. How does the frequency of the output compare with the frequency of the input? Increase the input-clock frequency to 1 kHz, and use a dual-trace oscilloscope to observe and draw the waveforms that show this frequency relationship.

 c. Summarize the operation of a T flip-flop. Describe the typical use of this circuit.

BINARY COUNTERS

REFERENCES

Hall: pages 104–114.

7493 and 74193 data sheets (in appendix).

OBJECTIVES

At the completion of this laboratory exercise, you should be able to:

1. Find the frequency ratios between the outputs of a 7493 four-bit binary counter.
2. Demonstrate the output count sequence of a 7493 four-bit binary counter.
3. Show how a 7493 counter can be modified with feedback to divide an input frequency by any integer.
4. Explain the operation of a 74193 presettable, up or down counter.

EQUIPMENT

1 Signal generator
1 Dual-trace oscilloscope
1 5-V power supply

MATERIALS

1 7493 four-bit binary ripple counter
4 LEDs
4 47-Ω 0.25-W resistors
1 Small audio speaker
2 74193 four-bit binary synchronous counters
1 100-Ω resistor

PROCEDURE

MODULE 1 The 7493 as a frequency divider.

1. Read pages 104–106 in Hall and the data sheet for the 7493 counter. From the logic diagram for the de-

vice, you can see that it contains four JK flip-flops with their J and K inputs internally tied high. This is often called a toggle, or T, flip-flop. Recall from Experiment 9 that the output of a toggle flip-flop changes state once for each input-clock pulse.

a. Draw a diagram to show that the output-clock frequency is one-half the input-clock frequency.

b. If the output of one T flip-flop is connected to the clock input of a second T flip-flop, how will the output frequency of the second compare with the clock-input frequency of the first?

c. With one external connection as specified in the 7493 data sheet, note *c*, the four T flip-flops can be connected in series. Predict the ratio of frequency out of each flip-flop to the input frequency.

d. The frequency ratios of the 7493 counter can be shown in several ways. To set up the 7493 for demonstrating its operation, use the data sheet in the appendix to draw the schematic, and build the circuit as follows:

   (1) Connect V_{CC} and ground to the proper pins.

   (2) Connect the QA output to the B clock input.

   (3) Connect R01 and R02 to ground.

2. Find the frequency ratios of the 7493 counter, using an audio test circuit.

a. Add the audio test circuitry shown in Fig. 10-1 to your schematic and circuit.

   (1) Note that the input of the audio test circuit will be touched to the various input and output pins of the 7493. So when you add this circuit section to the schematic, no connection needs to be drawn between the test probe and the rest of the circuit.

   (2) Make the connecting wire, which is the audio input test probe, long enough to reach and touch each of the input and output pins of the 7493.

b. Apply power to the 7493.

c. Connect a 1760-Hz TTL-level square-wave signal to the 7493 A input.

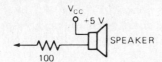

Fig. 10-1 An audio test circuit.

d. Touch the audio probe to this A input. You should hear a tone that in music is an "A."

e. Touch the audio probe to the QA output, then to the QB output, then to the QC output, and finally to the QD output. The series of decreasing frequencies you hear are A's in lower octaves. Each octave represents a change in frequency by a factor of 2.

3. A quieter way to demonstrate the frequency ratios of the 7493 is to use a dual-trace oscilloscope.

a. Apply power to the 7493.

b. Connect the 1760-Hz TTL-level square-wave signal to the 7493 A input.

c. Connect one channel of a dual-trace oscilloscope to the A input clock of the 7493 as a reference.

d. Use the other channel of the oscilloscope to look at the four Q outputs, one at a time.

(1) For best stability, trigger the oscilloscope on the negative edge of the lowest-frequency signal you are viewing.

(2) If you saved the oscilloscope multiplexer circuit from Experiment 7, you can look at all five signals at once.

e. Draw a timing diagram showing the relationship between the input clock and the four Q output signals.

f. On what edge of the input clock do the outputs change state?

MODULE 2 The 7493 as a binary counter.

1. In addition to dividing an input frequency by 2, 4, 8, and 16, the four outputs of a 7493 show a binary count of the number of pulses input to the device.

2. To set up the 7493 to demonstrate the binary count sequence, draw a schematic and connect the 7493 as follows:

a. Connect V_{CC} and ground to the proper pins.

b. Connect an LED and a 47-Ω resistor in series from each Q output of the 7493 to ground. For ease in viewing, wire the LEDs in binary weighted order with the one from the QA output on the right.

3. To observe the binary count:

a. Apply power.

b. Connect a 1-Hz TTL-level signal to the 7493 A input.

c. Observe the LEDs' pattern of lighting—they should show a binary count sequence.

d. Return to the timing diagram you drew for Module 1 (or draw a new one), and label the binary count for each state of the four Q outputs.

MODULE 3 The 7493 as a modulo-N divider.

1. Read the reference material in Hall, pages 104–106. Many applications require a circuit that divides an

input frequency by some integer such as 5, 10, or 12, rather than the powers of 2, such as 2, 4, 8, and 16.

a. The divisor, or ratio of frequency in to frequency out, of a frequency divider or counter is called its *modulo* (modulo $N = F_{IN}/F_{OUT}$).

b. For modulo-N dividers less than 16, a 7493 can be used.

(1) The count equal to the desired count (modulo N) is detected.

(2) The detected count is used to reset the counter to zero. It then starts the count over.

2. To demonstrate the 7493 as a modulo-10 divider:

a. Build the circuit shown in Fig. 10-2.

b. Apply power.

c. Connect a 1-kHz TTL-level signal to the A input.

d. Using an oscilloscope, compare the frequency of the QD output with that of the A input.

e. Draw a timing diagram for the A input and the Q outputs.

f. Through how many states do the Q outputs cycle?

g. Why is the binary count for 10 not visible on the outputs even though it must be present because it is being used to reset the counter to all zeros?

3. The 7493 as a modulo-12 divider.

a. Modify (redraw and rebuild) the circuit so that when the counter outputs reach 12 the counter is reset to zero.

b. Apply power and a 1-kHz TTL-level signal to the A input of the 7493.

c. Use an oscilloscope to determine the frequency ratio between the A input and the QD output.

d. Through how many states do the outputs step?

4. The 7493 as a modulo-N divider.

a. Draw and build a modified circuit to produce an output that is one-sixth the input clock frequency applied to input A.

(1) Which Q output will have the desired frequency?

(2) What signal will appear on the QD output?

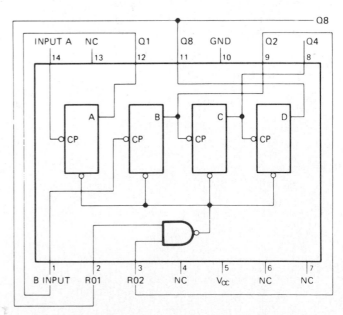

Fig. 10-2 A circuit showing the 7493 converted to a modulo-10 counter.

(3) Verify and record the output waveforms.

b. Draw a schematic for a circuit that will divide an input frequency by 13.

(1) Build and verify circuit operation.

(2) Draw the output waveforms.

MODULE 4 A presettable up or down counter, the 74193.

1. The 74193 is a synchronous, 4-bit binary, up or down counter, whereas the 7493 is an asynchronous, or ripple, counter.

   a. Read the reference material in Hall, pages 111–113, regarding synchronous counters.

   b. Study the 74193 data sheet (in appendix).

2. The 74193 as an up counter.

   a. Using the reference material and the data sheet, draw a circuit for a 74193 set to count up.

      (1) The data inputs can be left open.

      (2) What should be done with the clear input for normal counting?

      (3) What should be done with the load input?

   b. Build the circuit and test it, using a 1-kHz clock signal.

   c. Use an oscilloscope to observe the Q outputs and the carry-out pulse.

   d. On which edge of the input clock do the Q outputs change states?

3. The 74193 as a down counter.

   a. Modify the circuit for the 74193 to count down.

   b. Apply a 1-kHz clock, and observe the output count sequence with an oscilloscope or with LEDs and current-limiting resistors.

   c. Observe the borrow-out pulse. What states are present on the Q outputs when the pulse occurs?

4. The 74193 as a modulo-N divider. The modulo of this device can be changed to any number between 2 and 15 by using the borrow-out pulse to load in a number hard-wired on the four data inputs. For example, to make a divide-by-10 circuit, the binary number 1010 is hard-wired on the four data inputs and the borrow output is connected to the load input. Each time the borrow-out goes low, the load input is taken low also. This will load 1010 on the Q outputs and set the borrow output high again. On the next positive clock edge, the output will decrement to 9. Successive clock pulses will count the output down to zero and repeat the cycle.

   a. Draw and build a circuit to connect a 74193 as a decade divider.

   b. Apply a 1-kHz clock and verify its operation.

   c. Try to observe the load pulse. Why is it difficult to observe?

   d. Draw a timing diagram showing the input clock and all outputs (use the data sheet to help you).

   e. *Optional:* Wire and test some other divide ratios, using the 74193 counter. If a binary thumbwheel switch is available, this can be connected to the data inputs of the 74193 for ease in setting the modulo.

5. Cascading 74193s for larger-capacity modulo-N dividers.

   a. Draw a circuit showing how two 74193s can be used to divide an input frequency by a number such as 123.

   b. Build the circuit and verify its operation.

   c. Draw a set of output, clock, and borrow pulse waveforms illustrating the timing just before and just after the terminal count transition from 0 to reload 123.

PULSE SOURCES AND SHAPERS

REFERENCES

Hall: pages 42–47.
555, 74121, and 74122 data sheets (in appendix).

OBJECTIVES

At the conclusion of this laboratory exercise, you should be able to:

1. For a 555 timer IC:
   a. Calculate the circuit values for a given output frequency when it is used as a pulse source (astable multivibrator).
   b. Build and test a 555 astable multivibrator circuit.
   c. Frequency-modulate the output of the 555 circuit.
2. For a 74121 monostable multivibrator:
   a. Calculate the circuit values for a specified output pulse width.
   b. Build and test a 74121 circuit.
   c. Demonstrate the meaning of the term *nonretriggerable* multivibrator.
3. For a 74122 monostable multivibrator:
   a. Calculate the circuit values for a given output pulse width.
   b. Build and test the 74122 circuit.
   c. Demonstrate the meaning of the term *retriggerable* multivibrator.

EQUIPMENT

1 5-V power supply
1 Sine wave generator
1 Dual-trace oscilloscope

MATERIALS

1 555 timer IC
1 74121 monostable multivibrator
1 74122 monostable multivibrator
1 0.1-μF capacitor
1 0.01-μF capacitor
1 25-μF capacitor
1 small audio speaker
1 20-kΩ resistor
1 12-kΩ resistor
1 8.2-kΩ resistor
1 5.6-kΩ resistor
1 100-Ω resistor

PROCEDURE

MODULE 1 The 555 as a pulse source or an astable multivibrator.

1. Calculating component values for a given output frequency for a 555 astable multivibrator circuit.
   a. Read the reference material on the 555 timer IC in Hall, pages 43–44, and/or the 555 data sheet in the appendix.
   b. Given the formulas

   $$f = \frac{1}{T} = \frac{1.44}{(RA + 2RB)C}$$

   and

   $$\text{Duty cycle} = \frac{RA + RB}{RA + 2RB}$$

   calculate the values of RA and RB required with a 0.1-μF capacitor to give a 500-Hz output with a 60 percent (0.6) duty cycle.
   c. Draw a schematic diagram for the 555 circuit, using these values. Refer to Fig. 11-1 for the pin numbers.
      (1) Connect a 0.01-μF bypass capacitor from pin 5 to ground.

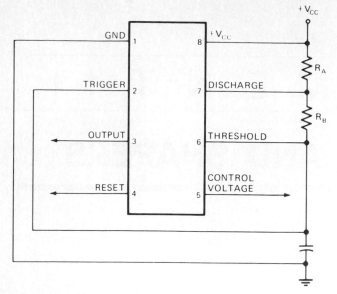

Fig. 11-1 Connection diagram for a 555 timer.

(2) Reset pin 4 may be connected directly to V_{CC} (5 V).

2. Building and testing the 555 astable multivibrator.
   a. Build the circuit as drawn.
   b. Apply power and observe the output waveform.
      (1) Measure the output frequency.
      (2) Give several plausible reasons why your measured frequency value may differ from the value on which your calculations were based.
   c. You may vary the frequency by replacing RA or RB with a potentiometer and a fixed 1-kΩ resistor in series with it to ensure the minimum resistance never becomes less than 1 kΩ.

3. Frequency-modulation of the 555 astable multivibrator. The output frequency of a 555 astable circuit can be changed or modulated by a signal applied to pin 5, the control voltage input. To show this, modify (redraw and rebuild) the 555 circuitry as follows:
   a. Remove the 0.01-μF bypass capacitor from the voltage control input pin 5.
   b. Connect a 0.5- to 1-Hz, 100-mV-peak sine wave signal to pin 5 through a 25-μF capacitor. (If the capacitor is a polar electrolytic one, watch the polarity—the positive side of the capacitor should be toward the 555 timer.)
   c. From the output of the 555, connect a 100-Ω resistor and a small audio speaker in series to V_{CC} = 5 V.
   d. Apply power. You should hear a vibrato effect.
   e. Vary the amplitude of the input signal, and observe the output waveform on an oscilloscope.
   f. Why does putting a signal on the control voltage input change the output frequency?

MODULE 2 The 74121 nonretriggerable monostable multivibrator.

1. Calculating the component values for obtaining a given output pulse width from a 74121 monostable multivibrator circuit.
   a. Read the data sheet for the 74121 (in appendix).
   b. Using a value of 0.1 μF for the timing capacitor, calculate the value of the timing resistor needed to give an output pulse width of 600 μs.
   c. Draw a schematic for the 74121, using these values and showing the proper connections to trigger on the rising edge of an input pulse.
   d. Why can the B input be used for slow risetime signals such as low-frequency sine waves?

2. Building and testing the 74121 monostable multivibrator.
   a. Build the circuit as drawn.
   b. Apply power.
   c. Connect a 1200-Hz TTL-level square wave to the input.
   d. Observe the input and output signals.
   e. If the output pulse width is not about 600 μs, change the value of R to correct it. Note the minimum value for R shown in the data sheet.

3. Demonstrating that the 74121 circuit is a *nonretriggerable* monostable multivibrator.
   a. Decrease the input frequency to 500 Hz.
      (1) Does the output high pulse width change?
      (2) Draw a timing diagram for the input and output at 500 Hz.
   b. Increase the input frequency to 1200 Hz.
      (1) Does the output high pulse width change? Why or why not?
      (2) Draw a timing diagram for the input and output at 1200 Hz.
   c. Increase the input frequency to 2400 Hz, and observe the output pulse width.
      (1) Compare this width to the output high pulse width with a 1200-Hz input.
      (2) Draw a timing diagram for the input and output with a 2400-Hz input.
   d. How does the 74121 respond to an input rising edge that occurs when the output is high?
   e. *Discussion:* This circuit is called a nonretriggerable monostable multivibrator because a new pulse time high cannot be triggered until the output first falls back low. (Module 3 will show the response of a retriggerable multivibrator, the 74122, for comparison.) A nonretriggerable multivibrator such as the 74121 is used to give out a fixed pulse width for a wide range of input pulse widths. The Schmitt trigger *B* input allows slow risetime signals, such as 60-Hz sine waves, to be converted to TTL pulses. Another application of the device takes advantage of the fact that if the width is set correctly, the circuit gives out the same frequency for two different input frequencies such as 1200 and 2400 Hz.

MODULE 3 The 74122 retriggerable monostable multivibrator.

1. Calculating the component values for obtaining a given output pulse width from a 74122 monostable multivibrator.
   a. Read the data sheet for the 74122 (in appendix).
   b. Calculate the value of R needed with a 0.1-μF capacitor to give it an output pulse width of 600 μs.
   c. Draw a schematic for a 74122 set to trigger on the rising edge of an input pulse.

2. Building and testing the 74122 monostable multi-vibrator.
   a. Build the circuit as drawn.
   b. Apply a 1200-Hz TTL-level sine wave input signal.
   c. Observe and measure the input and output pulses with a dual-trace oscilloscope.
      (1) If the output pulse width is not about 600 μs, change R to correct it.
      (2) Note the permitted range of R shown in the data sheet.
   d. Draw a timing diagram for the input and output with a 1200-Hz input.
3. Demonstrating that the 74122 circuit is a *retriggerable* monostable multivibrator.
   a. Increase the input frequency slowly from 1200 to 2400 Hz.
   b. What happens to the output pulse width as the input frequency approaches 2400 Hz?
   c. Draw a timing diagram for the input and output with a 2400-Hz input.
   d. *Discussion:* For a retriggerable monostable multi-vibrator such as the 74122, a new pulse time can be started at any time. Therefore, if a new trigger pulse occurs while the output pulse is still high, the device will start timing again from the new trigger. As long as pulses keep coming before the timing period is up, the output stays high.
   e. This circuit is useful as a missing-pulse detector. The output drops low if one or more pulses are missing from a train of pulses. For example, a machine may have to be sent through a restart sequence if one or more cycles of the 60-Hz power line voltage are missing. For what pulse width would you set a 74122 so that its output will drop low if one cycle of the 60-Hz power line voltage is missed?

A DIGITAL CLOCK

REFERENCE

Hall: pages 107–110.

OBJECTIVES

At the conclusion of this laboratory exercise, you should be able to:

1. Demonstrate how the functions performed in a digital-clock IC are accomplished with simple counters and gates.
2. Review the use of Karnaugh maps to simplify logic expressions.
3. Expand a block diagram for a basic digital clock to a schematic diagram of a circuit.
4. Build and test a basic digital-clock circuit.
5. Modify a basic digital-clock circuit to include a 60-Hz reference, a tenths-of-seconds display, an AM/PM indicator, and a time-set circuit.

EQUIPMENT

1 5-V power supply
1 Function generator

MATERIALS

6 Seven-segment common-anode displays
5 7447 BCD-to-seven-segment decoders
5 7493 counters
2 7400 quad two-input NAND gate ICs
1 7404 hex inverter IC
1 7420 dual four-input NAND gate IC
1 2N3904 transistor
1 3.3kΩ resistor
37 150-Ω resistors

PROCEDURE

MODULE 1 Converting a block diagram to a schematic for a basic digital-clock circuit.

1. System overview.
   a. Read the reference material in Hall, pages 107–110.
   b. Study the block diagram in Fig. 12-1. Note that the seconds section is on the left and the hours section is on the right, which is the reverse order of a standard digital-clock display.
   c. Use this same reverse, but standard, pattern when drawing your schematic, with the signal flow from left to right.
   d. When planning the circuit layout, set it up for a normal digital-clock display with the hours on the left and the displays of the minutes and seconds to the right of the hours display.
   e. For simplicity, the 1-Hz signal for the basic digital-clock circuit is provided by a signal generator set to produce a 1-Hz TTL-level square wave rather than by an on-board signal source.
2. Drawing the schematic for the seconds section of a digital clock.
   a. Refer to Fig. 12-1. The input counter on the left counts seconds. For this counter a 7490 or a 7493 wired to divide by 10 can be used. For each 10 input pulses, this counter gives one output pulse on its QD output.
   b. A 7447 can be used to convert the BCD output code to seven-segment code for the display. Remember to include current-limiting resistors in your circuit.
   c. The second counter records the 10s of seconds and should be wired to give one output pulse for each six input pulses from the QD output of the previous counter.

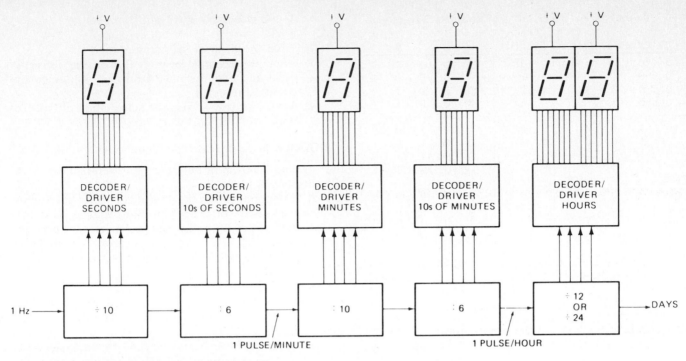

Fig. 12-1 A block diagram of a digital clock with a seven-segment read-out.

(1) What is the modulo of these two counters together?

(2) The divide-by-6 counter can be a 7493 also.

d. The output of the second counter can also use a 7447 decoder and resistors to drive its display.

3. Drawing the schematic for the minutes section of the digital clock.

a. The MSB output of the tens-of-seconds counter is 1 pulse per minute, which is the input-clock pulse for the minutes section.

b. The circuit for the minutes section of the clock is an exact repetition of the seconds section, so drawing the schematic for this section should be no problem.

4. Using truth tables and a Karnaugh map to simplify decoding logic for the hours section.

a. The output of the minutes section is 1 pulse per hour. To record these pulses, a modulo-12 counter is used. In hardware this can be done with a 7493 connected as a modulo-12 counter.

b. The decoding for the hours section presents a more complex problem than for the seconds and minutes sections. Think of the decimal numbers you wish to display, 1 through 12. Since they involve two digits, a single 7447 cannot be used for the decoding. Figure 12-2 shows a circuit that can be used to drive the two display digits.

(1) A 7447 drives the least significant digit of the hours display.

(2) The most significant digit needs to be only off, or a 1, so the driver transistor drives segment *b* and segment *c* of a seven-segment display in parallel for this.

c. Determine the contents of the black box in Fig. 12-2. In other words, you must find the combination of logic gates that will convert the 4-bit output

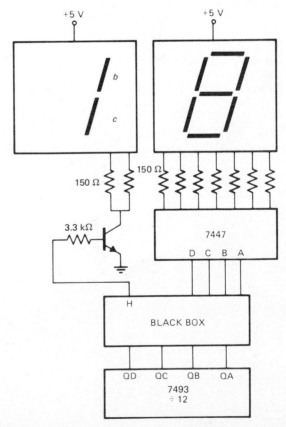

Fig. 12-2 An hours-display driver circuit for a digital clock.

7493 Outputs for ÷ 12				Display Digit Desired	Required Driver Inputs				
QD	QC	QB	QA		H	D	C	B	A
0	0	0	0	12	1	0	0	1	0
0	0	0	1	1	0	0	0	0	1
0	0	1	0	2	0	0	0	1	0
0	0	1	1	3	0	0	0	1	1
0	1	0	0	4	0	0	1	0	0
0	1	0	1	5	0	0	1	0	1
0	1	1	0	6	0	0	1	1	0
0	1	1	1	7	0	0	1	1	1
1	0	0	0	8	0	1	0	0	0
1	0	0	1	9	0	1	0	0	1
1	0	1	0	10	1	0	0	0	0
1	0	1	1	11	1	0	0	0	1

Fig. 12-3 The truth table for decoding the hours section of a digital-clock circuit.

code of the 7493 to the proper input code for the 7447 and the H transistor. The first step is to set up a truth table, as in Fig. 12-3.

d. You are now ready to review Hall, pages 62–66, if necessary, and use Karnaugh maps to produce the simplified logic expression for each driver input in terms of the 7493 Q outputs. In your Karnaugh maps, the unused states 1100, 1101, 1110, and 1111 are don't-care states because the counter never outputs them. Therefore, you can put X's in the boxes for these states on your Karnaugh map. The X's can be included in determining the simplified output expression if this produces a simpler result or ignored if it does not.

e. When you have found the correct logic expressions for each driver input, draw a logic diagram showing how you can implement them with common TTL gates.

5. Completing the digital clock.

a. Complete the schematic diagram for the entire digital clock. Show all pin numbers and connections.

b. Build the seconds section and test it.

c. When the seconds section is working correctly, build and add the next (minutes) section to the circuit and test it.

d. Work your way across the schematic until all sections are built and working.

MODULE 2 Improving the digital-clock circuit.

1. Adding a 60-Hz ac reference and tenths-of-seconds display.

a. A common reference-frequency input for digital clocks is the 60-Hz ac power line voltage. As shown in Hall, Fig. 2-33, this can be converted to produce 60-Hz TTL signal levels and can be rectified and filtered to provide the dc power supply for the entire digital-clock circuit.

b. Using a 60-Hz TTL input, draw a circuit that can be used to produce a tenths-of-seconds display and the 1-Hz input signal needed for the rest of the clock.

c. *Optional:* If the parts and time are available, build the power supply, the 60-Hz reference, and the tenths-of-seconds section to make a complete, self-powered digital clock.

2. Adding an AM/PM indicator.

a. Another improvement would be an indicator on the hours section that shows whether the hour is morning or evening.

b. Draw a circuit that changes its output every 12 hours and indicates evening by lighting an LED.

3. Setting the time—an update circuit.

a. Still another improvement would be to add some means of setting the outputs to the proper time.

b. Refer to Hall, Fig. 3-24. Draw a schematic for a circuit that can be used to gate either the 1-pulse/minute signal or the 2-Hz update signal into the minutes section.

c. The same circuit could be used to update the seconds or hours section.

A FREQUENCY COUNTER

REFERENCES

Hall: pages 113–119.

Data sheets for all ICs and displays.

OBJECTIVES

At the conclusion of this laboratory exercise, you should be able to:

1. Neatly draw a complete, large schematic for a complex digital system—an MSI frequency counter—showing all connections and pin numbers.
2. Plan and draw the layout for the construction of a complex digital system prototype circuit for an MSI frequency counter.
3. Systematically build and test a prototype circuit for a complex digital system—an MSI frequency counter.
4. Demonstrate the principle of operation of multiplexed displays.

EQUIPMENT

1 5-V power supply
1 TTL-level signal source
1 Oscilloscope
1 DVM

MATERIALS

1 7404 hex inverter
1 7476 dual JK flip-flop
1 7400 quad NAND gate
1 7447 decoder
1 7493 counter
1 74121 monostable multivibrator
1 74LS138 or 74138 decoder
4 74151 multiplexers

14 74160 decade counters
7 74175 quad D flip-flops
7 Seven-segment common-anode LED displays
1 1-MHz low-impedance crystal
7 3906 transistors
1 7- to 50-pF trimmer capacitor (optional)
10–20 0.1-μF ceramic bypass capacitors
1 10-kΩ resistor
2 1.3-kΩ resistors
7 1-kΩ resistors
2 390- or 470-Ω resistors
7 150-Ω resistors
1 Piece of 17 × 24 in 100-mil blue-grid drawing paper
9 Sections of 6-in solderless prototyping board
Assorted 22- to 24-gage solid-core, color-coded wire

PROCEDURE

MODULE 1 Planning a complex digital system circuit.

1. Drawing the schematic.
   a. Read the reference material.
   b. Plan the overall schematic layout for a complete multiplexed-display frequency counter.
      (1) Use the oscillator, divider chain, timing, and control circuitry from Fig. 13-1 and the entire counter and display circuitry of Fig. 13-2.
      (2) Remember to include bypass capacitors between V_{CC} and ground on the ICs such as the 74151s, 74160s, and so on.
   c. Draw a complete schematic showing all connections and pin numbers on a 17 × 24 in or larger piece of 100-mil blue-grid drawing paper.
2. Drawing the component layout.
   a. Plan and draw a physical layout for construction of the circuit, observing the following suggestions:
      (1) Try to follow the schematic layout as much as possible.

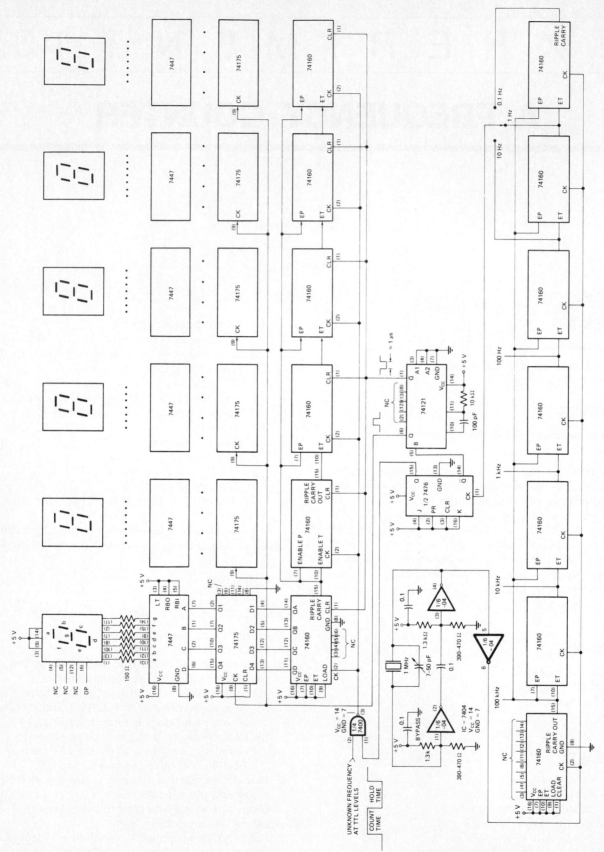

Fig. 13-1 A schematic for an MSI frequency counter with nonmultiplexed displays.

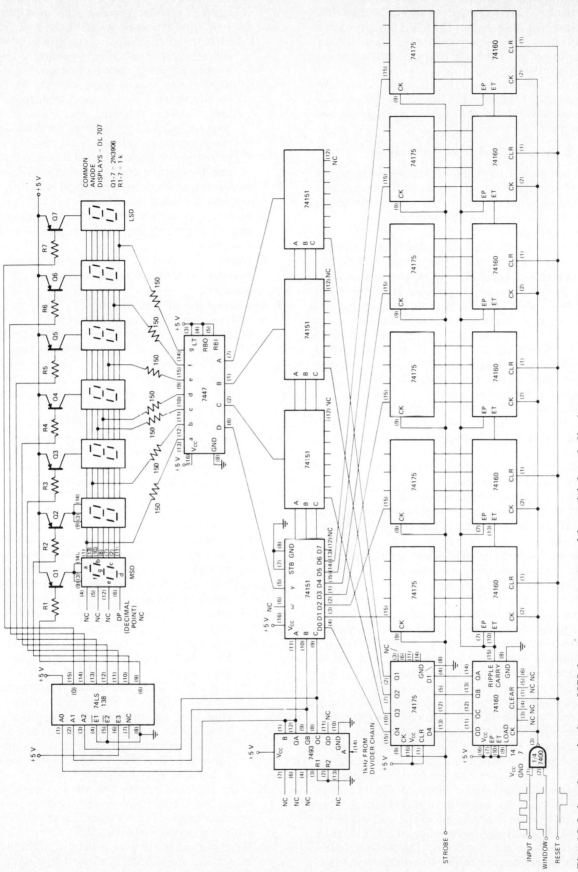

Fig. 13-2 A schematic for a MSI frequency counter with multiplexed displays.

(2) Try to minimize the number of wires that have to jump back and forth across the board.

(3) The ICs should all point in the same direction.

(4) Leave a space between the ICs so that the wires do not have to go over them. This makes it easier to get test probes in to the IC and to remove a defective IC.

b. When the overall layout is planned, choose the color codes for the wiring. This is especially important when several people are going to build one counter.

MODULE 2 Building and testing the circuit.

1. Look at the circuit to decide which sections can be built and easily tested individually. If a group of people are building one counter, then one or two people can build and test each major section.

a. Display section.

(1) First connect the displays, digit-driver transistors, and 7447. When this portion is built, the lamp test of the 7447 can be tied low and one digit-driver transistor enabled at a time. What pattern should the selected digit show?

(2) To determine whether the segments are wired correctly, temporarily hard-wire the BCD code for a 2 or 5 on the inputs of the 7447. As the end of each digit driver's base resistor is grounded or made low, that digit should display the correct number.

(3) Now add the 74LS138 and 7493 address counter circuitry. If you apply a 1-kHz clock to the 7493, all the displays should show this number.

b. Crystal oscillator, time-base divider chain, and control circuitry section.

(1) Start with the crystal oscillator.

(2) When the oscillator is working correctly, add and test each counter of the time-base divider chain.

(3) Build and test the 7476 window generator and the 74121 control-pulse generator.

c. Main counter chain section.

(1) First build the counter chain. The count window input can be temporarily tied high instead of to the 7476, and a 1-MHz signal applied to the unknown frequency input. Then the counters will count continuously and can be added and checked just as those in the time-base chain as described above.

(2) Next add the flip-flops. To verify their operation, first disable the counters' reset lines (tie them to +5 V). Tie the flip-flops' clock line to ground. Leave the count window lead open, and apply a 1-MHz signal to the count input to load a count into the counter. Then connect the window to ground. A count should now be present on the outputs of the counters. This count can be transferred to the outputs of the 74175 flip-flops by briefly lifting the clock input lead from ground. The counter logic states should now be present on the outputs of the 74175s and can be checked to see whether they correspond.

(3) Finally add the multiplexers. You may verify their operation by hard-wiring the A, B, and C address lines to ground. The multiplexer inputs should now be selecting the data from the least significant flip-flop (on the left). You can then perform the same sequence of steps described for verifying the flip-flops, but now the logic states of the least significant counter should be also present on the outputs of the four 74151s. You can step through all the counter outputs by successively hard-wiring the appropriate addresses on the 74151s and verifying the logic from each selected counter and flip-flop to the 74151 outputs.

2. When the major sections are all working, they can be joined and the whole unit tested.

a. Add the display section, oscillator, divider chain, count window, strobe, and reset signals to the correct points.

b. Input an unknown frequency, and compare your counter reading with a calibrated frequency counter.

3. Additional troubleshooting tips.

a. If the counter fails to function:

(1) Lift out the 7493 and temporarily hard-wire the QA, QB, and QC output wires (multiplexer address lines) to ground. The least significant digit of the display should now be enabled, and the multiplexer inputs should all point to the least significant counter on the left.

(2) Lift the strobe lead from the 74121 and connect it to ground. Lift the reset lead from the 74121 and connect it to +5 V.

(3) Lift the count window lead from the 7476 and apply a 1-MHz signal to the count input to load a count into the counters. Then connect the window input to ground. A count should now be present on the outputs of the counters.

(4) This count can be transferred to the outputs of the 74175 flip-flops by briefly lifting the clock input lead from ground. The logic states on the least significant counter should now be present on the outputs of the leftmost 74175 and on the outputs of the four 74151s. The decimal digit for this code should be displayed on the appropriate LED. Since these levels are all held fixed, they can be checked with a voltmeter or logic probe.

(5) The 74151 multiplexers can be stepped to pick up the outputs of the next 74175 by simply changing the jumpers you put in place of the 7493 to QA = +5 V, QB = ground, and QC = ground. In this way the connections from each counter to the 7447 inputs can be checked on a dc basis with a logic probe.

b. If the counter counts but shows erratic counts, check that the power-supply voltage is within specifications. TTL devices function erratically with low supply voltages.

c. If one digit of the display is brightly lighted but the others are dark, this is caused by failure of the 74L138 digit-scanning circuitry.

(1) Either the 74LS138 is defective, or the 7493 is

not supplying sequential addresses to it. An oscilloscope will quickly show whether the problem is in the 74LS138, the 7493, or the clock pulse coming to the 7493.

(2) Since the clock signal to the 7493 comes from the time-base divider chain, no signal here will lead you back to a malfunction of the divider chain or possibly the master oscillator.

d. If all digits are lighted equally but the numbers do not change when the input frequency is changed, the problem may be no count window or no clock pulse to the 74175 flip-flops. If the digits are all lighted equally but the count constantly changes to random numbers, the counters may not be getting a reset pulse. Use the delayed sweep function of an oscilloscope to find and verify these narrow pulse timing signals. Using the QD outputs of the time-base counter chain (rather than the carry-out pulses) to clock the 7476 and 7493 may solve this problem, since the QD outputs have a much longer duty cycle than the carry-out pulses.

e. Some other questions to consider:

(1) What symptom would the counter show if the inputs to the 7447 were connected incorrectly?

(2) What symptom would the counter show if the digit-driver transistors were connected to the 74LS138 in reverse order?

4. Describe the operation of each section of the counter. Include a timing diagram for the count window and control circuitry.

MODULE 3 Improving the frequency counter.

1. You may wish to add to the counter a high-speed decade prescaler such as the 11C90 and a high-speed comparator such as the NE529A. These improvements extend the input frequency range of the counter to 100 MHz and allow it to detect non-TTL-level signals.

2. Decimal points in the LED display can be wired with the time-window switch to indicate kilohertz or megahertz or fractions of hertz.

SHIFT REGISTER COUNTERS

REFERENCES

Hall: pages 121–128.

74175 data sheet (in appendix).

74194 data sheet (in appendix).

OBJECTIVES

At the conclusion of this laboratory exercise, you should be able to:

1. Demonstrate how the 74194 universal shift register can be connected to parallel-load, shift left, or shift right.
2. Show how the 74194 shift register can be connected to form a ring counter.
3. Explain the operation of a twisted-ring, or Johnson, counter.

EQUIPMENT

1 5-V power supply
1 TTL signal generator
1 Dual-trace oscilloscope

MATERIALS

1 74194 universal 4-bit shift register
2 7476 JK flip-flops
4 LEDs
4 47-Ω resistors
1 74175 quad D flip-flop

PROCEDURE

MODULE 1 The 74194 shift register.

1. Interpreting the data sheet for the 74194.
   a. Read the reference material in Hall on shift regis-

ters and the data sheet for the 74194 in the appendix.
   b. How many stages does the 74194 have?
   c. On which edge of the input clock does a shift take place?
   d. What logic level should be on the clear input for normal shifting?
   e. What logic level should be on mode inputs S1 and S0 to parallel-load a number?
   f. What logic levels should be on the S1 and S0 inputs for a shift-right operation?
   g. What logic level should be present on the clock when mode inputs are being changed?
   h. Remember to establish the proper conditions on each of the above inputs for each separate operation you implement on the 74194 shift register.
2. Drawing a circuit diagram.
   a. Draw a circuit diagram for a 74194 connected to load $A = 1$, $B = 0$, $C = 0$, and $D = 0$.
   b. Connect an LED and a 47-Ω current-limiting resistor from each Q output to ground.
   c. Connect the shift-right serial input to ground.
   d. Connect the power supply and ground to the proper pins.
   e. Connect the clear input to permit proper loading and shifting.
3. Building and testing the 74194 shift register.
   a. Build the circuit as drawn.
   b. Apply V_{CC} and observe the output LEDs. Why do the parallel inputs not appear on the Q outputs?
   c. Apply a 1-Hz TTL-level clock to the clock input. The desired pattern should now load and be visible on the LEDs.
   d. What changes in the mode inputs must be made to get the output pattern to shift right?
      (1) You can make this change with the power on so that the loaded pattern is not lost.
      (2) How many clock pulses does it take for the loaded 1 to get to the QD output?
      (3) What happens to the 1 you loaded after four clock pulses?

MODULE 2 A ring counter.

1. To prevent a 1 that you load into a shift register from being lost off the end of the register, you can route it back to the A flip-flop. It will then shift through again. This connection is known as a *recirculating* shift register. To modify the normal 74194 shift register circuit to produce a recirculating shift register:
   a. Remove the shift-right serial input from ground, and connect it to the QD output.
   b. Connect the mode inputs to reload the parallel input pattern.
   c. Apply power and the clock.
   d. Set the mode inputs for shift right.
   e. Observe the output shifts on the LEDs.
   f. What happens to the 1 after four clock pulses?
2. To use an oscilloscope to map the timing of the recirculating shift register:
   a. Increase the input-clock frequency to about 10 kHz, and observe the clock input and the Q outputs with an oscilloscope.
   b. Draw a timing diagram showing the clock input and the four Q outputs.
   c. Connect the QA output to the shift-left serial input.
   d. Load in 0001.
   e. Set the mode inputs for serial shift left.
   f. Observe and record the output waveforms with the oscilloscope.
3. Other pulse patterns can be produced by changing the word loaded. Try loading 0101 or 0011 and observing the output waveforms.
4. When the parallel outputs of a recirculating shift register such as this are used, it is often called a *ring counter*.

MODULE 3 A twisted-ring, or Johnson, counter.

1. Another useful shift register counter is the twisted ring, Johnson, or walking ring. It can be made with either JK or D flip-flops.
   a. Figure 14-1 shows a circuit for a Johnson counter using a 74175 quad D flip-flop IC. Note that the $\bar{Q}$ output of the last stage is fed back into the D input of the first stage.
   b. Assuming the Q outputs are initially reset to zero by momentarily touching the clear input to ground, write a truth table for the expected outputs for eight clock pulses.
   c. Draw a timing diagram for the input clock and the Q outputs from the truth table for this counter.
   d. Which edge of the input clock causes the shift?
2. Building and testing the Johnson counter.
   a. Build the circuit of Fig. 14-1.

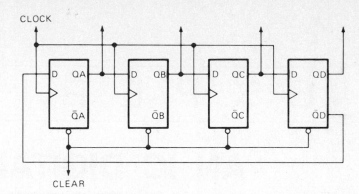

Fig. 14-1 A schematic for a Johnson counter using a 74175 quad D flip-flop.

   b. Apply power and a 5-kHz clock.
   c. Observe the outputs with an oscilloscope.
   d. Compare the observed waveforms with the timing diagram you drew. You may have to think a little bit about what to trigger on to make the two pictures correspond.
   e. What is the ratio of the frequency of the input clock to the frequency of each Q output?
   f. What, then, is the modulo of this counter?
   g. What is the duty cycle of each output?
3. Decoding a Johnson counter.
   a. *Discussion:* As you saw in your truth table (output-state table), this counter has eight distinct states. Decoding the counter involves detecting each of these unique states and producing a separate output signal for each state, such as a one-of-eight high (or low) output. These outputs could be quite useful in controlling or enabling sequential operations in an industrial system. The advantage of decoding a Johnson counter is that it does not produce the glitches that are created by decoding a ripple binary counter.
   b. To decode the Johnson counter, examine your output-state table and/or timing diagram. Observe that state 0 is decoded by $\bar{A} \cdot \bar{D}$, state 1 by $A \cdot \bar{B}$, state 2 by $B \cdot \bar{C}$, and so on. Use the timing diagram or table to determine the decoded outputs for the other five states. As you can see, decoding the Johnson requires only a two-input AND gate for each state. This simplicity is another advantage over the more complicated decoding circuitry required for other counters.
   c. Step *b* is an intuitive approach to decoding, but you may verify these results by using Karnaugh maps. Remember to include eight don't-care states.

AN IC DIGITAL-TO-ANALOG CONVERTER—THE 1408

REFERENCES

Hall: pages 161–166.

MC1408 D/A converter data sheet (in appendix).

OBJECTIVES

At the conclusion of this laboratory exercise, you should be able to:

1. Describe the theory of operation of a monolithic digital-to-analog (D/A) converter, the MC1408.
2. Build, calibrate, and test a voltage output D/A circuit using the MC1408.
3. Demonstrate the meaning of the terms *resolution* and *accuracy* for a D/A converter.
4. Show the output waveforms produced by using an up or down counter on the inputs of a D/A converter.

EQUIPMENT

1 Triple-output dc power supply of 5, 15, and −15 V (or three separate power supplies to provide these three output voltages)
1 Dual-trace oscilloscope
1 TTL-level signal generator
1 Digital voltmeter

MATERIALS

1 MC1408L8 D/A converter (or equivalent)
1 74193 binary up or down counter
1 741 operational amplifier
5 0.1-μF capacitors
1 15-pF capacitor
1 10-kΩ multiturn trim potentiometer
2 1.0-kΩ resistors
2 510-Ω resistors

PROCEDURE

MODULE 1 A monolithic D/A converter.

1. Using the data sheet to determine the operating characteristics of the MC1408 D/A converter.
   a. Read the reference material and the data sheet for the MC1408 D/A converter (in the appendix).
   b. For the MC1408 answer the following questions:
      (1) How many bits does it have?
      (2) What is its resolution?
      (3) What are the maximum values for V_{CC} and V_{EE}?
      (4) What are the typical operating values for V_{CC} and V_{EE}?
      (5) Are the digital inputs TTL-compatible?
      (6) For values of V_{EE} below −10 V, what should be done with pin 1?
      (7) With a V_{REF} of 2 V and $R14 = 1$ kΩ, what is the typical full-scale output current?
2. Building a D/A circuit.
   a. Examine the circuit shown in Fig. 15-1. What is the purpose of the operational amplifier connected to the output of the MC1408?
   b. Build the circuit and temporarily connect all the data inputs to ground.
   c. Check all connections carefully.
3. Verifying the operating voltages.
   a. Apply power.
   b. Verify the circuit voltages V_{CC}, V_{EE}, and V_{REF}.
   c. Pins 14 and 15 of the MC1408 should be at or near 0 V.
   d. What voltage should be present on pin 2 of the amplifier?
   e. With all data inputs of the MC1408 low, what voltage should be present on the output of the amplifier?
4. Calibrating the D/A converter.
   a. If all operating voltages check out, tie all the data inputs of the MC1408 to 5 V.

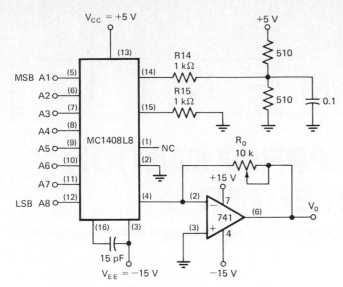

Fig. 15-1 A schematic for a voltage output D/A converter using the MC1408L8.

b. Adjust $R0$ until the output voltage from the amplifer is as near 9.961 V as possible.

5. Calculating the resolution of the D/A converter.

a. All 1s on the inputs represent a binary count of 255. This converter puts out 256 voltage levels, 0 to 9.961 V. To find the size of each step in volts, divide 10.000 V by 256 or 9.961 V by 255.

b. The top level is 9.961 rather than 10.000 V because 0 V counts as a level. As another example, the numbers 0, 1, 2, 3 define four levels but only three increments. If these were volts out of a 2-bit D/A converter, it would be referred to as a 4-V, full-scale output.

c. For this nominal 10-V-output converter, what is the resolution in volts?

6. Determining the accuracy of the D/A converter.

a. Calculate the voltage out that should be produced by each of the eight inputs.

b. Make one data input at a time high, and measure the actual output voltage for each.

c. Ideally the maximum error for any output should be no greater than $\pm \frac{1}{2}$ the LSB output voltage. Do all your readings fall within this limit of accuracy?

d. With all data inputs at ground, the output voltage should be 0 V. Any difference from this value is an offset error. Does your D/A converter show any offset error?

e. How does this circuit adjust for gain error?

MODULE 2 An up or down counter with a D/A converter.

1. Setting up the counter.
a. Draw a circuit for two 74193 binary counters cascaded to make an 8-bit up or down counter.
b. Build the circuit as drawn.
c. Tie the count-down input high.
d. Apply a 5-kHz TTL square wave to the count-up input.
e. Test the circuit to verify its operation.

2. Adding a counter to the D/A converter, and observing the output waveforms.
a. Connect the Q outputs of the counter to the data inputs of the MC1408 D/A converter.
b. Observe the output of the amplifier with an oscilloscope. What waveform is displayed?
c. Expand the display so that you can see the steps in the waveform. How many millivolts does each step represent?
d. Observe the output waveform closely with the intensity turned down and the focus finely tuned. Is the converter output monotonic?
e. Move the 5-kHz signal to the count-down input of the counter, and tie the count-up input high. How does this change the output waveform of the D/A converter?
f. What is the ratio of the frequency of the input pulses to that of the output waveform?

3. Using an audio circuit to demonstrate the counter circuit of the D/A converter.
a. Connect the circuit shown in Fig. 15-2 to the output of the amplifier (observe the capacitor's polarity).
b. Apply power and a 100-kHz TTL square wave to the count-up input of the counter. You should hear a tone that sounds close to a "G" in music.
c. Use the oscilloscope to observe the output waveform, and measure its frequency.
d. Vary the frequency of the signal down in steps of 10 kHz, and note changes in output tones and waveforms.

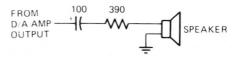

Fig. 15-2 An audio output test circuit for a D/A converter with a counter.

EXPERIMENT 16

A SUCCESSIVE-APPROXIMATION A/D CONVERTER

REFERENCE

Hall: pages 169–172.

OBJECTIVES

At the conclusion of this laboratory exercise, you should be able to:

1. Explain the theory of operation of a successive-approximation A/D converter.
2. Build and test an 8-bit successive-approximation A/D converter.
3. Draw a complete timing diagram for a successive-approximation A/D converter.
4. Add a D/A converter on the output of the A/D converter, and observe that a sine wave signal can be digitized and then converted to a replica of its analog form.
5. Observe the effect of the A/D sampling rate on the fidelity of the replicated sine wave.

EQUIPMENT

4 Power-supply outputs of 5, −5, 15, and −15 V
1 Dual-trace oscilloscope
1 Digital voltmeter
1 TTL-level signal source
1 3-V-peak sine wave signal source

MATERIALS

1 MC14549 or MC14559 successive-approximation register
2 MC1408 D/A converters (or equivalent)
1 74LS374 octal D flip-flop
2 LM741 operational amplifiers (or equivalent)
1 LM319 high-speed comparator

2 0.1-μF capacitors
3 50-pF capacitors
2 10-kΩ multiturn trim potentiometers
1 100-kΩ resistor
1 10-kΩ resistor
4 2.4-kΩ resistors
1 2.2-kΩ resistor
1 100-Ω resistor

PROCEDURE

MODULE 1 Circuit analysis from given data.

1. Reference material.
   a. Read the reference material on A/D converters in Hall, pages 169–172.
   b. Study the circuit in Fig. 16-1, which is a successive-approximation A/D converter using an MC1408 D/A converter, an MC14549 or MC14559 successive-approximation register, an LM741 operational amplifier, an LM319 high-speed comparator, and a 74LS374 octal D flip-flop.
2. Notes on theoretical circuit operation.
   a. What is the purpose of the LM741 operational amplifier on the output of the MC1408 D/A converter?
   b. Note that the reference voltage for the D/A converter is connected through a resistor to pin 15 rather than to pin 14 of the MC1408 D/A converter, as in Experiment 15. This is because a negative reference voltage is being used in the circuit of Fig. 16-1, so the input range is −5 to +5 V.
   c. Note also that the noninverting input of the op amp is connected to −5 V instead of to ground, to accommodate this same voltage range.
   d. The LM319 comparator gives TTL or CMOS output levels when pin 3 is connected to ground and the output is pulled to 5 V with a resistor, as shown.

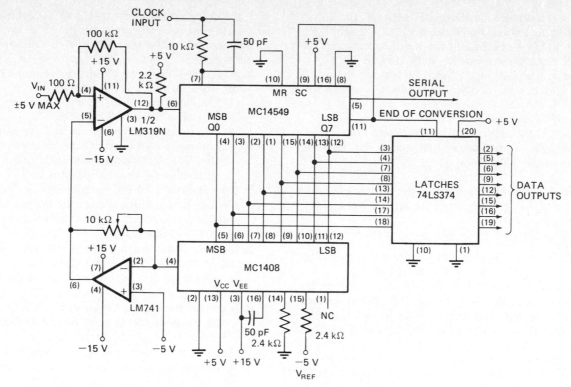

Fig. 16-1 A schematic for a successive-approximation A/D converter.

e. The MC14549 or MC14559 is a CMOS successive-approximation register (SAR). What is its purpose?

f. Why are the 10-kΩ resistor and 50-pF capacitor included on the clock input of the A/D converter for prototyping board construction?

g. Why do you suppose that a 74LS device was used for the output latches rather than a standard 7400 series part?

h. Note that Q0 of the MC14549 or MC14559 is the MSB output.

MODULE 2 Building and testing a successive-approximation A/D converter.

1. Circuit layout.
  a. Plan the layout of this circuit to minimize the number of wires that have to jump from one end of the board to the other.
  b. Leave space for another MC1408 and LM741 which you may wish to add to the latch outputs for the last part of this experiment.

2. Building and testing the D/A section.
  a. Build the MC1408 and LM741 sections of the circuit carefully with short leads.
  b. Temporarily connect all the MC1408 data inputs to ground.
  c. Apply power and adjust V_{REF} to −5 V.
  d. The output of the amplifier should be −5.00 V. Verify this voltage.
  e. Connect all data inputs of the MC1408 to 5 V, and adjust the 10-kΩ trimpot until the voltage on the output of the amplifier is 4.961 V.

3. Adding the A/D section and demonstrating the output for a full-scale positive input.

a. Add the LM319 comparator, the MC14549 or MC14559, and the 74LS374 circuitry. Use color-coded wiring.

b. Connect a 5-kHz, 5-V CMOS-level square wave to the converter clock input.

c. With the LM319 comparator input temporarily connected to 5 V, observe the output of the op amp with an oscilloscope.
  (1) You should see a pattern of increasing voltage steps as each bit is tried by the SAR and kept or reset.
  (2) Since 5 V is at the top of the range, all bits should be turned on and left on.
  (3) Draw the output pattern.

4. Demonstrating the A/D output for a full-scale negative input.
  a. Connect the LM319 comparator input to the −5-V reference voltage.
  b. Observe the output of the LM741 op amp.
    (1) What does this waveform represent?
    (2) Which bit is tried first?
    (3) How large is the largest voltage step?
    (4) How large is the smallest voltage step?

5. A/D operation for an "unknown" input, not full-scale.
  a. Predict the digital word that should be produced by an input of 2.4 V.
  b. Try this value to test your prediction.
  c. Where in the circuit is a convenient place to read the output digital word?
  d. What are some sources of error for this converter?

MODULE 3 A successive-approximation A/D timing diagram.

1. Observe the timing waveforms as follows.

a. On a dual-trace oscilloscope, observe the input clock and the end-of-conversion (EOC) pulse.

b. How many clock pulses are actually required for each complete conversion with this circuit?

c. Observe the $Q0$ output and the input clock.

d. On which edge of the input clock is a new bit tried?

e. Which bit is tried first?

2. Draw a timing diagram for a complete conversion, showing the input clock, EOC, and the eight Q outputs of the MC14549.

MODULE 4 Adding a D/A converter to demonstrate the effect of the A/D sampling rate on the fidelity of a replicated waveform.

1. Adding the second D/A converter.

a. Build another D/A section identical to that in Fig. 16-1, using the MC1408 and an LM741.

b. Test this D/A section by first tying all the data inputs of the MC1408 to ground. What voltage should the output of the amplifier show? (Remember that the amplifier is referenced to -5 V rather than to ground.)

c. Connect all the data inputs of the MC1408 to 5 V.

d. Adjust the 10-kΩ trimpot until the output voltage of the LM741 op amp is 4.961 V.

e. When this D/A section works correctly, connect the data outputs of the 74LS374 to the corresponding data inputs of the MC1408.

2. Demonstrating the effect of the A/D sampling rate on the output.

a. Apply a 3-V-peak, 10-Hz sine wave to the comparator input of the A/D converter.

(1) Display this A/D input waveform on channel 1 of a dual-trace oscilloscope.

(2) If you do not have two signal generators, you can use a 555 timer IC set for about 5 kHz for the A/D clock input and then use the signal generator for the comparator input.

b. Use channel 2 of the oscilloscope to observe the reconstructed sine wave on the output of the D/A section you just added. How does it compare with the A/D input signal?

c. Increase the frequency of the sine wave input signal to 100 Hz. What effect does this have on the waveform on the output of the second D/A converter?

d. Increase the input frequency to 1000 Hz, and again observe the output of the D/A converter. (You may have to adjust the variable time/div setting of the oscilloscope to get a stable display.)

e. What conclusion can you draw about the sampling rate and the fidelity of the output?

EXPERIMENT 17

ARITHMETIC LOGIC UNIT

REFERENCE

Hall: pages 185–188.

OBJECTIVES

At the conclusion of this laboratory exercise, you should be able to:

1. Show how a 74181 arithmetic logic unit (ALU) IC can be programmed with a binary instruction on its select inputs to perform arithmetic or logic operations on two 4-bit binary words.
2. Predict, and use a 74181 ALU to verify, the results of performing various arithmetic and logic functions on two 4-bit binary words.
3. Demonstrate how two 74181 ALUs can be cascaded to perform arithmetic and logic operations on two 8-bit binary words.

EQUIPMENT

1 5-V power supply

MATERIALS

2 74181 ALU ICs
10 LEDs
10 47-Ω resistors

PROCEDURE

MODULE 1 Reference and discussion.

1. Carefully read the reference material in Hall, pages 185–188, for the 74181 ALU.
2. Refer to Fig. 17-1.

a. A refers to a 4-bit binary word on the four A inputs, B represents a 4-bit binary word on the four B inputs, and F represents a 4-bit binary word on the four F outputs.
b. Note that the tables show the output functions produced for both positive and negative logic conventions.
c. What determines the function performed on the input words?

MODULE 2 The 74181 ALU in logic mode.

1. Predicting logic functions. Predict the output word produced by each of the 16 logic functions of a 74181 ALU with an A input of 1001 and a B input of 1010. (Assume positive logic conventions.)
2. Building the test circuit of the ALU logic function.
   a. Connect V_{CC} and ground to a 74181 ALU.
   b. Apply the input words 1001 to the A inputs and 1010 to the B inputs.
   c. For logic functions, what connections should be made to the M input and the C_n input? Make these connections.
   d. Connect a 47-Ω resistor and an LED in series from each F output and from the C_{n+4} output to ground to make it easier to see the output words.
3. Verifying logic function predictions.
   a. For each of the 16 instructions, observe the output word and compare it with your predictions made in step 1.
   b. Note that each function is performed on a bit-by-bit basis.

MODULE 3 The 74181 ALU in arithmetic mode.

1. Predicting arithmetic operations. Again, assume positive logic. Note that a low on C_n in positive logic means "with carry," or do carry, while a high on C_n means "no carry," or do not carry.
   a. For arithmetic operation without a carry-in, deter-

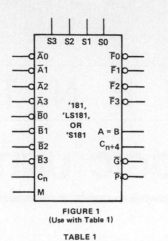 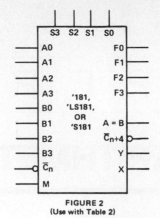

FIGURE 1
(Use with Table 1)

FIGURE 2
(Use with Table 2)

TABLE 1

SELECTION				ACTIVE-LOW DATA		
				M = H	M = L; ARITHMETIC OPERATIONS	
S3	S2	S1	S0	LOGIC FUNCTIONS	C_n = L (no carry)	C_n = H (with carry)
L	L	L	L	$F = \bar{A}$	F = A MINUS 1	F = A
L	L	L	H	$F = \overline{AB}$	F = AB MINUS 1	F = AB
L	L	H	L	$F = \bar{A} + B$	$F = A\bar{B}$ MINUS 1	$F = A\bar{B}$
L	L	H	H	F = 1	F = MINUS 1 (2's COMP)	F = ZERO
L	H	L	L	$F = \overline{A + B}$	$F = A$ PLUS $(A + \bar{B})$	$F = A$ PLUS $(A + \bar{B})$ PLUS 1
L	H	L	H	$F = \bar{B}$	F = AB PLUS $(A + \bar{B})$	F = AB PLUS $(A + \bar{B})$ PLUS 1
L	H	H	L	$F = A \oplus B$	F = A MINUS B MINUS 1	F = A MINUS B
L	H	H	H	$F = A + \bar{B}$	$F = A + \bar{B}$	$F = (A + \bar{B})$ PLUS 1
H	L	L	L	$F = \overline{A}B$	F = A PLUS (A + B)	F = A PLUS (A + B) PLUS 1
H	L	L	H	$F = A \oplus B$	F = A PLUS B	F = A PLUS B PLUS 1
H	L	H	L	F = B	$F = A\bar{B}$ PLUS (A + B)	$F = A\bar{B}$ PLUS (A + B) PLUS 1
H	L	H	H	F = A + B	F = (A + B)	F = (A + B) PLUS 1
H	H	L	L	F = 0	F = A PLUS A*	F = A PLUS A PLUS 1
H	H	L	H	$F = A\bar{B}$	F = AB PLUS A	F = AB PLUS A PLUS 1
H	H	H	L	F = AB	$F = A\bar{B}$ PLUS A	$F = A\bar{B}$ PLUS A PLUS 1
H	H	H	H	F = A	F = A	F = A PLUS 1

TABLE 2

SELECTION				ACTIVE-HIGH DATA		
				M = H	M = L; ARITHMETIC OPERATIONS	
S3	S2	S1	S0	LOGIC FUNCTIONS	$\bar{C}_n$ = H (no carry)	$\bar{C}_n$ = L (with carry)
L	L	L	L	$F = \bar{A}$	F = A	F = A PLUS 1
L	L	L	H	$F = \overline{A + B}$	F = A + B	F = (A + B) PLUS 1
L	L	H	L	$F = \bar{A}B$	$F = A + \bar{B}$	$F = (A + \bar{B})$ PLUS 1
L	L	H	H	F = 0	F = MINUS 1 (2's COMPL)	F = ZERO
L	H	L	L	$F = \overline{AB}$	$F = A$ PLUS $A\bar{B}$	$F = A$ PLUS $A\bar{B}$ PLUS 1
L	H	L	H	$F = \bar{B}$	$F = (A + B)$ PLUS $A\bar{B}$	$F = (A + B)$ PLUS $A\bar{B}$ PLUS 1
L	H	H	L	$F = A \oplus B$	F = A MINUS B MINUS 1	F = A MINUS B
L	H	H	H	$F = A\bar{B}$	$F = A\bar{B}$ MINUS 1	$F = A\bar{B}$
H	L	L	L	$F = \bar{A} + B$	F = A PLUS AB	F = A PLUS AB PLUS 1
H	L	L	H	$F = \overline{A \oplus B}$	F = A PLUS B	F = A PLUS B PLUS 1
H	L	H	L	F = B	$F = (A + \bar{B})$ PLUS AB	$F = (A + \bar{B})$ PLUS AB PLUS 1
H	L	H	H	F = AB	F = AB MINUS 1	F = AB
H	H	L	L	F = 1	F = A PLUS A*	F = A PLUS A PLUS 1
H	H	L	H	$F = A + \bar{B}$	F = (A + B) PLUS A	F = (A + B) PLUS A PLUS 1
H	H	H	L	F = A + B	$F = (A + \bar{B})$ PLUS A	$F = (A + \bar{B})$ PLUS A PLUS 1
H	H	H	H	F = A	F = A MINUS 1	F = A

*Each bit is shifted to the next more significant position.

Fig. 17-1 74181 ALU truth tables for negative and positive logic. *(Courtesy Texas Instruments, Inc.)*

mine what connections should be made to the M and C_n inputs.

b. For an A input of 0110 and a B input of 0011, predict the output word produced for each of the 16 possible arithmetic instructions on the S inputs, with no carry-in.

2. Verifying the arithmetic function predictions.

  a. To check your predictions, make the proper connections to a 74181 for arithmetic operations.

  b. Apply the specified input words, and observe the output word for each instruction.

3. Determine the proper connections to perform arithmetic operations by using a carry-in.

  a. Using an A input of 0110 and a B input of 0011, predict the output word produced for each of the 16 arithmetic operations, *with* a carry-in.

b. Make the proper connections and verify your predictions.

MODULE 4   Cascading 74181 ALUs.

1. Draw a schematic showing how two 74181 ALUs can be cascaded to perform arithmetic or logic functions on two 8-bit binary words in positive logic.

  a. Is C_{n+4} an active high or active low output?

  b. For positive logic, is C_n active high or active low?

2. Connect the two 74181 ALUs as drawn.

  a. Try adding two 8-bit words to test your circuit in arithmetic mode.

  b. Try ORing two 8-bit words to test your circuit in logic mode.

MICROCOMPUTER PROJECT DOCUMENTATION

Documentation is a very important part of the development of any electronic project. Experts indicate that approximately 30 percent of the time spent in developing a successful product should be spent on documentation. This is especially true for any microcomputer project such as those in the rest of this book.

Document each laboratory as if you were giving it to your boss just before your yearly evaluation. Following are some recommended items to include in your documentation package for each project.

1. Schematic and description of hardware.
   a. The schematic should show the significant parts added to your microcomputer. In most cases the laboratory directions in the book show the schematics of the added hardware, so you just have to add the specific port addresses and pin numbers for your microcomputer.
   b. Describe how the hardware works. Explain what inputs are required to produce a particular output.
2. List of where everything is located.
   a. You should provide a memory map or list of memory locations used.
   b. Define the port addresses used for this project.
3. Description of what the program does (purpose).
   a. Where does the program get its data?
   b. How is data manipulated?
   c. Where is data sent?

Partial example: This program sends characters from a table in memory out bit 0 of port 0 at 300 baud with 1 stop bit.
4. Description of how the program works (algorithm).
   a. Flowcharts and/or word descriptions should be provided for the main program.
   b. Separate flowcharts and/or word descriptions should be added for significant subroutines.
5. Assembly language program.
   a. Each page should have the programmer's name, program title, and page number in one-of-four, two-of-four, three-of-four, or four-of-four format.
   b. Before the start of the program, there should be:
      (1) A list of EQUATES with descriptions.
      (2) A list of subroutines called.
   c. Each instruction or functional group of instructions should have a comment explaining what it does. Comments should not just repeat the instruction mnemonic.
   d. A section before each subroutine should tell for that subroutine:
      (1) Which registers are used.
      (2) Which flags are affected.
      (3) Other subroutines called.
Note: The monitor listing for your microcomputer is usually a good example of how to document your programs.

BINARY AND BCD ARITHMETIC WITH A MICROCOMPUTER

REFERENCES

Hall: pages 194–211.

User's handbook or assembly language programming manual for the microcomputer used.

OBJECTIVES

At the conclusion of this laboratory exercise, you should be able to:

1. Describe some of the instructions available in a microprocessor instruction set.
2. Write and test assembly language microcomputer programs to:
   a. Add or subtract two 8-bit binary numbers.
   b. Add two two-digit BCD numbers.
   c. Mask and move nibbles.
   d. Add two multiple-byte binary or BCD numbers.
   e. Multiply two 8-bit binary numbers by successive addition.

EQUIPMENT

1 Microcomputer with monitor program (examples are the MMD-I, SDK-85, MEK6800D2)

MATERIALS

5–10 Sheets of assembly language programming paper

PROCEDURE

INTRODUCTION In Experiment 17 we showed that an arithmetic logic unit (ALU) can perform a wide variety of operations on two binary words. The operation performed is determined by the binary-coded instruction applied to the instruction inputs.

As shown by the block diagrams in Hall, Figs. 8-1 and 8-3, the heart of a microprocessor or microcomputer is an ALU. The other parts of a microcomputer are registers and RAM, to store the operands and results of various operations; ROM or RAM, to store binary-coded instructions; input ports, to allow data from the outside to get in; output ports, to send data to the outside world; and three major buses, to link all these elements.

Having these elements linked with an ALU allows a programmed sequence of operations to be executed. Data can be input and operated on, and the results can be stored in memory (RAM or registers) or output. This first microprocessor experiment is intended to give a small glimpse of what you can program a microcomputer to do.

MODULE 1 A method for learning a new processor. When you are first learning about microprocessors or learning about one that is new to you, the following sequence of steps may help you get started.

1. Study the block diagram.
   a. Find out how many bits are in the data bus and how many in the address bus.
   b. Check how many accumulators the microprocessor has.
   c. Determine whether the device has internal registers or must always use external RAM for data storage.
   d. Does it have a stack pointer register?
   e. Does it have one or more index registers?
   f. Does it have an internal timer?
   g. Does it have built-in I/O ports?
2. Examine the instruction set to get an overview.
   a. How many addressing modes does the processor have?
   b. What instructions does it have for moving data between ports, registers, and memory?
   c. What arithmetic and logic instructions does it have? Look for AND, OR, XOR, add, subtract, compare, and rotate or shift instructions.

int./ext. clock
data bus -
address bus
memory mapped
   in
port decoding   ports
power supply
ACC.s
s P ?
I. R
Flags
addressing modes
  # instr.
  inter.
can buses be floating
      DMA

d. Look for jump or branch instructions, and find out what conditions can cause a jump or branch.

e. Look to see what instructions the processor has to call or branch to a subroutine.

3. Next obtain a single-board microcomputer or system using that microprocessor.

  a. Read the manual to learn commands to do the following:

  (1) Examine and change the contents of memory locations.

  (2) Examine and change the contents of registers or accumulators.

  (3) Examine flags or condition code registers.

  (4) Execute or run programs.

  b. Check the memory map for the board or system to find the addresses occupied by the monitor program.

  c. Find out which addresses contain RAM that you can use for programs.

  d. Find the addresses for input and output ports.

4. Perform a simple initial operation.

  a. Use the memory-examine-and-change command to load a few bytes of data into RAM.

  b. Then read them back to make sure they were written correctly.

5. Write, enter, execute, and verify a simple program as follows:

  a. Write a simple assembly language program for the microcomputer.

  b. Code the program into machine language.

  c. Load the machine code for the program into the system's RAM.

  d. Execute the program and examine the results, using the monitor commands.

6. Writing and testing more complex programs.

  a. Arithmetic programs are good to use for starting programs because they do not require any special input or output devices and because the results are easily verified.

  b. The remaining modules of this experiment are some suggested programs to help you become familiar with the operation of a single-board computer or system and to learn how simple arithmetic programs are written.

MODULE 2 Binary addition.

1. Defining the program problem.

  a. For the microcomputer available, plan, outline, or flowchart an assembly language program to add an 8-bit binary number stored at one RAM address to an 8-bit binary number stored at the next-higher address.

  b. Store the main part of the result in the next-higher address and any carry produced in the least significant bit of the address after that.

  c. Think about which instruction can be used to move a carry from the carry flip-flop to the least significant bit of the accumulator, so it can then be moved to memory.

2. Writing and coding the program.

  a. For writing this program, use assembly language programming paper.

b. Make sure that each part of the program is in the correct field, as shown in Hall, Fig. 8-19.

c. For each instruction, write a comment to explain for future reference what that instruction does.

d. It is very important to develop from the start an orderly, systematic way of writing programs. Programs scribbled on brown paper bags are very difficult to debug.

e. Assign addresses and machine codes to each instruction.

3. Testing the program.

  a. Enter the machine code in your system RAM.

  b. Run the program and check your results.

  c. Try adding two numbers that produce a carry and then two numbers that do not.

4. Questions:

  a. What are the largest numbers that can be added with this program?

  b. How can the program be modified to subtract two 8-bit binary numbers?

  c. In what form will the answer be if the result of the subtraction is negative?

MODULE 3 BCD addition.

1. Defining the program problem.

  a. Plan an assembly language program to add two two-digit BCD numbers to give a BCD result.

  b. The numbers to be added are stored in two successive memory locations.

  c. Store the BCD result at the next address and any resultant carry in the least significant bit of the next address.

2. In writing the program, consider the following:

  a. What conditions in BCD addition require a correction factor? [Review Hall, pages 179–180, if necessary.]

  b. What instruction will make this correction automatically, if required?

3. Enter and execute your program, and verify the results.

MODULE 4 Masking and moving nibbles.

1. Masking.

  a. ANDing an 8-bit binary number with 11110000 is sometimes referred to as *masking* the lower 4 bits (nibble).

  b. In what logic state will the lower 4 bits always be after this operation?

  c. What effect will this operation have on the upper 4 bits?

  d. Any number of bits in a word can be masked. With what word would you AND to mask the upper bit only?

2. Creating a program which masks and moves nibbles.

  a. Masking is often used with shift or rotate instructions to create an 8-bit word from two nibbles.

  b. Given a memory location containing the two nibbles W and X and another memory location containing nibbles Y and Z, write a program to produce the word XZ in a third memory location.

  c. Assemble and test your program.

MODULE 5 Multiple-byte addition.

1. Defining the program problem.
- **a.** Plan an assembly language program to add two 5-byte binary numbers.
- **b.** The least significant byte of one number is stored in a memory location, and the next 4 bytes are stored in ascending order in the next four locations.
- **c.** The other number is stored in the next five memory addresses with the least significant byte first.
- **d.** Store the result and any carry in the next six addresses after the second number's addresses.

2. In writing the program, consider the following:
- **a.** How can you "point" to the byte to be moved into the accumulator from memory, the byte to be added to the accumulator, and the memory location where the result will be stored?
- **b.** How can you keep track of how many bytes have been added?
- **c.** How do you make sure that any carry which results from adding, for example, the two least significant bytes is included when the next-higher bytes are added?

3. Testing the program.
- **a.** Enter and execute the program, and verify the results.
- **b.** How can this program be modified to add multiple-byte BCD numbers?

MODULE 6 Multiplication by successive addition.

1. Defining and writing the program.
- **a.** Write an assembly language program to multiply two 8-bit binary numbers.
- **b.** Use the methods of successive addition. [Review Hall, pages 187–188, if necessary.]

2. Testing the program.
- **a.** Enter and execute your program, and verify the results.
- **b.** If the multiplier and multiplicand each have 8 bits, what is the largest number of bits that the product can have?
- **c.** What is a major disadvantage of this method of multiplication?

MODULE 7 Debugging assembly language programs.

1. Most microcomputers intended for laboratory use have monitor programs that include software single-step, examine-register, and examine-memory commands.
- **a.** The single-step function allows you to execute one instruction of your program and return control to the monitor.
- **b.** You can then use the examine-register and examine-memory commands to see whether the instruction produced the desired effect.
- **c.** If it did, the single-step command can be used to execute the next instruction and to check the results in the registers and memory.
- **d.** Usually from this step-by-step analysis you can figure out the errors in your program.

2. If your microcomputer has the single-step, examine-memory, and examine-register commands:
- **a.** Introduce a small error such as a wrong bit of data, interchanged instructions, a jump to a wrong address, or omission of a branch or return instruction.
- **b.** Then use the debug procedure outlined above to locate and correct the error.

E X P E R I M E N T 19

POLLED KEYBOARD INPUT

REFERENCES

Hall: pages 211–212.

User's handbook or assembly language programming manual for the microcomputer used.

OBJECTIVES

At the conclusion of this laboratory exercise, you should be able to:

1. Write and test a program to read in parallel ASCII code from an encoded keyboard when a key-pressed strobe is present, mask the parity bit, and store the ASCII code in an array or a table in memory.
2. Write assembly language routines that use program loops for polled input to a microcomputer.
3. Write and test an assembly language program to insert the ASCII character for carriage return (CR) after every 80 characters if it has not been previously entered.
4. Write and test a short routine to convert the ASCII character codes for 0 to 9 and A to F to their 4-bit hexadecimal values.
5. Write assembly language routines that use compare and conditional jump or branch instructions.
6. Use the single-step and examine-register commands of a microcomputer to debug programs.

EQUIPMENT

1 Microcomputer with two 8-bit input ports

MATERIAL

1 Parallel-output, ASCII-encoded keyboard with key-pressed strobe (example: Jameco JE610)

If an encoded keyboard is not available, the data inputs can be simulated with eight single-pole, double-throw (SPDT) toggle switches. The key-pressed strobe can be simulated with a debounced pushbutton switch.

PROCEDURE

MODULE 1 A polled keyboard program.

1. Circuit description.
   a. Many computer-type keyboards have on-board encoder ICs that detect and debounce a key press and then give a 7- or 8-bit, parallel-output, ASCII code for the key pressed.
   b. In addition, the on-board encoder ICs such as the AY-5-2376 give out a pulse or key-pressed strobe to indicate when the valid ASCII character code for the key pressed is present on the parallel outputs.
   c. Figure 19-1 shows how these outputs can be connected to two microcomputer input ports.
      (1) The connections shown are for 7-bit, parallel-output ASCII plus a parity bit.
      (2) Assume the key-pressed strobe goes to a logic high when valid data is on the outputs of the keyboard.
2. Defining the problem. The purpose of this program is to:
   a. Read in parallel ASCII code from an encoded keyboard when a key-pressed strobe is present.
   b. Mask the parity bit.
   c. Put the ASCII code in an array in memory. An array is just an ordered set of data such as a list. In this case it simply means that the ASCII character codes will be placed in successive memory locations.
3. Breaking down the problem into a machine-independent task list or flowchart.
   a. To write all but the very simplest program, first list the tasks (jobs) that the program must perform. Each task can then be dealt with individually. In

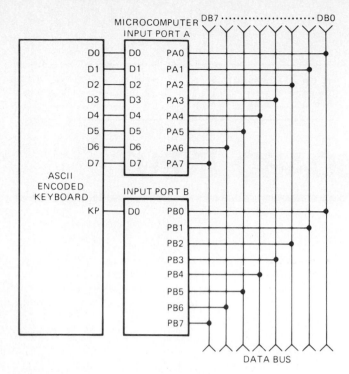

Fig. 19-1 The microcomputer port connections for an ASCII-encoded keyboard.

the long run, this method is much more effective than starting right off writing in assembly language.

  b. A list for this program might include:
  (1) Initialize the ports, if necessary.
  (2) Set the memory pointer to the starting address of the array.
  (3) Detect the key-pressed strobe.
  (4) Read in the ASCII.
  (5) Mask the parity bit (make the parity bit always zero).
  (6) Store the ASCII in an array or a table.
  (7) Increment the memory pointer.
  (8) Detect the end of the key-pressed strobe.
  (9) Loop back to detect the next key-pressed strobe.
  c. Note that the list of tasks is machine-independent. This means that it does not use the mnemonics for any specific microcomputer. Therefore, it can be easily expanded into the assembly language of any machine.
  d. Some programmers write this list in the form of a flowchart such as those shown in the references. Draw a flowchart for this program.
4. Using your flowchart and/or list to write the assembly language program.
  a. Think carefully about the instruction or group of instructions that will accomplish each task in your list or box in your flowchart.
  b. Write the instructions sequentially on programming paper. After every 16 or so instructions, put in three or four NOP instructions. If you accidentally leave out an instruction, you only have to move a few instructions to insert it rather than having to shift the rest of your program.

  c. Include comments that tell what each instruction or functional group of instructions does.
  d. For the program in this module, consider the following points:
  (1) The ports of most programmable I/O port ICs are automatically set as inputs after a reset instruction. If this is the case for the microcomputer you are using, you will not have to initialize them.
  (2) How can the parity bit be made to be always zero (masked) without the other 7 bits being affected?
  (3) Why is it necessary to detect the end of one key-pressed strobe before looping back to detect the key-pressed strobe high again?
  e. After you have written all the mnemonics for the program, check carefully that you have not left out any instructions. Then write the machine code for each instruction.
5. Testing the program.
  a. Enter the machine-code program in your microcomputer RAM and test it.
  b. Debug the program until it works correctly.
  c. How would you alter this program to work with an active low key-pressed strobe?
  d. The process of testing a signal line over and over until some desired state is present is called *polling.*

MODULE 2 A subroutine to display the ASCII code for each key pressed.

1. If your microcomputer has on-board, seven-segment displays and a monitor program with a readily accessible display subroutine, rewrite your polled keyboard program so that the ASCII code for each key is displayed as the key is pressed.
2. Assemble, enter, test, and debug your modified program.

MODULE 3 An ASCII-to-hexidecimal code conversion program.

1. Write a job list and/or flowchart for a short program to convert the ASCII character codes for 0 to 9 and A to F to their 4-bit hexadecimal values.
  a. The character to be converted is initially in the accumulator.
  b. The presence of any ASCII character other than those for 0 to 9 and A to F should cause a jump (branch) to an error routine.
  (1) What are the ASCII character codes for 0 to 9 and A to F?
  (2) What are the illegal ASCII character code ranges for this program?

	Carry	Zero
A = Compared	0	1
A > Compared	0	0
A < Compared	1	0

Fig. 19-2 The effect of compare instructions on 8080A or 8085A zero and carry flags.

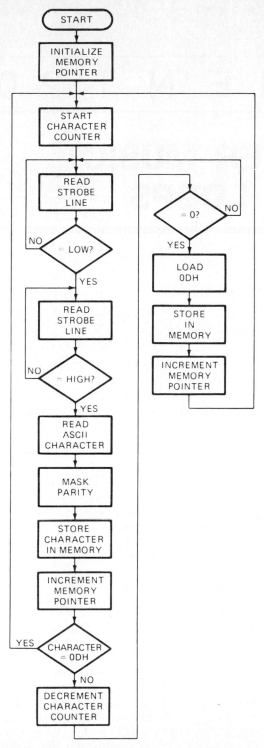

Fig. 19-3 A flowchart for the automatic-carriage-return program.

2. Write a well-documented assembly language program for this conversion, after noting the following. This program is a good exercise in using compare and conditional jump or branch instructions. Compare instructions do not affect the data being examined; they just set flags according to the results of the comparison. For 8080A and 8085A processors, the zero and carry flags are used to indicate whether the contents of the accumulator are equal to, less than, or greater than a compared byte. The chart in Fig. 19-2 shows how the 8080A and 8085A flags will be set for each of these cases.

3. Assemble the program, enter it into your microcomputer, and test it.

MODULE 4 An automatic-carriage-return program.

1. Figure 19-3 is a flowchart for a program to insert the ASCII code for carriage return (CR) after 80 characters have been entered from the keyboard.
   a. Any time that a CR is sent from the keyboard, the character counter is started over.
   b. One purpose of such a program is to enter text into memory, from which it can either be used to create a display on a CRT monitor or be sent to a printer.

2. Write a well-documented assembly language program for this job. To simplify testing, reduce to five the character count before each CR.

3. Assemble the program, enter it into your microcomputer, and test it.

MICROCOMPUTER MUSIC AND TIMING LOOPS

REFERENCES

Hall: pages 212–216.

Assembly language programming manual for the microcomputer used.

User's handbook for the microcomputer used.

OBJECTIVES

At the conclusion of this laboratory exercise, you should be able to:

1. Use delay loops and nested delay loops.
2. Write a program to output a square-wave pulse train of a given frequency (musical tone).
3. Create a program to output a pulse train for a given time (musical note).
4. Devise a program to output a series of different-frequency pulses (musical song).

EQUIPMENT

1 Microcomputer with latched 8-bit output port
1 5-V power supply
1 Oscilloscope

MATERIALS

1 2N3904 (or equivalent) NPN transistor
1 2.2-kΩ resistor
1 100-Ω resistor
1 Audio test speaker

PROCEDURE

MODULE 1 A microcomputer program to produce a square-wave pulse train of a given frequency and demonstrate it as a musical tone.

1. Planning a short assembly language program to produce a 7040-Hz square-wave pulse train on the least significant bit of an output port on a microcomputer.
   a. Draw a section of the desired waveform.
      (1) For how many microseconds is the waveform high during each cycle?
      (2) For how many microseconds is it low?
   b. As perhaps you can see, this waveform can be produced by outputting a 1 to the LSB position of the port, delaying for the desired time high, outputting a 0 to the LSB position, and delaying for the desired time low. The procedure is repeated to give a continuous pulse train.
   c. Draw a flowchart for this program.
2. Rough out the assembly language program for the pulse train as follows:
   a. Remember to initialize the output port, if required.
   b. Recall that in any program using subroutines, the stack pointer must be initialized before the subroutine is called.
   c. If the accumulator is initially loaded with 01H, then the complement accumulator instruction can be used to change the LSB for each half cycle.
   d. A subroutine delay loop such as that in Hall, Fig. 8-25b, can be used.
   e. After the program is roughed out, the exact delay constant can be calculated for your microcomputer based on its clock frequency and the number of clock cycles required for each instruction.
3. Use the following procedure to calculate the delay constant.
   a. Find the number of clock cycles required for each instruction in the delay loop, as shown in Hall, Fig. 8-23. The number of clock cycles or states is shown for 8080A and 8085A instructions in Hall, Table 8-2; for the MC6800 in Hall, Table 10-1; and for the 6502 in Hall, Table 10-2.
   b. Find the period (1 divided by the frequency) of your microcomputer clock.

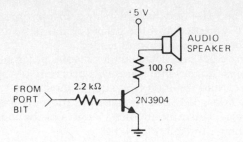

Fig. 20-1 A transistor-buffered audio test speaker circuit.

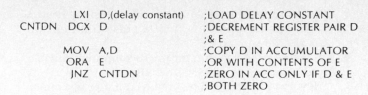

```
         LXI   D,(delay constant)    ;LOAD DELAY CONSTANT
CNTDN   DCX   D                      ;DECREMENT REGISTER PAIR D
                                     ;& E
        MOV   A,D                    ;COPY D IN ACCUMULATOR
        ORA   E                      ;OR WITH CONTENTS OF E
        JNZ   CNTDN                  ;ZERO IN ACC ONLY IF D & E
                                     ;BOTH ZERO
```

Fig. 20-2 An 8080A or 8085A assembly language routine for a delay loop using a 16-bit register pair.

c. Add the number of cycles required for instructions that will only be executed once per loop. Multiply the number of cycles times the time per cycle for your microcomputer (clock period). This can be thought of as a fixed *overhead* time.

d. Add the number of cycles for the instructions that will be repeated each time the delay loop executes. Multiply this total by the time per cycle for your microcomputer. This gives the time for once through the actual loop.

e. To find the delay constant, subtract the overhead time from the desired delay time and divide the result by the delay time produced by each execution of the actual loop:

$$\text{Delay constant} = \frac{\text{total time} - \text{overhead}}{\text{loop cycles} \times \text{clock period}}$$

f. Make sure to convert the delay constant to hexadecimal for entry into your microcomputer.

4. Testing the program both visually and aurally.

a. Enter the program in your microcomputer RAM and run it.

b. Observe the output on the least significant bit of the output port with an oscilloscope or frequency counter.

c. You may need to fine-tune the delay constant to get the frequency exact.

d. Connect the transistor buffer circuit shown in Fig. 20-1 with an audio test speaker to the LSB of the output port. You should hear a sound that is an "A" in music.

5. Modifying the output to obtain eight different frequencies or octaves.

a. Substitute the increment accumulator instruction in place of the complement accumulator instruction you used in this program.

b. Connect the test-speaker buffer input to each of the output port bits, one at a time.

c. What is the relationship between the frequencies you hear? (If you cannot hear the relationship, use an oscilloscope to determine it.)

d. How does the program produce all these different frequencies?

MODULE 2 Longer delay times—nested loops.

1. In many cases, such as for making lower frequencies, a longer delay is needed than can be achieved by counting down a single 8-bit register or memory location. One way to do this is to count down a 16-bit register if the microcomputer has one.

For 8080A and 8085A processors, the DCX instruction decrements the indicated 16-bit register. However, the DCX instruction does not set the zero flag, so JNZ cannot be used directly to tell whether the countdown is complete. Figure 20-2 is an 8080A or 8085A assembly language routine that shows how ORing the two halves of a register pair can be used with countdown to test for 0 in a 16-bit register pair. The accumulator will be 0 only if the contents of D and E are both 0.

2. Another method of creating longer delays is with nested loops. In this case, a register or memory location is counted down not just once, as in the program of Fig. 20-2, but *N* times. Another register or memory location is used to keep track of how many times the first register or memory location has been counted down. The flowchart in Fig. 20-3 shows how nested loops are done.

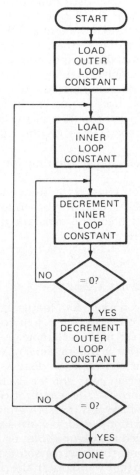

Fig. 20-3 A flowchart of nested loops.

3. Write an assembly language program using nested delay loops to produce a 2.5-Hz pulse train on the LSB of an output port.
4. Enter your program into the microcomputer, and use an oscilloscope to observe the output.

   How long a delay will be produced if a programmer accidentally jumps back and reloads the inner delay constant again after decrementing it? Watch for this common error.
5. Several delay loops can be nested to create even longer delays. Draw a flowchart for three nested loops.

MODULE 3 A musical note.

1. A musical note is just a tone, such as the sounds the Module 1 program produced, which is turned on and then off. Nested countdown or delay loops can be used to produce a musical note. The inner loop determines the frequency of the note, as was done in Module 1. The outer loop counts how many cycles of the tone have been output. For example, suppose the inner loop is set to produce a 1-kHz tone and you want it to be on for 0.2 s. Each cycle of the 1-kHz tone takes 1 ms, so 200 cycles is equal to the desired on time of 0.2 s, or 200 ms. A second register or memory location is initially loaded with 200_{10} (C8H). After each cycle of the 1-kHz tone, this counter is decremented. If the count is not down to zero, then the program should loop back and output another cycle of the 1-kHz tone. If the count is down to zero, the program should turn the output off.
2. Draw a flowchart for a program to produce a note of 7040 Hz that lasts 0.2 s and, after 0.2 s off, repeats.
3. Write the assembly language program for the on-and-off 7040-Hz note, and test it with the buffered speaker. If you use the increment accumulator instruction, then you should hear the note "A" for each of eight different octaves on the eight output port lines.
   a. How can you change the time for which the note plays?
   b. How can you change the frequency of the note?
   c. Does the delay constant chosen for the frequency of the note affect the constant required for the time that the note plays?

MODULE 4 Playing a song.

1. The program you wrote for Module 3 produces a one-note song. In other words, it just repeats the same note with a rest after each note. An improvement would be to have the program create a series of different notes. This can easily be done as follows:
   a. Store the delay constant for each note and the delay constant for the length of each note in sequential memory locations. (A group of sequential memory locations used to store data such as this is often called a *look-up table*, or just a table.)
   b. To play a song, the delay constants for one note are read from memory and put in the proper registers.

c. When the note is finished, a memory pointer is incremented and the delay constants for the next note are read out and loaded.
2. Figure 20-4 is a flowchart for a song program. Write and test an assembly language program for this flowchart. Note the following suggestions:
   a. It is a good idea to calculate the note-frequency delay constants for the 12 notes of the top octave shown in Hall, Fig. 4-14.
   b. The delay constants for notes in lower octaves will be approximate multiples of these.

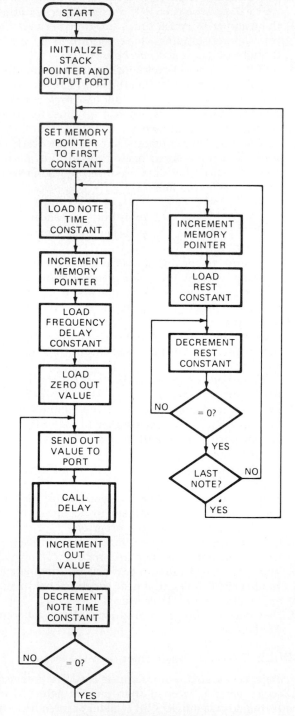

Fig. 20-4 A flowchart for a song.

   c. The length of note delay constant can then be calculated for each note.

   d. For your first song choose just a 5- to 10-note sequence. For example, you might use the following 5-note frequencies for an interesting song theme: 7040, 7902, 6272, 3136, and 4699 Hz.

3. Another approach to playing music with a microcomputer is to use a top-octave synthesizer and dividers to produce all the required note frequencies at once. CMOS transmission gate switches, such as the CD4016, with their enable inputs tied to output port lines can be used to gate the desired notes into an op amp mixer. This approach is *polyphonic*, which means that several notes can be played at once. The microcomputer controls which notes get played and their timing.

MEASURING REACTION TIME WITH A MICROCOMPUTER

REFERENCES

Hall: pages 212–216.

Assembly language programming manual for the microcomputer used.

User's manual for the microcomputer used.

OBJECTIVES

At the conclusion of this laboratory exercise, you should be able to use a microcomputer delay loop and counter to measure the time between two events.

EQUIPMENT

1 Microcomputer with one output port line and one input port line

MATERIALS

1 7400 quad two-input NAND gate

1 LED
2 2.2-kΩ resistors
1 150-Ω resistor
1 Spring-loaded, pushbutton switch, single-pole double-throw switch

PROCEDURE

Experiment 20 used delay loops to time the output of pulses. Here you measure the time between two events by counting the number of times that a delay loop executes during the time between the two events. You measure the time it takes you to press a pushbutton switch after you see an LED light.

MODULE 1

1. If they are not already built as a laboratory module, build and test the switch debouncer and the LED drive circuits shown in Fig. 21-1.
2. Connect the debounced switch to an input port line and the LED driver to an output port line.

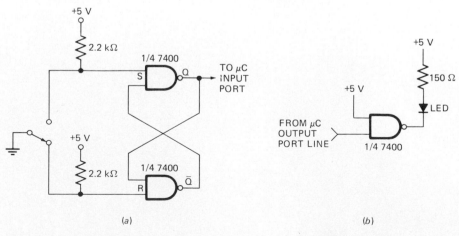

Fig. 21-1 (a) NAND gate switch debouncer. (b) LED driver circuit.

3. Draw a flowchart for an assembly language program to:
   a. Initialize ports.
   b. Wait 2 s for you to get ready.
   c. Turn on the LED.
   d. Execute a 1-ms delay loop over and over until a high from the switch debouncer is detected, which indicates that you have pressed the button.
   e. Keep a count in memory of how many times the 1-ms delay loop executes before the button is pressed.
   f. Display the count (number of milliseconds) on the LED of your microcomputer if the display routine is readily accessible.
4. Write an assembly language program for the flowchart.
5. Enter the program into the microcomputer and test it. To get a true test of your reaction time, have some- one else start the program running so you can con- centrate on pushing the button as soon as you see the light.

MODULE 2 Averaging several trials.

1. Rewrite your program so that it:
   a. Measures your reaction time for eight successive trials and stores the results in eight successive memory locations.
   b. Adds the eight results.
   c. Divides the sum by 8 to get the average for eight trials. *Note:* Dividing a binary number by 8 can be done by simply shifting it right three bit positions and masking the upper 3 bits.
2. Enter the program in your microcomputer and test it. Is the average value comparable with the individ- ual results you got?

LIGHTING AN LED MATRIX: TIMED OUTPUT AND MULTIPLEXING

REFERENCES

Hall: pages 117–119, 212–216.

Assembly language programming manual for the microcomputer used.

User's manual for the microcomputer used.

OBJECTIVES

At the conclusion of this laboratory exercise, you should be able to:

1. Use delay and nested delay loops for the timed output of data.
2. Demonstrate the use of a rotate instruction.
3. Use a look-up table and memory pointer to output a sequence of data bytes.
4. Show how any desired pattern can be displayed on an 8×8 LED matrix by multiplexing.

EQUIPMENT

1 Microcomputer with two 8-bit latched output ports
1 5-V power supply

MATERIALS

1 8×8 LED matrix with driver transistors
Parts for matrix:
    64 LEDs, minimum 25-mA capacity
    64 150-Ω, 0.25-W resistors
    8 2N2907 transistors
    8 2N3904 transistors
    8 2N2222 transistors
    16 1-kΩ resistors
    8 10-kΩ resistors
    8 2.2-kΩ resistors
    1 4×6 in piece of 100-mil vector board

PROCEDURE

MODULE 1 Programming a microcomputer to light and blink a specified LED in an 8×8 LED matrix.

1. By the end of this experiment, you should be able to display any pattern you desire on the LED matrix. However, as with any system or program, you should start with some simple experiments to get the feel of it and then build up to a "Times Square" display.
2. Study the schematic in Fig. 22-1 for the LED matrix and driver transistors. The matrix is made up of horizontal rows and vertical columns. Note that to light an LED, both the row driver transistor supplying the current to its anode and the column driver transistor sinking the current from its cathode must be on.
   a. Is a logic high or a logic low required on a bit of port A to turn on a row?
   b. What logic level is required from a bit of port B to turn on a column?
   c. What word should be output to port A and what word to port B to light the LED in the upper right corner of the matrix?
   d. What word should be output to each port to light the entire top row of LEDs?
   e. What word should be output to each port to light the entire leftmost column of LEDs?
3. Lighting an LED.
   a. Determine from your instructor or from the user's manual for your microcomputer the sequence of instructions required to initialize the ports for output operations.
   b. Write and test an assembly language program to light the LED in the upper right corner of the matrix.
4. Making an LED blink.
   a. When the program to light the upper right LED works correctly, add a delay routine to turn the LED on for 0.5 s and off for 0.5 s.
   b. Assign addresses for the delay routine far enough into memory to be out of the way of future additions and modifications.

MODULE 2 Programming a microcomputer to produce rotating patterns of lighted LEDs in an 8×8 LED matrix.

1. Rewrite the program of Module 1, section 4, to light

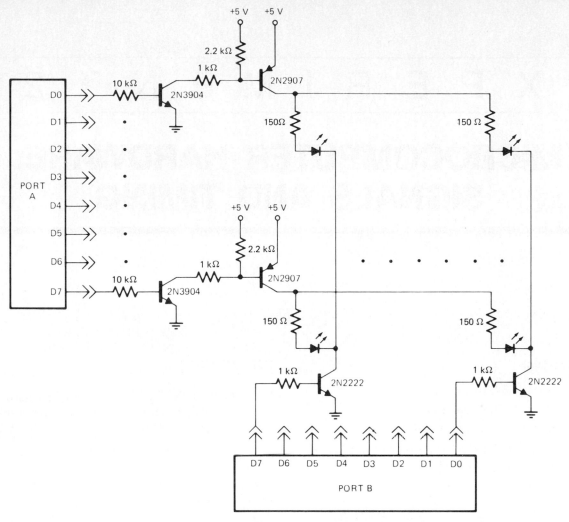

Fig. 22-1 A schematic for an 8 × 8 LED matrix with driver transistors.

single LEDs in sequence according to the following directions:

a. After each 0.5 s, the lighted LED shifts down one place.

b. When the lighting reaches the bottom LED of the matrix, it returns to the top and starts over.

2. Lighting groups of LEDs in sequence.

a. What small modification can you make to the program in step 1 so that an entire row of LEDs lights sequentially from top to bottom of the matrix and then repeats?

b. How would you modify the program so that the LEDs only in columns 0, 2, 4, and 6 light sequentially?

3. Try the three modifications to your program.

MODULE 3 Programming a microcomputer to display letters and numbers in an 8 × 8 LED matrix by using multiplexing.

1. Producing any desired pattern on this matrix:

a. The pattern of lighted LEDs desired in the top row is sent to the columns from the B port.

b. A word is sent to the A port to light the top row.

c. After a delay, the pattern of LEDs desired in the next row down is sent to the columns from the B

port. Then a word is sent to the A port to light this next row.

d. Each row is lighted with the desired pattern, one after another, until all have been lighted.

e. After the bottom row is lighted, the program loops back and steps down through the rows again.

f. The patterns for the rows are stored in eight successive memory locations.

2. Draw a flowchart for a program to display the letter X on the matrix.

3. Write and test the assembly language program for this flowchart.

4. Determining the optimum rate for multiplexing.

a. If you use a long delay time for each row (0.5 s), when you run the program you can see this multiplexing in slow motion.

b. When the program steps through the pattern correctly, keep decreasing the delay loop time constant until the display appears continuously lighted (does not blink).

c. How fast does the multiplexing have to be for this to happen? (Use your delay constant to calculate the optimum multiplexing frequency.)

5. How could you modify this program to display a series of letters or numbers, one after the other?

MICROCOMPUTER HARDWARE: SIGNALS AND TIMING

REFERENCES

For the 8080A: Hall: pages 222–228.

For the 8085A: Hall: pages 228–235.

For the 6800: Hall: pages 256–278.

User's manual for the microcomputer used.

Logic analyzer: Hall: pages 156–159.

OBJECTIVES

At the conclusion of this laboratory exercise, you should be able to:

1. Equate the ICs on a printed-circuit board with their schematic representations.
2. Observe the address-, data-, and control-bus signals of a microcomputer as it executes a simple instruction.

EQUIPMENT

1 Single-board microcomputer or system
1 Dual-trace oscilloscope
1 Power supply
1 Logic analyzer (optional)

MATERIALS

1 40-pin glomper clip (type with a metal spring and hinge pin is recommended)

For the 8080A or 8085A single-stepper:

1 7400 NAND gate
1 74121 monostable multivibrator
1 100-pF capacitor
1 10-kΩ resistor
2 1-kΩ resistors
1 Spring-loaded SPDT switch

PROCEDURE

INTRODUCTION Because of the many hardware differences among microprocessors, it is necessary to give a separate procedure module for each of three common microcomputers, the 8080A, 8085A, and 6800. If you are not working with one of these, use Modules 1 to 3 as models to devise a procedure for the machine you are using. For example, the Z80 is similar to the 8080A, and the 6502 is similar to the 6800.

MODULE 1 Microcomputer hardware.

1. Read the reference material, and study the schematic for your microcomputer.
   a. Find the major parts such as the microprocessor, clock generator, ROM, RAM, address decoders, address-bus buffers, data-bus buffers, and I/O ports.
   b. Look at the printed-circuit board in your microcomputer, and identify the ICs that perform these functions.
2. Proceed to the appropriate module for your microcomputer:
   a. 8080A: Module 2, then Module 3.
   b. 8085A: Module 4, then Module 3.
   c. 6800: Module 5.

MODULE 2 The 8080A microcomputer.

1. Supply voltages.
   a. Put a 40-pin glomper clip carefully on the 8080A, and turn on power to the board.
   b. How many supply voltages does the 8080A require?
   c. Measure and record the supply voltages.
2. Clock signals.
   a. How many clock signals does the 8080A require?
   b. Observe these clock signals with a dual-trace oscilloscope. (Be careful not to short-circuit the

glomper-clip pins when attaching the oscilloscope probe.)

c. What frequency is Φ1?

d. What frequency is Φ2?

e. What are the voltage levels for these waveforms?

f. Are the clock signals TTL-compatible?

g. Sketch the waveforms and compare them with those in the reference.

h. Why is it important that the clock edges not overlap?

3. Some control-signal waveforms under monitor program execution.

a. Predict the logic levels that should be present on the RESET, INT, INTE, WAIT, READY, and HLDA pins of an 8080A during normal operation. (Record your predictions.)

b. Press the reset button so that your microcomputer executes its monitor program.

c. Measure and record the logic levels on these pins to check your predictions.

4. Observing the timing sequence for an instruction cycle by using a single-instruction program.

a. The elusive SYNC signal.

(1) Use an oscilloscope to observe the SYNC signal coming from the 8080A.

(2) It is difficult to get a stable trace of more than one pulse of this signal because it does not usually come at fixed intervals.

b. The one-instruction program.

(1) To get a good picture of the SYNC signal and others, enter the following one-instruction program in RAM and run it:

HERE: JMP HERE.

(2) This program cycles the microcomputer in a tight loop so that the signals repeat at regular intervals.

c. The SYNC and Φ2 relationship.

(1) With this program running, observe the SYNC and Φ2 signals.

(2) You may have to adjust the variable horizontal time/div control of the oscilloscope to get a clear, stable pattern.

(3) Sketch the relationship of SYNC to Φ2.

d. The STSTB, SYNC, and Φ2 relationship.

(1) Observe the SYNC signal from the 8080A and the STSTB signal from the 8224.

(2) Sketch the relationship of these signals.

(3) What is the purpose of the STSTB signal?

e. Data-bus contents with STSTB low.

(1) With the oscilloscope, determine the logic level on each of the eight data lines when STSTB is low.

(2) The word present should be either A2H (the status word for an instruction fetch) or 82H (the status word for a memory read).

f. Data bus with memory read low (instruction cycle).

(1) The jump instruction is a 3-byte instruction which requires three memory reads to execute once.

(2) Predict the contents of the data bus during each of these three reads from memory.

(3) With the oscilloscope, observe Φ2 and one of the data lines that changes during program execution.

(4) How many clock cycles are needed to fetch and execute this instruction? (How many clock cycles occur before the pattern on the data line repeats?)

(5) Measure T_{DS2}, the time that data is present before the next rising edge of Φ2.

5. Single-stepping. Use the procedure in Module 3 to single-step the 8080A.

6. Logic analyzer.

a. If you have a logic analyzer, the single-step circuit may not be needed.

b. The analyzer can be clocked on the MEM R signal from the 8228 and set to start taking samples (trigger) when the first address of a program is present on the address bus. The logic analyzer trace then shows the series of addresses and the series of bytes read in from memory to the 8080A.

MODULE 3   Single-stepping on 8080A or 8085A.

1. As explained in the reference, an 8080A or 8085A can be single-stepped from machine cycle to machine cycle by inserting wait states. The circuit shown in Fig. 23-1 can be used to do this.

a. The output of this circuit is normally low. What effect does this low on its READY input have on an 8080A or 8085A?

b. When the monostable is triggered, it produces an output high pulse of a few hundred nanoseconds. This is long enough for the 8080A or 8085A to finish one machine cycle and start the next.

c. During which state of a machine cycle will the 8080A or 8085A enter a wait state?

d. What conditions are on the data and address bus during a wait state?

e. Since the processor can keep inserting wait states forever and since the contents of the buses are held stable during a wait state, these contents can be read 1 bit at a time with an oscilloscope, a voltmeter, or a logic probe.

2. Build the single-step circuit. (Note that it is connected differently to the 8080A than to the 8085A.)

a. For the 8080A, connect the output of the single-stepper to the RDYIN input of the 8224 in your microcomputer.

b. For the 8085A, connect the output of the single-stepper directly to the READY pin of the 8085A.

3. Using the single-stepper.

a. Press the reset button.

b. Measure the logic levels on the address bus and the data bus.

(1) The address bus should show 0000H.

(2) The data bus should show the code for the first instruction of the monitor program for your microcomputer.

c. Toggle the single-step switch, and recheck the address- and data-bus contents.

(1) The address bus should show 0001H.

(2) The data bus should show the code for the next instruction or data in the monitor program.

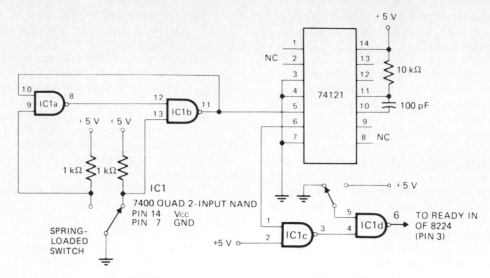

Fig. 23-1 A single-stepper circuit for 8080A and 8085A systems.

4. Additional notes regarding single-stepper application:
   a. LEDS with driver transistors can be connected to the data bus to more easily monitor the data-bus contents as you single-step through a program.
   b. This single-stepping technique is powerful for debugging hardware problems in a microcomputer.

MODULE 4 The 8085A microcomputer.

1. Supply voltages.
   a. Put a 40-pin glomper clip gently on the 8085A, and turn on the power to the board.
   b. How many supply voltages does the 8085A require?
   c. Measure and record the supply voltages.
2. Clock signals.
   a. How is the clock signal for the 8085A produced?
   b. Observe the clock output with an oscilloscope. (Be careful not to short-circuit the glomper-clip pins as you attach the oscilloscope probes.)
   c. Calculate the frequency of the clock.
3. Observing some control-signal waveforms under monitor program execution.
   a. Predict the logic levels that should be present on the INTR, INTA, RST 5.5, RST 6.5, RST 7.5, TRAP, READY, HOLD, HLDA, RESET IN, and RESET OUT pins of the 8085A during operation of a simple program. Record your predictions.
   b. Press the reset button so that your microcomputer executes its monitor program.
   c. Measure and record the logic levels on these pins to check your predictions.
4. Timing sequence under execution of a single-instruction program.
   a. The elusive ALE.
      (1) An important signal for the 8085A is ALE. Observe this signal.
      (2) It is difficult to get a stable trace of this signal for more than one or two pulses because it does not occur at fixed intervals.
   b. The one-instruction program.

(1) To get a good picture of this signal and others, enter the following one-instruction program in RAM and run it:

HERE: JMP HERE

(2) This cycles the microcomputer in a tight loop so that the signals repeat at regular intervals close enough together to be seen on an oscilloscope.
   c. The clock-ALE relationship.
      (1) With this program running, observe the clock and the ALE signals.
      (2) You may have to adjust the variable horizontal time/div to get a clear, stable trace. Adjust for 9 or 10 ALE pulses on the screen.
      (3) Note that the ALE pulses are not evenly spaced.
      (4) Sketch the relationship between the clock and ALE.
      (5) After how many clock cycles does the pattern of ALE pulses repeat? (How many clock cycles does the JMP instruction require?)
   d. Observing the relationships of control-bus signals during execution of a single instruction.
      (1) What is the purpose of the ALE signal?
      (2) During which state of a machine cycle does it occur?
      (3) How many machine cycles does the JMP instruction require?
      (4) How many states (clock cycles) are in each machine cycle?
      (5) From these facts, identify the starting point for execution of this instruction on your sketch of clock and ALE.
      (6) Observe and draw the $\overline{RD}$ pulses, the $IO/\overline{M}$ line, $S1$, and $S0$.
      (7) What operation do the states of these lines indicate is occurring?
   e. Observing the relationship of control-bus signals to data-bus contents during a read operation.
      (1) Predict the contents of the address and data buses for each state during execution of the

JMP HERE instruction. Remember that *A0* through *A7* are multiplexed on the data bus, so these lines will contain both addresses and data.

(2) Observe ALE and AD0.

(3) What levels are present on AD0 during the three ALE pulses of each execution?

(4) Compare these with your predictions.

(5) Observe the $\overline{RD}$ and AD0 signals.

(6) What levels are present on AD0 during the three $\overline{RD}$ pulses of each execution?

(7) Compare this with your predictions.

5. Single-stepping. Use the procedure in Module 3 to single-step the 8085A.

6. Logic analyzer.

    a. If you have a logic analyzer, the single-step circuit may not be needed.

    b. The analyzer can be clocked on $\overline{RD}$ from the 8085A and set to start taking samples (trigger) when the first address of a program is present on the address bus. The analyzer trace will show the sequence of memory addresses and the series of data bytes read in from memory or ports as the program executes.

MODULE 5   The 6800 microcomputer.

1. Supply voltages.

    a. Put a 40-pin glomper clip carefully on the 6800.

    b. How many supply voltages does the 6800 require?

    c. Measure and record the supply voltages.

2. Clock signals.

    a. How many clock signals does the 6800 require?

    b. With an oscilloscope, observe the clock signals.

       (1) Are they TTL-compatible?

       (2) What is the period of each?

       (3) What is the frequency of each?

    c. Draw a timing diagram showing the relationship of these clock signals, and compare it with that in the reference.

    d. Why is it important that these clock edges not overlap?

3. Some control signals.

    a. Predict the logic levels that should be present on the $\overline{RESET}$, $\overline{NMI}$, $\overline{HALT}$, $\overline{IRQ}$, TSC, and BA pins of the 6800 during simple program execution.

    b. Press the reset button so that your microcomputer executes its monitor program.

    c. Measure the logic levels on these pins to check your predictions.

    d. Observe the DBE signal. To what other signal is this almost identical?

4. Observing the timing sequence for an instruction cycle by using a single-instruction program.

    a. The elusive data-bus signals.

       (1) With an oscilloscope, observe the signal on the data-bus *D0* pin.

       (2) It is difficult to get a stable trace of this signal because the pulses are not occurring at regular intervals.

    b. The single-instruction program.

       (1) To get a good picture of this signal and others, enter the following one-instruction program in RAM at address 0000H and run it:

          7E 00 00 HERE: JMP HERE

       (2) This cycles the microcomputer in a tight loop so that the signals repeat at regular intervals often enough to produce a stable display.

    c. Predicting the data- and address-bus contents for an instruction cycle.

       (1) The JMP instruction is a 3-byte instruction requiring three memory read operations.

       (2) Predict the contents of the address and data buses during each of the three reads from memory.

       (3) Note that *A0* is high only once during each execution of this instruction.

    d. Verifying the relationship of Φ1 and *A0*.

       (1) Observe the Φ1 clock and *A0* with a dual-trace oscilloscope.

       (2) Trigger on the rising edge of Φ1.

       (3) How many clock cycles are required for each execution of this instruction?

       (4) How long after Φ1 goes high does *A0* go high (T_{AD})?

    e. Measuring the access time for a RAM read operation

       (1) Leave one probe on Φ1, and move the other to one of the data bits that goes high only once during execution of this instruction.

       (2) How long after Φ1 goes high does this data bit go high? This time is approximately equal to T_{AD} plus the T_{ACC} of the RAM being used.

       (3) Calculate the access time T_{ACC} for your RAM from the measurements just made.

    f. Observe and record the logic state of the $R/\overline{W}$ output of the 6800.

5. Idling the 6800.

    a. Tie pin 2 of the 6800 to ground.

    b. Into what state does this put the 6800?

    c. Observe and record the logic level on the BA pin.

    d. For what operation is this state used?

6. Logic analyzer. If you have a logic analyzer, it can be clocked on the falling edge of Φ2 and triggered on the first instruction word of the program being run. Then the analyzer will show the contents of the data and, if enough inputs are available, the address bus as the first section of the program executes.

MICROCOMPUTER TROUBLESHOOTING

REFERENCES

Hall: pages 246–249, 278.

Operator's manual for the microcomputer used.

Schematic for the microcomputer used.

OBJECTIVE

At the conclusion of this laboratory exercise, you should be able to develop and use a systematic method of troubleshooting a microcomputer or microcomputer-based product.

EQUIPMENT

1 Single-board microcomputer or system
1 Digital voltmeter
1 Dual-trace triggered oscilloscope
1 Logic analyzer (optional)

PROCEDURE

INTRODUCTION In troubleshooting a microcomputer or microcomputer-based instrument, in the long run a sequential approach is more effective than random poking, probing, and hoping. For either a gross failure or a subtle malfunction, it is best to work your way down from the start of the debugging procedure described below. For practice, work through this procedure on the microcomputer you are using.

MODULE 1 Initial checks and signal "roll call."

1. Identify the symptom.
   a. List the symptoms that you find or a customer describes.
   b. If someone else describes the symptoms to you, check them yourself or have that person demonstrate the symptoms to ensure the problem is not just an operator error.
2. Make a careful visual and tactile inspection of your microcomputer.
   a. Check for signs of excessive heat.
   b. Check that all ICs are firmly seated in their sockets and that the ICs have no bent pins.
      (1) Sometimes a bent pin will make contact for a while, but after heating, cooling, and vibration it no longer does.
      (2) Also, inexpensive IC sockets may oxidize with age and no longer make contact.
   c. Check that PCB edge connectors are clean and seated fully. A film that may be present on edge-connector fingers can be removed with a clean pencil eraser.
   d. Check the ribbon-cable connectors.
      (1) If they have been moved around a lot and do not have stress relief, they may no longer make dependable contact.
      (2) If moving the cable around changes the operation of the machine, this indicates another possible problem.
3. Check the power supplies.
   a. From the operation manual determine the power-supply specifications for your microcomputer.
   b. Measure the power-supply voltages, and check that they are within specifications.
   c. Also check with an oscilloscope to make sure the power supplies do not have excessive noise on them. Power supplies are a very common source of problems. Low voltage or excessive ripple may lead you to believe an IC is bad.
4. Using an oscilloscope, check that the clock signals are present and correct.
5. Verify the input control signals.
   a. If everything thus far seems correct but the unit still has problems, check that the CPU input control signals, such as RESET, READY, HOLD, INT,

and NMI, are at the proper level for normal operation. (Refer to the CPU data book or manual for proper levels.)

  b. A common problem is that, because of some other hardware problem, the processor will get stuck in a wait, hold, reset, or interrupt condition.

  c. If one of these signals is at the wrong level, find out from the schematic what is connected to that input and track down the problem.

6. Verify the CPU output signals.

  a. If the input signals are correct, check the active CPU or CPU group output signals such as SYNC, ALE, DBIN, VMA, STATUS STROBE, $\overline{\text{MEMR}}$, $\overline{\text{RD}}$, and so on to see whether they are present.

  b. The absence of these signals probably indicates a bad CPU or CPU group IC. Try replacing the one that is the source of the missing signal.

  c. Also quickly check whether pulses are present on lower address lines and data lines. With a normal oscilloscope these pulses will appear random, but at least it is a quick way to know whether the CPU is sending out addresses and whether the data bus is active.

  d. Also use an oscilloscope to see whether the memory decoders are producing chip select signals ($\overline{\text{CS}}$).

MODULE 2

Verifying the step-by-step CPU operation during instruction execution. If the CPU or one of the CPU group ICs is not bad, then the next step is to find out whether the correct instructions are coming into the CPU in proper order from memory.

1. A logic analyzer is a good way to check detailed CPU operation.

  a. Connect eight of the signal inputs of the analyzer to the data bus, and connect any remaining signal inputs to the address bus.

  b. The analyzer can be clocked on $\overline{\text{MEMR}}$ for an 8080A, $\overline{\text{RD}}$ for an 8085A, or DBE for a 6800.

  c. The analyzer should be set to trigger on the first instruction word to be read in from memory and the address of that word.

  d. The analyzer trace should show the first 256 or so address and data words after the trigger word.

  e. If the words read back are not correct, there are several possible sources for the problem.

  (1) An address or data line that should change but never does may be short-circuited to V_{CC} or ground.

  (2) An address-bus buffer or data-bus buffer IC may be bad or may not be getting enabled.

  (3) Two address lines or two data lines might be short-circuited. Watch for this pattern in the logic-analyzer trace.

2. Single-stepping is another way to check detailed CPU operation.

  a. If a logic analyzer is not available, then for 8080A, 8085A, and Z80 processors, the hardware single-step method described in Experiment 23, Module 3, can be used to let you obtain this same information.

  b. LEDs with driver transistors can be connected to the address data lines to help you see their con-

tents as you step through a program from machine cycle to machine cycle.

MODULE 3

Testing address- and data-bus buffers.

In microcomputer systems that use address- and data-bus buffers, these buffers are a common cause of failure. Two common methods of finding a problem with a buffer follow.

1. Using a logic analyzer, or the hardware single-step method and an oscilloscope or voltmeter, you can check the inputs and outputs of each buffer for proper levels.

  a. If a signal is getting to the input pin of a buffer but not appearing on the output pin:

  (1) First, check that the buffer is getting enabled. If it is not, find the problem with an enable.

  (2) If the buffer is enabled, then it may be defective. So try replacing it, and again check the output.

  (3) If the output level of the suspected buffer is still incorrect after it is replaced, probably some other device on that bus line has an internally short-circuited input or output. To find the short-circuited device, use the schematic to locate all devices with inputs or outputs connected to the malfunctioning line. Remove these ICs one at a time, or lift the pins until the line goes to the correct logic level. The last pin lifted, then, is defective. This IC should be replaced.

  (4) Unfortunately, it is not uncommon for more than one input or output on a bus line to be short-circuited. So after you replace the malfunctioning IC, reconnect the other ICs one at a time to make sure none of them is also defective.

  b. If the input signal to a buffer is not correct:

  (1) Remove the buffer. If the signal input line now has the correct value, then the buffer input probably was short-circuited and the buffer should be replaced.

  (2) If after you remove the buffer the input signal line is still incorrect, probably some other device on that line is short-circuited. Remove the other devices (or pins) on this line, one at a time, as described in Section 1a(3) above until the signal level is correct. Replace the defective IC. Also use a procedure similar to that described in Section 1a(4) to reconnect the other ICs and verify their proper operation.

  (3) If removing all devices on the line does not correct the problem, the signal source may be faulty.

  c. Remember that the cost of simply replacing a few inexpensive buffer or decoder ICs may be much less than the cost of labor involved in unsoldering and lifting pins to find a defective one.

2. If you have a pulser probe such as the Hewlett-Packard 546A and a current-tracing probe such as the Hewlett-Packard 547A [see Hall, Fig. 1-5], a short-circuited IC can usually be found quite quickly. The 546A is used to pulse current into the short-circuited line. The current probe is then moved along the

short-circuited line, as shown in Hall, Fig. 1-5. When the probe passes the IC with a short-circuited input, the light in the probe tip will go out.

MODULE 4 Testing RAM.

If the microcomputer reads in instructions and data properly from ROM but still does not perform all its functions correctly, the remaining sections to test are RAM and I/O parts. To test RAM, use either step 1 or step 2 below, depending on the capabilities of your specific microcomputer.

1. Using the monitor program.
   a. If the system has a monitor program, it can be used to write to RAM and read back to ascertain whether the write was successful.
   b. For your microcomputer, write and try a routine that tests its RAM by first writing all 1s (FF) to each address and reading them back, then writing and reading all 0s, and finally writing and reading alternating 1s and 0s (55 or AA).
2. Using a test PROM.
   a. If the system does not have a monitor program, the system ROM can be replaced with a test PROM that contains a routine to test all the RAM in the system and indicates an error when the test fails.
   b. For your microcomputer, write a program that tests its RAM by first writing all 1s (FF) to each

address and reading them back, then writing and reading all 0s, and finally writing and reading alternating 1s and 0s (55 or AA). Burn your test program into a PROM, and try it in place of your system ROM.

MODULE 5 Test I/O ports.

1. If RAM works correctly, then program routines can be used to exercise I/O ports and help you track down a problem with them.
   a. To check an input port, for example, a routine is written to initialize and read over and over from that port.
   b. Then a standard oscilloscope can be used to find out whether the port is getting addressed (enabled) and whether the data on the inputs of the port device are getting onto the system data bus when the device is enabled.
2. For your microcomputer, write and run a program to initialize an input port and read from it over and over.
   a. Hard-wire a data word such as 55 onto the inputs.
   b. Use an oscilloscope to observe the CS input of the port and D0 of the data bus.
   c. How long after the device is selected do input data appear on the data bus?

USING MICROCOMPUTER INTERRUPTS

REFERENCES

Hall: pages 291–295.

Hardware reference manual for your microcomputer.

OBJECTIVES

At the conclusion of this laboratory exercise, you should be able to:

1. Use the hardware reference manual to determine the response of your microcomputer to active interrupt input(s).
2. Demonstrate the use of an interrupt input to tell a microcomputer to read in data from an encoded keyboard.
3. For your microcomputer write an interrupt service routine which reads in data from an encoded keyboard.
4. Demonstrate the use of an external clock source with an interrupt input for a timing reference in place of delay loops.
5. Write a routine to service an interrupt from an external clock source.

EQUIPMENT

1 Microcomputer board with interrupt capability, input port, and output port
1 5-V power supply
1 Oscilloscope

MATERIALS

1 Encoded keyboard with key-pressed strobe
1 74121 one-shot multivibrator
1 2N3904 transistor
1 LED
1 0.001-μF capacitor
1 10-kΩ resistor
1 4.7-kΩ resistor
1 220-Ω resistor

PROCEDURE

INTRODUCTION Almost all microcomputers have one or more interrupt inputs. An interrupt input, if enabled, allows an external signal to tell the microcomputer to finish the instruction that it is executing and then jump to a program that responds to the need indicated by the interrupt.

Interrupts have several important functions and advantages. They can relieve the microcomputer of the burden of polling an input over and over to see whether a signal such as a key-pressed strobe is present. They allow a microcomputer to respond very quickly to a catastrophe or a situation requiring immediate attention. They can also relieve the microcomputer of the burden of timing and delay loops.

MODULE 1 Determining the interrupt capabilities of a microcomputer.

1. The number of interrupt inputs and the response of the CPU to these inputs vary greatly from one CPU to another.
   a. Read the reference material in Hall, and/or the hardware reference manual for your microcomputer to determine its interrupt capability.
   b. For your microcomputer, answer the questions in sections 2 and 3.
2. These hardware considerations are important:
   a. How many interrupt inputs does the microcomputer have?
   b. Do these inputs require active high, active low, or edge signals?
   c. Do these inputs have priorities?

d. Is external hardware required to insert the first instruction of the interrupt service routine, or does the CPU do this automatically when it responds to the interrupt input?

3. These are some software considerations:

a. What instructions, if any, are required to enable and unmask the interrupts?

b. Does the CPU automatically save register contents and flags by pushing them onto the stack, or does the interrupt program have to use push instructions at its start to do this?

c. What instructions are used to return from the interrupt routine to the main program?

MODULE 2 Using an interrupt input to detect a key-pressed strobe and read in parallel data.

1. Defining the problem

a. In Experiment 19, a polling technique is used to detect the key-pressed strobe from an ASCII-encoded keyboard. The key-pressed strobe is connected to an input port line, and this line is read over and over until an active key-pressed strobe is found. The parallel ASCII data then is read in from another port.

This polling technique is simple and works well, but it has the disadvantage of preventing the microcomputer from doing anything else while it is waiting for a key to be pressed. In many applications it is desirable to have the microcomputer totally ignore the keyboard until a key is pressed. This is easily done by servicing the keyboard on an interrupt basis.

2. Keyboard interrupt hardware.

a. Connect the parallel ASCII output of an encoded keyboard to an input port on your microcomputer.

b. Connect the key-pressed strobe from the keyboard to the 74121 pulse-narrower circuit shown in Fig. 25-1.

(1) If the key-pressed strobe is active low, connect it to pins 3 and 4 and tie pin 5 to V_{CC}.

(2) If the key-pressed strobe is active high, connect it to pin 5 and tie pins 3 and 4 to ground.

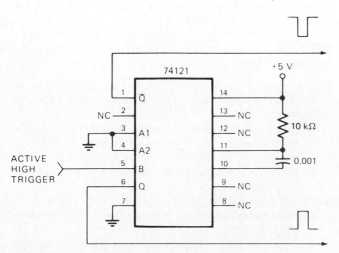

Fig. 25-1 A pulse-narrower circuit for an interrupt input.

c. Connect the correct active level output from the 74121 to an interrupt input on your microcomputer. (For an SDK-85, RST 6.5 is available; for an MEK6800D2, use $\overline{\text{IRQ}}$.)

3. Keyboard interrupt software.

a. First write an assembly language program to:

(1) Initialize ports, if necessary.

(2) Initialize the stack pointer.

(3) Load a jump vector to the interrupt service routine, if required.

(4) Initialize a memory pointer to the starting address in memory where the ASCII characters will be located.

(5) Store this pointer in two dedicated memory locations (pointer store).

(6) Unmask the interrupt used.

(7) Enable the interrupts.

(8) Sit in an endless loop waiting for an interrupt. This endless loop can be produced with the instruction:

WAIT:　JMP WAIT

This endless loop simulates a mainline program, such as controlling a machine, that the microcomputer might be doing while waiting for an interrupt.

b. Write an interrupt service subroutine which, when called by a hardware interrupt signal, will:

(1) Push all registers used in the routine onto the stack if the CPU has not already done this in response to the interrupt signal.

(2) Get the memory pointer from the pointer store.

(3) Read in the parallel ASCII code from the port.

(4) Mask the parity bit.

(5) Put the ASCII code in the memory table.

(6) Increment the pointer and put the incremented pointer back in the pointer store.

(7) Display the hex code for the ASCII on the LED displays of your microcomputer if the monitor has a readily accessible display routine.

(8) Pop registers.

(9) Enable interrupts.

(10) Return to the main program (endless loop).

4. Testing and analyzing the keyboard interrupt program.

a. Enter the initialization program and the interrupt service subroutine into memory, and run the initialization program.

b. Press a few keys on the keyboard.

c. Stop the program and see whether the ASCII data reached the table in memory.

d. What is a possible cause of only the code for the first key pressed getting read but all the following key presses being ignored?

e. Why is the 74121 circuit necessary to decrease the width of the key-pressed strobe? (*Hint:* How long does it take the microcomputer to read in a character, reenable interrupts, and return?)

f. What are the advantages and disadvantages of the polled and interrupt methods of detecting a key-pressed strobe?

MODULE 3 Using an interrupt input for counting and timing applications.

1. Defining the problem. Another important application of interrupts is to relieve a microcomputer of the burden of counting down timing loops. An example might be a machine being controlled by a microcomputer that needs a pulse which is on for 4 min and off for 4 min with an accuracy of 1 s. Nested delay loops could be used to produce the required delay, but this ties up the microcomputer with just one small task. During one 4-min interval, the processor could execute 100 million instructions, doing many other jobs. To avoid this waste, a 1-Hz signal can be applied to an interrupt input of the CPU. An internal register or a memory location can be used to keep the count of how many times the CPU has been interrupted. This number will correspond to the number of seconds that have passed.

   This same interrupt principle could be used to keep a running count of the number of cans of applesauce that come by on a conveyor belt or for any other counting application.

2. Clock sources for interrupt timing.
   a. A stable 1-Hz signal can be produced from a signal generator or from the 60-Hz ac power lines. The 120-V ac, 60-Hz line voltage is stepped down to 6.3 V with a transformer and then converted to TTL levels with a Schmitt trigger. This 60-Hz TTL signal is divided by 6 and then by 10 to give a stable 1-Hz signal. The 1-Hz signal is passed through the pulse narrower in Fig. 25-1 to give the required interrupt input signal.
   b. A stable 1-kHz signal can be produced by dividing down the processor clock with a programmable timer or counter such as the 8155. The 1-kHz signal is passed through the pulse narrower of Fig. 25-1 to give the required interrupt input signal. This signal will interrupt the processor every 1 ms. The interrupt service routine can count these interrupts and only increment the seconds count after every 1000 interrupts. This latter method has the advantage that it uses the on-board crystal-controlled clock.

3. An interrupt-based interval timer.
   a. Hardware.
      (1) Connect a 1-Hz TTL signal to the 74121 pulse-narrower circuit shown in Fig. 25-1.
      (2) Connect the correct output of the 74121 to an interrupt input of your processor.
      (3) Connect the LED driver circuit shown in Fig. 25-2 to an output port line.
   b. Software.
      (1) Write a short assembly language program to initialize the output ports, initialize the stack pointer, initialize the register or memory loca-

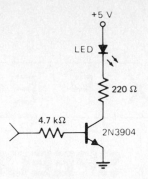

Fig. 25-2 An LED driver circuit.

tion used as a seconds counter, enable interrupts, and unmask interrupts. End this program with WAIT: JMP WAIT.
      (2) Devise an interrupt service routine that increments the seconds count after each interrupt and after each 4-min interval toggles the output port bit and resets the counter. End this routine with an enable interrupt instruction and a return instruction.
   c. Test the clock interrupt program for a 4-min-interval timer.
      (1) Load the initialization program and the interrupt service subroutine into memory.
      (2) Run the initialization program, and observe the LED on the output port. It should blink on for 4 min and off for 4 min. To simplify testing, reduce the terminal count to 5 s instead of 4 min.

MODULE 4 A real-time clock.

Many computer systems and programs need a clock or real-time reference. This can easily be done on an interrupt basis.

1. Write and test an interrupt service routine that uses a 1-Hz interrupt signal to count seconds, minutes, and hours in three successive memory locations. (*Hint:* Do not forget the DAA instruction to keep the count in BCD format.)
2. If your microcomputer monitor has readily accessible display routines, call them to display the time on the microcomputer LED displays.
3. Modify the program to use a 1-kHz interrupt input signal such as one that might come from a programmable timer driven by the processor clock. (*Hint:* Count 1000 interrupts before incrementing the seconds count.)
4. To check the accuracy of the processor clock, set the time and let the program run for 24 h. Check how much time your software clock has gained or lost. Compute the percentage error. How could this error be reduced?

E X P E R I M E N T 2 6

SPEECH SYNTHESIS AND HANDSHAKE DATA TRANSFER

REFERENCES

Hall: pages 296–301.

SC-01 data sheet (in appendix).

OBJECTIVES

At the conclusion of this laboratory exercise, you should be able to:

1. Write an assembly language program to output data by using a software handshake.
2. Create an assembly language program to output data by using an interrupt-driven handshake method.

EQUIPMENT

1 Microcomputer with one 8-bit output port, one additional output port line, and one additional input port line

MATERIALS

1 Votrax SC-01 speech synthesis IC
1 74C906 CMOS hex buffer
1 LM380 audio amplifier
2 2N3904 NPN transistors
1 small audio speaker
1 220-μF capacitor
1 100-μF capacitor
3 0.1-μF capacitors
1 0.022-μF capacitor
1 0.01-μF capacitor
1 150-pF capacitor
1 10-kΩ potentiometer
10 4.7-kΩ resistors
1 47-kΩ resistor
1 6.8-kΩ resistor

1 3.3-kΩ resistor
1 10-kΩ resistor
1 10-Ω resistor

PROCEDURE

INTRODUCTION As explained in the reference, parallel data transfer to and from many peripherals must be done on a handshake basis. By handshake we mean that the receiving device must first send a signal indicating that it is ready to receive data. The sending device must then send the data and a signal indicating that it has sent the data. Finally, the receiving device must send an acknowledge signal to indicate that it has received the data and is ready for the sender to start the next data transfer. Handshake signals can be created by software (programming) or by hardware.

An interesting example of a peripheral device that requires handshake data transfer is the Votrax SC-01 speech synthesizer IC. The appendix contains portions of the data sheets for this device. The SC-01 creates speech by outputting a sequence of *phonemes* sent to it. As shown in Table 1 in the data sheet, each phoneme is specified by a 6-bit binary code. An additional 2 bits determines the inflection (pitch) of a phoneme.

Figure 26-1 shows how an SC-01 can be connected to microcomputer ports to generate speech under program control. Figure 26-2 shows the timing waveforms for the transfer of a phoneme to the SC-01.

The SC-01 first indicates that it is ready to receive a phoneme by raising its $\overline{A}/R$ output high. Then some external device sends a phoneme and inflection code to the SC-01. After a setup time T_S, the external device sends a STROBE signal to latch the phoneme code into the SC-01. When the STROBE signal goes low, the SC-01 automatically resets its $\overline{A}/R$ output. When the SC-01 completes sounding one phoneme and is ready for the next phoneme, it raises its $\overline{A}/R$ line high again.

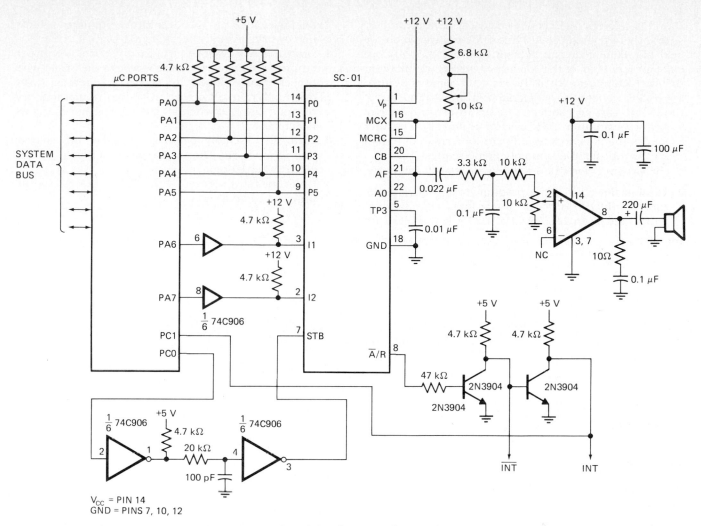

Fig. 26-1 Connection of Voltrax SC-01 speech synthesizer to microcomputer ports.

This experiment shows two ways to output a sequence of phonemes from a table in memory to the SC-01 with proper timing.

MODULE 1 Software handshake with polling.

1. If the circuit shown in Fig. 26-1 is not available as an already built module, build the circuit. The audio amplifier can be tested independently.
2. List the phoneme codes for a couple of simple words.

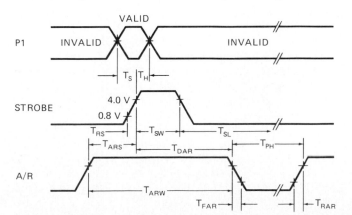

Fig. 26-2 Timing waveforms for transfer of a phoneme to an SC-01.

Use 3F (no sound) to separate words. To start, let the inflection bits be 00. Later you can experiment with these bits to improve the accuracy of the sounds. Use a code such as FFH as an end-of-message indicator.

3. From Fig. 26-1 determine which port to send the phoneme codes to, which port line you will read to find out when the SC-01 is ready to receive a phoneme, and which port line you will send the strobe pulse out on.
4. Use the timing values in the SC-01 data sheet in the appendix to determine for how long the phoneme and inflection code must be present before the strobe signal can be sent.
5. Draw a flowchart or write a sequential task list for a program to poll $\overline{A/R}$, send a phoneme, and send a strobe pulse over and over until the end-of-message code is detected.
6. Write the assembly language program for this flowchart. Enter the program in your microcomputer and test it.
7. Experiment with different phoneme codes and different values for the inflection bits. As with any new language, it takes a while to get it to say what you mean.

MODULE 2 Software Handshake with Interrupt.

Because phonemes take between 47 and 250 ms to

81
SPEECH SYNTHESIS AND HANDSHAKE DATA TRANSFER

sound, it is often inefficient to have the microcomputer sitting there polling the $\overline{A/R}$ line to determine when the next phoneme code can be sent to the SC-01. A more efficient way is to let the $\overline{A/R}$ line of the SC-01 interrupt the microcomputer when the next phoneme is needed. Figure 26-1 shows how a signal from the $\overline{A/R}$ output of the SC-01 can be connected to an interrupt input of your microcomputer. $\overline{A/R}$ goes low at most 500 ns after STB goes high. Therefore, $\overline{A/R}$ cannot cause more than one interrupt for the same phoneme request.

The program for this module consists of two parts.

1. Draw a flowchart for a program to initialize ports, table pointers, unmask interrupts, enable interrupts, and sit in a HERE: JMP HERE loop while waiting for an interrupt. This program simulates a main-line or background program.

2. Draw a flowchart for an interrupt service routine to output a phoneme code and strobe to the SC-01 with proper timing, enable interrupts, and return to the main program. This section should return with interrupts disabled when an end-of-message character is detected.

3. Write an assembly language program for each of these flowcharts. Do not forget to include interrupt vector instructions.

4. Enter the two program sections into your microcomputer and test them.

INTERFACING AN UNENCODED KEYBOARD TO A MICROCOMPUTER

REFERENCE

Hall: pages 123–125, 302–305.

OBJECTIVES

At the conclusion of this laboratory exercise, you should be able to:

1. Write and test an assembly language subroutine to scan a matrix keyboard, detect a key pressed, debounce it, and read in the code for the key pressed.
2. Demonstrate the use of a look-up table to convert the key-pressed code to ASCII.

EQUIPMENT

1 Microcomputer with 8-bit input port and 8-bit latched output port

MATERIALS

1 63-key matrix-type keyboard (optional)
8 Germanium or small-signal silicon diodes
16 4.7-kΩ resistors
1 74148 eight-line to three-line priority encoder

PROCEDURE

INTRODUCTION The reference material in Hall, pages 123–125, describes how a key press on a matrix keyboard can be detected, debounced, and encoded (sometimes referred to as decoded for keyboards) by using hardware. Experiment 19 shows how a fully encoded keyboard with a key-pressed strobe can be interfaced to a microcomputer by detecting the key-pressed strobe on a polled or an interrupt basis. The hardware encoder approach of Experiment 19 is used to minimize the software load on the microcomputer.

For applications in which the microcomputer is not heavily burdened, it is feasible to detect a key press, debounce it, and convert the key-pressed code to a desired code with a software subroutine. Hall, pages 302–305, describes how this is done for a 4 × 4 matrix keyboard. The purpose of this experiment is to extend the software encoding technique to an 8 × 8 matrix keyboard and to demonstrate a faster, more efficient method of using look-up tables for code conversions.

MODULE 1 Developing and testing a software keyboard encoder.

1. Analyzing the keyboard and interface circuitry.
   a. Figure 27-1 shows the connections for an 8 × 8 matrix to an output port and an input port.
   b. The eight rows of the matrix are connected to eight output port lines.
   c. Diodes prevent a high output and a low output from being short-circuited when two keys in a column are pressed at the same time.
   d. Instead of connecting the eight column lines directly to an input port, as was done with the 4 × 4 matrix, they are connected to a 74148.
      (1) Using this inexpensive external IC makes the program simpler and reduces the overall cost because a separate port is not needed for the shift input.
      (2) The 74148 puts out a 3-bit binary code which corresponds to the number of an input that has a low on it.
      (3) The $\overline{GS}$ output is high when no columns have a low on them and low when any column has a low. The $\overline{GS}$ output, then, functions as a key-pressed strobe. It can be polled to detect a key press.
      (4) The output code from the 74148 is inverted. This small problem can be solved by connecting the columns to the 74148 inputs in reverse order, as shown. As connected, the 74148 will output 000 on $\overline{A2}$, $\overline{A1}$, and $\overline{A0}$ if a low is present on column 0.

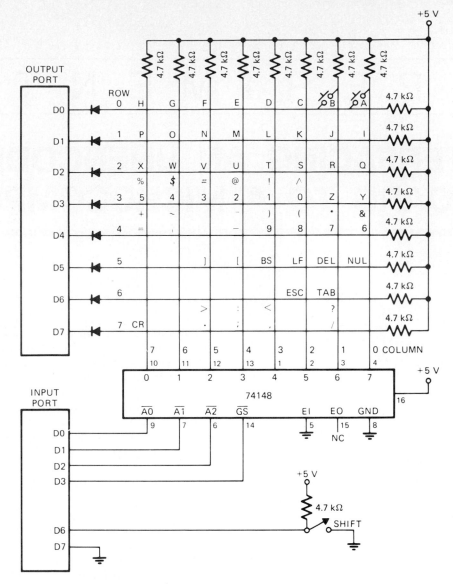

Fig. 27-1 Connections for an unencoded keyboard to a microcomputer.

2. Draw a flowchart for a subroutine to do the following:
   a. Check that all keys are open, detect a key press, wait the 20-ms debounce time, and check whether key is still pressed.
   b. If a key is pressed, the program should search the matrix to find the row and column where the key is pressed.
   c. The row and column key-pressed code should then be converted to ASCII.
   d. This is similar to the flowchart in Hall, Fig. 11-12, except for the addition of a second key-press check after the 20-ms debounce time. This second check is included to ensure that the first check did not detect just a noise pulse.

3. Setting up the hardware.
   a. If the hardware shown in Fig. 27-1 is connected to an output port and an input port, the assembly language program for this flowchart can be written and tested one section at a time.
   b. If a matrix keyboard is not available, build the circuit as shown. Use a jumper wire to temporarily short-circuit a row to a column to simulate a key press.

4. Write a short program to initialize the stack pointer, initialize the ports, and call the keyboard scan and encoder routine.

5. Write and test the section of the keyboard routine to detect all keys open, detect a key press, wait 20 ms, and check again for a key press.

6. Write and test the section to locate the row and column of a key press as follows:
   a. Use a register or memory location as a row counter

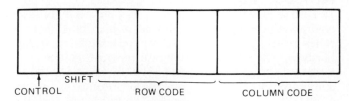

Fig. 27-2 Word format of the shift, row, and column codes.

to produce a 3-bit binary code for the number of the row in which the pressed key was found.

   b. The 74148 sends a 3-bit binary code for the column containing the key press.

   c. Combine the 3-bit row code, the 3-bit column code, and the shift input into a word with the format shown in Fig. 27-2. This word is used in Module 2 to access the correct location in the look-up table.

   (1) What code will be output if two keys in the same row are pressed at the same time?

   (2) What code will be output if two keys in the same column are pressed at the same time?

MODULE 2 Developing a look-up table for a key-press-to-ASCII conversion.

1. When your program thus far produces the correct shift, row, and column word for a key press, the next step is to make the look-up table. The table is used as follows:

   a. A memory pointer is pointed at the first location in the table.

   b. The shift, row, column (SRC) code word is added to the memory-pointer value.

   c. The pointer then points to the desired ASCII value you put in the table.

   (1) For example, if the A key is pressed and the shift key is pressed, the SRC word will be 0000 0000.

   (2) This 0000 0000, when added to the memory pointer, will point to the first memory location in the table.

   (3) Since the ASCII code for an uppercase capital A is 41II, insert this value in the first memory location in the table.

   d. If the shift key and the B key are pressed, what SRC word will be produced?

   (1) What table location will this address?

   (2) What ASCII code should be placed in this location? (Table 3-2 in Hall contains the complete 7-bit ASCII code.)

   e. If the shift key is not pressed and the A key is pressed, what SRC word will be produced?

   (1) What address in the table will be pointed to?

   (2) What ASCII code should be placed in this address?

2. Writing the table and program for conversion to ASCII.

   a. Make up a table for at least the uppercase and lowercase letters.

   b. Load this table into memory.

   c. Write and run the assembly language steps for your program to convert the SRC code to ASCII and to return to the calling program with the ASCII code in the accumulator.

   d. Use the register-examine command of your microcomputer to verify the ASCII code in the accumulator for each key press.

   e. If your microcomputer board has a readily available display routine, use it to display the ASCII code on its LED displays.

3. Discuss the following:

   a. Bit 7 of the input port was left available for a control key input. What effect would including this input have on the size of the look-up table?

   b. Why is this method of using a look-up table faster than the method shown in Hall, Fig. 11-13?

   c. How could this program be modified to give an EBCDIC output for each key press?

STEPPER MOTORS

REFERENCES

Hall: page 315.

74194 data sheet (see appendix).

OBJECTIVES

At the conclusion of this laboratory exercise, you should be able to:

1. Demonstrate the operation of a stepper motor.
2. Develop two methods of controlling a stepper motor with a microcomputer.
3. Write and test assembly language programs for each of these methods of controlling a stepper motor.

EQUIPMENT

1 Microcomputer with 8-bit latched output port
1 Oscilloscope
1 5-V power supply
1 12- or 15-V power supply with 2-A capability
1 Digital voltmeter

MATERIALS

1 Stepper motor such as Superior Electric MO61-FD302 or IMC Magnetics Corp. Tormax 200
1 74194 universal 4-bit shift register
1 7400 quad NAND gate
3 10-kΩ resistors
1 Stepper-motor power driver board (see Fig. 28-1a)
Parts for stepper-motor power driver board:
  1 7406 hex inverter
  4 MJE2955 power transistors
  4 1N4002 diodes
  4 1-kΩ resistors
  4 470-Ω resistors
  1 4-Ω, 20-W resistor

PROCEDURE

INTRODUCTION As described in the reference, stepper motors rotate, or "step," from one fixed position to another, instead of spinning smoothly as most motors do. Many of these motors have four coils. At any given time, current is flowing through two of them. The motor is stepped by changing which two coils have current flowing through them.

Figure 28-1a shows a schematic for logic-controlled current switches for a four-coil stepper motor. Figure 28-1b shows the switch sequence for clockwise and counterclockwise stepping. This switching sequence can be produced by several means, ranging from purely hardware to mostly software.

MODULE 1 Hardware operation of the stepper motor.

1. Examine the schematic of Fig. 28-2, which shows a 74194 universal shift register connected as a 4-bit ring counter.
   a. The NAND gates and switches on the control inputs of the register allow it to be loaded with the starting pattern, shifted left, shifted right, started, and stopped.
   b. Analyze the data sheet for the 74194 in the appendix, and the logic shown in Fig. 28-2, to determine the effect of each position of the three switches.
   c. What inputs are required on S1 and S0 for load, shift right, and shift left? *Note:* The S1 and S0 inputs of the 74194 should only be changed while the clock input is high! The clock input will be high when the RUN/STOP switch is closed (STOP position).
2. Building and testing the ring counter circuit.
   a. Build the circuit of Fig. 28-2. Jumper wires can be used for switches.
   b. Apply power and a 100-Hz TTL input-clock signal.
   c. With the RUN/STOP switch in the STOP position, set the LOAD switch for LOAD. Momentarily put the RUN/STOP switch in the RUN position.

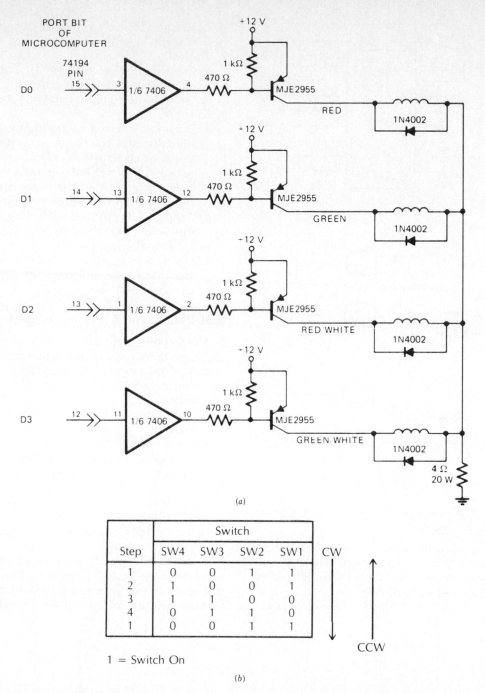

(a)

		Switch			
Step	SW4	SW3	SW2	SW1	
1	0	0	1	1	
2	1	0	0	1	
3	1	1	0	0	
4	0	1	1	0	
1	0	0	1	1	

CW ↑ ↓ CCW

1 = Switch On

(b)

Fig. 28-1 *(a)* **Schematic of a stepper motor power driver board.** *(b)* **Switch sequence for a stepper motor.**

d. Open the LOAD switch and select the desired direction of shift with the clockwise/counterclockwise switch.

e. Put the RUN/STOP switch in the RUN position.

f. Observe the output waveforms. They should correspond to the switch chart shown in Fig. 28-1*b*.

3. Adding and running the stepper motor.

a. If the ring counter operates correctly, turn off the power and connect the four outputs of the 74194 to the inputs of the stepper-motor driver board.

b. Apply power. Use the switches to load the starting values, set for shift right, and run. The motor should be stepping clockwise.

c. Put the RUN/STOP switch in the STOP position; change the direction switch to counterclockwise and the RUN/STOP switch to RUN again. The motor should be stepping counterclockwise.

d. Vary the input-clock frequency slowly from 1 Hz to 1 kHz.

e. Note that in a certain frequency range (usually 90 to 160 steps per second) the motor makes more noise as it steps. This is called its *natural resonant frequency.*

f. As the frequency of the input clock approaches 1 kHz, what happens to the stepping motion of the motor? Why?

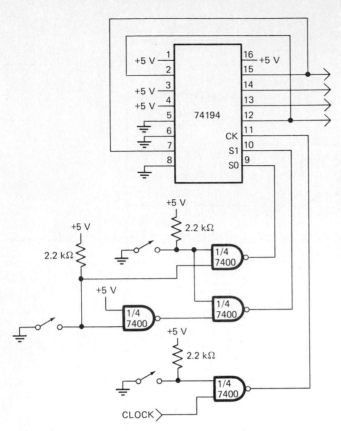

Fig. 28-2 A 74194 ring-counter circuit for stepper-motor control.

MODULE 2 Combination of hardware and software control of the stepper motor.

1. Controlling the direction, speed, and number of steps of a stepper motor with a microcomputer.
   a. The first example uses the 74194 to produce the stepping sequence in hardware.
   b. The microcomputer is used to load the initial pattern and control the direction, speed, and number of steps in software.
2. Hardware.
   a. Connect the clock input of the 74194 to D0 of your microcomputer output port.
   b. Connect the S0 input to D1 and the S1 input to D2.
3. Software.
   a. Draw a flowchart for a program to load the starting word and step the motor a given number of steps in a clockwise direction at a given number of steps per second. *Note:* A delay must be introduced between steps because the motor cannot step as fast as the microprocessor can output pulses.
   b. Write and test the assembly language program for this flowchart. Try 50 steps at 10 steps per second for your first trial.
   c. Modify the program so that the motor will step 50 steps clockwise and then 50 steps counterclockwise over and over.

MODULE 3 Full software control of a stepper motor.

1. The stepping-sequence waveforms can easily be produced directly by a microcomputer.
   a. The four inputs of the stepper driver board are connected to the lower 4 bits of an output port in order.
   b. The pattern 0011 0011 is loaded into the accumulator.
   c. An output, delay, rotate, output, delay, . . . sequence is then used to step the motor at the proper rate.
2. Write and test an assembly language program to step the motor a given number of steps clockwise or counterclockwise at a given rate, using this method.
   a. Try 50 steps clockwise at 10 steps per second for your first trial.
   b. Try some other values such as 100 steps counterclockwise at 200 steps per second.
3. List the advantages and disadvantages of each of the three methods of controlling a stepper motor.

USING A D/A CONVERTER WITH A MICROCOMPUTER

REFERENCES

Hall: pages 161–166, 315–316.

Laboratory manual, Experiment 15.

OBJECTIVES

At the conclusion of this laboratory exercise, you should be able to:

1. Interface an IC D/A converter to a microcomputer.
2. Demonstrate how a D/A converter can be used with a microcomputer to produce a programmable power supply.
3. Show how a D/A converter can be used with a microcomputer to produce any desired output waveform.

EQUIPMENT

1 Microcomputer with latched 8-bit output port
1 Oscilloscope
1 Digital voltmeter
4 Power supplies with outputs of 5, 15, −5, and −15 V

MATERIALS

1 741 op amp
1 2N2907 transistor, TO-18 case
1 2N2222 transistor, TO-18 case
2 0.1-μF capacitors
1 470-Ω resistor
1 100-Ω resistor
2 82-Ω, 1-W resistors
1 Audio test speaker
1 8-bit D/A circuit module, or these parts:
    1 MC1408L8 D/A converter
    1 741 op amp
    1 0.1-μF capacitor
    1 50-pF capacitor

1 10-pF capacitor
1 10-kΩ multiturn trimpot
1 5.1-kΩ resistor
2 2.4-kΩ resistors

PROCEDURE

MODULE 1 Interface an IC D/A converter to a microcomputer.

1. D/A circuit module.
   a. If it is not already built as a laboratory module, build the D/A converter circuit with a current-to-voltage converter as shown in Fig. 29-1.
   b. Connect the data inputs of the D/A converter to an 8-bit latched output port on your microcomputer.
2. Programming the D/A converter.
   a. Write an assembly language program to initialize the output port of your microcomputer and to output 0s to all bits of the port.

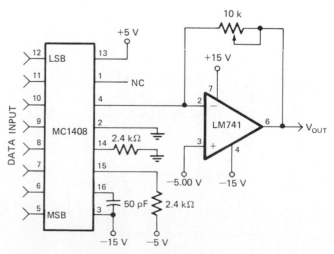

Fig. 29-1 Schematic for an 8-bit D/A converter circuit with voltage output.

b. Run the program, and measure the voltage on the output of the LM741 voltage-to-current converter. It should be −5 V. If it is not, check whether the correct bits were output, check voltages, and so on until it works correctly.

c. Change the program to output all 1s.

d. Run the program and adjust the 10-kΩ trimpot until the output voltage measures 4.961 V.

e. Answer the following questions:
   (1) What is the resolution of an 8-bit D/A converter?
   (2) What is the resolution of this converter in volts?
   (3) What binary word should be output from the microcomputer to give 0 V out of the D/A converter? Try this.

MODULE 2 Using a microcomputer and D/A converter as a programmable power supply.

1. Many applications require a programmable power supply, or, in other words, a voltage source that can supply considerable current. The output of the D/A converter is programmable from −5 to +5 V, but the output current is limited by the output-current capability of the op amp, usually only a few milliamperes. The output-current drive of the basic D/A converter can be increased by adding a buffer stage such as that shown in Fig. 29-2, in order to make a programmable power supply (PPS) that is practical.

2. *PPS circuit description.* The op amp is connected in a voltage-follower configuration so that the voltage on the output will always be within a few millivolts of the voltage on the noninverting input, regardless of the load. The transistors supply the current gain. This buffer will supply at least 75 mA over the full output-voltage range. Large power transistors such as the MJE3055 and MJE2955 could be added to these transistors in a Darlington configuration to boost the output current to several amperes.

3. Building, programming, and operating the PPS circuit.

a. Build this buffer and connect it to the voltage output of the D/A converter.

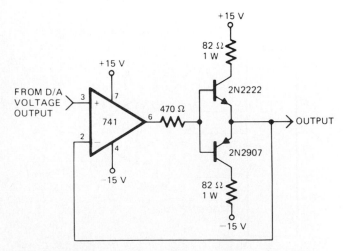

Fig. 29-2 Schematic for a buffer circuit for a D/A voltage output.

b. Add a 100-Ω resistor from the buffer output to ground.

c. For several programmed inputs, compare the voltage into the buffer and the voltage on the 100-Ω resistor.
   (1) How much error is there?
   (2) Is this significant compared with the resolution of the converter?

MODULE 3 Programmed linear waveform generation.

A microcomputer program can be used to generate almost any desired voltage waveform on the output of the D/A converter.

1. Write an assembly language program loop to output an incrementing 8-bit count to the D/A converter over and over.

a. What waveform should this produce?

b. Run the program and observe the output waveform with an oscilloscope.
   (1) What frequency does the output waveform have?
   (2) What limits the frequency of the output?

c. If you wish to also hear the quality and pitch of this waveform, you can connect a small audio test speaker between the 100-Ω resistor and ground on the buffer output.

2. Revise the program to increment the count twice before each output.

a. What effect does this have on the output frequency?

b. What effect does this have on the resolution of the waveform?

3. Revise the program to use a decrementing count.

a. What waveform should this produce?

b. Run the program and observe the waveform.

4. Write and test an assembly language routine to produce a symmetric triangular output waveform.

5. How could you produce an asymmetric triangular waveform?

MODULE 4 Programmed nonlinear waveform generation: sine waves.

1. Almost any desired nonlinear waveform can be produced with a microcomputer and D/A converter. The desired values for each point on a waveform are stored in a table in memory and then sent out to the D/A converter in proper order. Complex waveforms require lengthy tables which are somewhat tedious to produce. Therefore, as an example of this powerful technique, a sine wave is used.

2. Defining the structure of a sine-wave table. To trace a sine wave, you need to make up a table of values to send to the D/A converter at selected intervals. Table 29-1 shows the values for the sines of angles between 0° and 90° at 5° intervals. For angles between 90° and 180°, these values repeat but in the reverse order. For example, the sine of 95° is the same as the sine of 85°, the sine of 100° is the same as the sine of 80°, and so on.

For a sine wave centered on zero, the values for 180° to 270° have the same magnitude as those for 0° to 90°, but are negative in sign. For example, the sine of 10° is 0.174, and the sine of 190° is −0.174.

TABLE 29-1 Sine values converted to integer hexadecimal equivalents

$\theta°$	$\sin \theta$	$127 \sin \theta$	Hex
0	0	0	00
5	0.087	11	0B
10	0.174	22	16
15	0.259	33	21
20	0.342	43	2B
25	0.423	54	36
30	0.500	64	40
35	0.574	73	49
40	0.643	82	52
45	0.707	90	5A
50	0.766	97	61
55	0.819	104	68
60	0.866	110	6E
65	0.906	115	73
70	0.940	119	77
75	0.966	123	7B
80	0.985	125	7D
85	0.996	126	7E
90	1.000	127	7F

For angles from 270° to 360°, the values repeat those of 180° to 270° but in reverse order.

All this repeating of values and symmetry means that only the 19 values for one quadrant of the waveform have to be stored in the table in memory.

3. Determining the sequence, range, and scale of the values in the sine table.

    a. Scaling the sine wave values.

        (1) The table must contain values proportional to the sine of the angles and in the range of 0 to 127.

        (2) Since the sine function ranges from 0.000 to 1.000, the values can be calculated by simply multiplying the sines of the angles by 127, as shown in Table 29-1.

        (3) The resulting decimal values are then converted to hexadecimal or binary for loading into the memory table.

    b. Figure 29-3 shows the order in which the table values are read out to produce a complete sine wave.

        (1) Note how the locations must be read so that peak values and zero values are not read out twice.

        (2) To approximately center the output waveform on zero, an offset value of 80H is added to the values read from the table for the first two quadrants.

        (3) For the third and fourth quadrants, the values read from the table are subtracted from 80H.

    c. Defining the range of sine wave values.

        (1) For the first and second quadrants, the sine wave ranges from the zero value of 80H to the maximum value of FFH.

        (2) For a symmetric sine wave, the third and fourth quadrants vary from the zero line of 80H to 01H.

        (3) This implies 7FH (127) levels above the zero line and 7FH (127) levels below.

4. Developing the software for sine wave generation by the D/A converter.

    a. Draw a flowchart for a program to output the values determined in Table 29-1 to the D/A converter to produce a continuous sine wave output.

    b. Write and test an assembly language program for this flowchart.

MODULE 5 Programming any complex, nonlinear waveform.

1. The method used in Module 4 may seem to be a difficult way to produce a sine wave, but for many complex waveforms it is one of the easiest.

    a. An example of a waveform that is difficult to produce by analog means is the amplitude envelope of a musical note as played by, for example, a guitar. Figure 29-4a shows such a complex waveform.

    b. The programming problem here is to use the D/A converter to vary the amplitude of the sine wave. Note that the sine wave itself is not being gener-

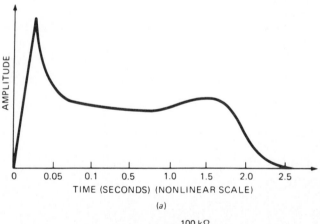

(a)

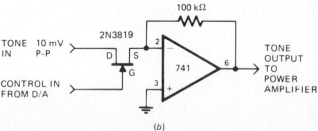

(b)

Fig. 29-4 (a) Graph of amplitude versus time for a guitar note. (b) Schematic for a circuit to control the amplitude envelope of an input tone.

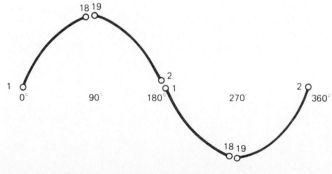

Fig. 29-3 Diagram showing which table values to use to generate each quadrant of a sine wave.

ated by the D/A converter, but is provided by some other source, such as a signal generator.

2. To use the D/A converter to control the amplitude (volume) of a sine wave requires the addition of a voltage-controlled amplifier circuit to the D/A converter.

   a. Figure 29-4h shows a circuit for an electronic volume control which can be controlled by the output of a D/A converter.

   b. The D/A converter you have been using will work if you adjust the current-to-voltage converter feedback resistor so that the output goes only from −5 V to 0 V. The N-channel JFET gate should never be made positive.

   c. At very low drain-signal levels, the JFET acts as a resistor whose value is controlled by the voltage on its gate.

   d. The gain of the amplifier is $R_F/(R_{IN} + R_{FET})$.

   e. With −5 V on the gate, the JFET has a very high resistance, so the gain is near zero.

   f. As the voltage on the gate of the JFET approaches zero, the JFET resistance drops to a few hundred ohms. Therefore, the gain goes way up and the output is much larger.

3. Using the D/A volume-control circuit, you can write a program to create the desired amplitude envelope, point by point.

E X P E R I M E N T 3 0

ANALOG-TO-DIGITAL CONVERSION WITH A MICROCOMPUTER

REFERENCE

Hall: pages 316–317.

OBJECTIVES

At the conclusion of this laboratory exercise, you should be able to:

1. Interface a D/A converter and comparator to a microcomputer to make a counter or a successive-approximation analog-to-digital converter.
2. Write and test a program for a counter type of A/D converter.
3. Create and test a program for a successive-approximation A/D converter.

EQUIPMENT

1 Microcomputer with one 8-bit latched output port and one input port line

1 Oscilloscope
1 Digital voltmeter
1 Power supply with outputs of 5, 15, −5, and −15 V

MATERIALS

1 D/A circuit with current-to-voltage conversion and comparator (see Fig. 30-1) or these parts:
  1 MC1408L8 D/A converter
  1 741 op amp
  1 LM319 comparator
  1 15-pF capacitor
  1 10-kΩ trimpot
  1 2.2-kΩ resistor
  2 1-kΩ resistors

PROCEDURE

MODULE 1 The D/A circuit module with a comparator.

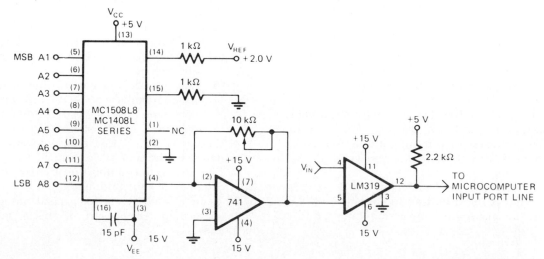

Fig. 30-1 D/A converter and comparator circuit for a microcomputer-controlled A/D converter module.

1. As described in the reference, a D/A converter is a major part of several types of A/D converters. The inputs for the D/A converter can come from a counter, a successive-approximation register, or a microcomputer.
2. Figure 30-1 shows the schematic for a D/A circuit that can be connected to an output port and an input port to perform A/D conversion under microcomputer control.
   a. If this circuit is not already built as a laboratory module, then build it.
   b. Test the D/A section with simulated inputs of zero, half of full scale, and full scale.
   c. Adjust the 10-kΩ trimpot until the full-scale output is 9.961 V. This makes the converter a 10.000-V unit.
   d. Test the comparator section. The output of the comparator should be high if the input from the D/A output is less than V_{IN} and low if the D/A output is greater than V_{IN}.
3. When the D/A comparator circuit works correctly, connect the D/A inputs to an output port on your microcomputer and the comparator output to the least significant bit of an input port.

MODULE 2 Counter-type A/D converter with a microcomputer.

1. The simplest type of A/D converter with a D/A output is the counter type. This is done with a microcomputer in nearly the same way as with a hardware counter.
   a. An incrementing count is outputted to the D/A converter.
   b. After each increment the comparator output is checked to find out whether the D/A output is equal to or greater than V_{IN}.
   c. If it is greater than or equal to V_{IN}, the process is stopped and the count is proportional to the voltage in.
   d. If the D/A converter output is not greater than or equal to V_{IN}, then the count is incremented and output.
   e. The comparator output is checked again.
2. Draw a flowchart for a program to perform A/D conversion with this counter method.
   a. Write an assembly language program for this flowchart. Have your program put the result in a register or memory location so you can check it with a monitor command when the conversion is complete.
   b. Enter the machine code for the program into your microcomputer, and run the program. Try running the converter with inputs of 0, 5, and 10 V, and compare the binary value you get with the expected value.
   c. This is essentially a voltmeter with a 0- to 10-V range. What is its resolution in volts?
3. Measuring the maximum conversion time for this A/D converter.

a. Make your program into an endless loop so the conversion takes place over and over.
b. With V_{IN} = 10 V, run the program.
c. Observe the output waveform from the 741 with an oscilloscope.
   (1) How long does each complete conversion take?
   (2) What effect does V_{IN} have on conversion time for this type of converter?

MODULE 3 Successive-approximation A/D conversion with a microcomputer.

1. A faster but slightly more complicated method of A/D conversion is successive approximation. The circuit for this is the same as that in Fig. 30-1, but the programming approach is different.
   a. As discussed in the reference, a high on the most significant bit alone is first output to the D/A converter.
   b. If the comparator indicates that the resultant voltage is greater than V_{IN}, this bit is turned off and the next bit is tried.
   c. If the resultant voltage is less than V_{IN}, this bit is kept on and a high on the next most significant bit is added to it.
   d. The sum is tried, and this bit is kept or reset based on the output of the comparator.
   e. The process continues until all eight bit positions have been made a high, tried, and either kept or rejected.
2. Draw a flowchart for a program to perform A/D conversion by successive approximation. To keep the program reasonably short, think of how this can be done as a loop.
3. Write the assembly language program for this flowchart. Make the program into an endless loop so it will do the conversion over and over.
4. Testing the program and measuring the conversion time.
   a. Run the program with V_{IN} = 10 V.
   b. Observe the output of the 741 with an oscilloscope.
      (1) How many steps are required for each conversion?
      (2) Explain what each step represents.
      (3) How long is required for each conversion?
      (4) How many conversions per second does the unit perform?
      (5) Compare the conversion time of this successive-approximation A/D converter with the conversion time for the counter type of A/D converter with the same V_{IN}.
   c. Change V_{IN} to 5 V. How many conversions per second does the unit perform now?
   d. Change V_{IN} to 0 V and find the conversion time.
   e. Summarize your findings.
5. Give one advantage and one disadvantage of using a microcomputer as part of the A/D conversion process.

SERIAL DATA INPUT AND OUTPUT WITH SOFTWARE

REFERENCE

Hall: pages 325–335.

OBJECTIVES

At the conclusion of this laboratory exercise, you should be able to write and test assembly language programs or subroutines to:

1. Send serial data to a teletype at 110 baud, using an output port line.
2. Receive serial data from a teletype at 110 baud, using an input port line.
3. Output serial data to a tape recorder in Kansas City standard (KCS) format.
4. Input KCS serial data from a tape recorder.

EQUIPMENT

1 Microcomputer with latched output port and input port
1 Oscilloscope
1 Teletype (optional)
1 Tape recorder (optional)

MATERIALS

Parts for current-loop circuits:
2 2N2907 transistors
1 2N3904 transistor
1 1-μF, 15-V capacitor
2 4.7-kΩ resistors
1 2.7-kΩ resistor
1 1.6-kΩ resistor
1 1-kΩ resistor
1 100-Ω, 0.5-W resistor
1 430-Ω, 1-W resistor
1 200-Ω, 1-W resistor
Parts for KCS circuits:
1 74123 dual monostable multivibrator
1 LM319 comparator
1 0.15-μF capacitor
1 0.1-μF capacitor
1 0.05-μF capacitor
1 10-kΩ trimpot
1 100-kΩ resistor
2 39-kΩ resistors
1 10-kΩ resistor
2 1-kΩ resistors
1 100-Ω resistor

PROCEDURE

MODULE 1 TTY output.

Data usually is sent to a teletype in a serial format such as that shown in Fig. 31-1. Parallel data in a microcomputer can be converted to serial form and sent to a teletype either by a UART or by a program routine. This

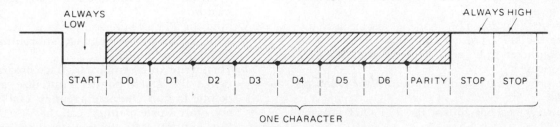

Fig. 31-1 Format for asynchronous serial-data transmission.

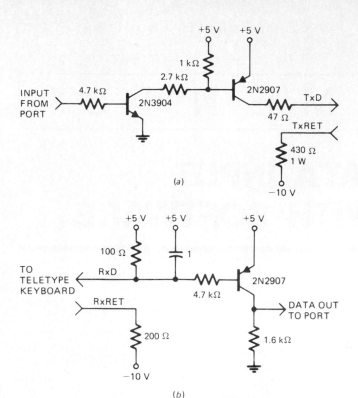

(a)

(b)

Fig. 31-2 *(a)* Schematic for a converter from a logic level to a 20-mA current loop. *(b)* Schematic for a converter from a 20-mA current loop to a logic level.

module explores how data can be converted and sent by using the software method.

1. Communication to and from a teletype is done by current loops. Figure 31-2a shows a circuit that converts standard TTL logic levels, such as those from a microcomputer output port, to a nominal 20-mA current loop to send to a teletype. A high on the input of the 20-mA driver, for example, produces a nominal output current of 20 mA, which is a high for the current loop.

   Figure 31-2b shows a circuit that converts a 20-mA current-loop signal from a teletype to logic levels suitable for a microcomputer input port.

2. Data often is sent to a teletype at 110 baud. What is the time in milliseconds for each bit at this rate?

3. Draw a flowchart for a subroutine to send 1 data byte serially out the least significant bit of a port at 110 baud with 2 stop bits. Note that the LSB of the data byte is sent first and the MSB, or parity bit, is sent last before the stop bits.

4. Write the TTY output program in two parts.
   a. Write the assembly language subroutine program for your flowchart. Save all flags and registers used in the routine.
   b. Then write an assembly language program to initialize the stack pointer, initialize the port, load the character to be sent, and call the TTY OUT subroutine.

5. Test the program, using one or more of the following methods.

6. Using an oscilloscope to test the TTY OUT subroutine.
   a. Make the program into an endless loop that sends

the same character over and over.
   b. An oscilloscope can then be connected to the output port line to check the format and timing of the output data word.

7. Use a teletype to test the TTY OUT subroutine.
   a. If the TTY OUT subroutine checks out with the oscilloscope and if a teletype is available, build the 20-mA current-loop driver shown in Fig. 31-2a.
   b. Connect it to the output port line and the teletype.
   c. When the routine is run, the teletype should print out the character sent.

8. Using two microcomputers to test the TTY OUT subroutine.
   a. If a teletype is not available but you have two microcomputers, one can be programmed with the TTY OUT subroutine that you write in this module.
   b. The other microcomputer can be programmed with the TTY IN subroutine developed in Module 2.
   c. Run both programs and check for a successful transfer of a block of data.

9. Consider these possible modifications:
   a. How would you modify this program to send the data bytes at 300 baud?
   b. How would you modify the initialization program so that it sends a block of 256 bytes of data from a table in memory and then returns control to the monitor?

MODULE 2 Teletype input.

1. Serial data can also be read in from a teletype or some other source by using a software routine.
   a. Figure 31-3 shows a flowchart for a routine to read in serial data in the format shown in Fig. 31-1.
   b. As is done in a UART, this routine waits for a low on the input line.
   c. It then checks again after a 0.5-bit time to find out whether the low was a valid start bit or just a noise transient.
   d. If the start bit was valid, the routine waits 1 full bit time and reads the first data bit. At what position in the data bit will this read take place? Why is this desirable?
   e. As bits are read in, they are rotated into a register or memory location to build the data word.
   f. When all the bits are collected, the routine waits for a stop bit, restores registers, and returns. It is important that the routine actually detect the stop bit. If the routine did not wait for a stop bit, then when the last data bit was a 0, the routine might return and be recalled while this bit was still low. If the timing was slightly off, this low might get treated as a start bit, and the wrong bits would be read in.

2. Writing the TTY IN subroutine.
   a. Write an assembly language subroutine for the flowchart in Fig. 31-3.
   b. Then write an assembly language program to initialize the stack pointer, initialize a memory pointer to store characters read in a table in memory, start a byte counter, call the TTY IN subroutine, and return to the monitor when the desired number of bytes is read in.

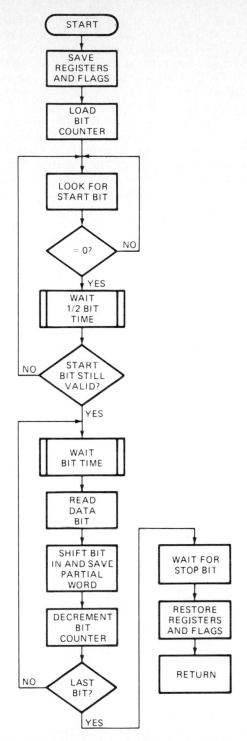

Fig. 31-3 Flowchart for a program to read data from a teletype.

3. Using two microcomputers to test the TTY IN subroutine.

a. Connect the input line of the microcomputer containing the TTY IN subroutine to the output port line of another microcomputer that contains the TTY subroutine OUT from Module 1. Connect a 4.7-kΩ pull-up resistor from the input port line to V_{CC}. This is necessary so that the receiver "sees" a high when the transmitter port line is floating, as it is before the output routine is run.

b. Start the input program running first and then the output program. The input program should read in the number of characters you loaded in the byte counter and then return control to the monitor. You can use the monitor commands to examine memory to find out whether the characters sent were properly received.

4. Using a teletype to test the TTY IN subroutine.

a. If a teletype is available, add the current-loop adapter from Fig. 31-1b to your input port line.

b. Use the data sent from the teletype to test the program.

MODULE 3 Sending and storing data on tape by using a KCS tape interface.

1. An inexpensive way to store microcomputer programs is on magnetic tape. Cassette or reel-to-reel recorders can be used. A problem with these machines is that their frequency response is too poor to record digital pulses directly. Digital data often is recorded on these tapes by using frequency shift keying (FSK), which uses one frequency tone to represent a digital 1 and another frequency to represent a digital 0.

2. Kansas City standard.

a. The KCS for 300-baud transmission uses 8 cycles of 2400 Hz to represent a 1 and 4 cycles of 1200 Hz to represent a 0.

b. The KCS also specifies the format for serial-data recording.

(1) It states that a recording should start with 30 s of all 1s (2400 Hz).

(2) Data is sent in blocks of 256 characters separated by 5 s of all 1s (2400 Hz).

(3) Each data character consists of 1 low start bit, 8 data bits including parity, and 2 high stop bits.

3. Writing the KCS send program.

a. Figure 31-4 shows a flowchart for a subroutine to send a block of data out the least significant bit of a port in KCS format.

b. Note that this is very similar to the TTY OUT subroutine except for the subroutines that send a 0 as 4 cycles of 1200 Hz or a 1 as 8 cycles of 2400 Hz.

c. First write and test the assembly language subroutines to send 0 and 1.

(1) The principle is to send a low, wait a half-cycle time, send a high, wait a half-cycle time, and repeat the desired number of times.

(2) What is the time low for 1200 Hz?

(3) What is the time high for 2400 Hz?

d. When these routines work properly, write an assembly language program for the rest of the subroutine in Fig. 31-4. Note that these programs provide a good example of the use of nested subroutines.

e. Then write an assembly language program to initialize the stack pointer, the output port, the memory pointer, and the byte counter. This program should call the KCS output routine and return control to the monitor when the entire block of data has been sent.

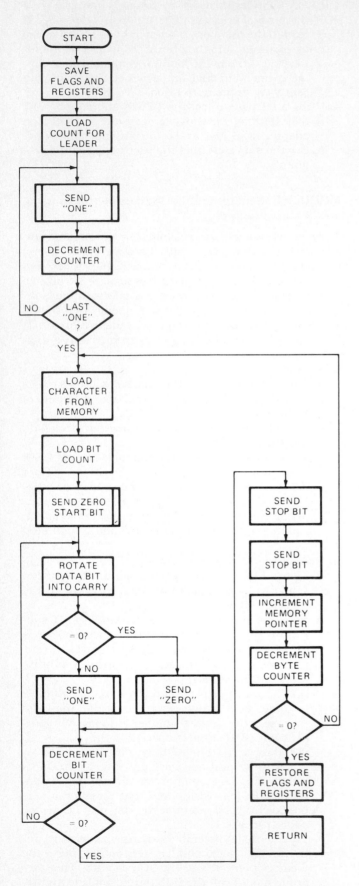

Fig. 31-4 Flowchart for a subroutine to output data in KCS format.

4. Testing the KCS send program. For testing purposes, the KCS output subroutine can be made into an endless loop that sends out the same byte, 55H for example, over and over. The output waveforms can then be checked with a standard oscilloscope. The variable horizontal time/div control of the oscilloscope may need adjusting to obtain a stable display.

5. Using the KCS program to store data on tape.
   a. To make it compatible with a tape recorder microphone input, the signal from the port line must be attenuated and filtered. The circuit in Fig. 31-5a will do this reasonably well for most recorders. The simple filtering is required because the harmonic content of the square waves produced by the microcomputer often generates strange waveforms when an attempt is made to record them on tape.
   b. If a tape recorder is available, build the circuit of Fig. 31-5a and use it with Module 4 to record and play back a block of data.

MODULE 4 Receiving KCS format from tape.

1. To simplify the reading of data stored on tape in KCS format by a microcomputer, some external hardware

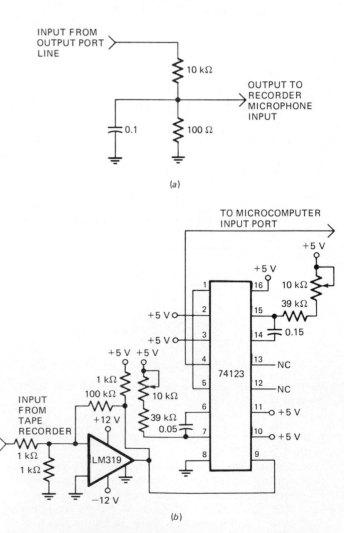

Fig. 31-5 (a) Schematic for an attenuator and filter circuitry for a KCS tape output. (b) Schematic for a KCS converter from FSK to logic level.

is used. Figure 31-5*b* shows a simple circuit to convert the audio tone signals from the tape recorder to a simple high or low for each bit. In this form the data can be read in with a subroutine very similar to the TTY IN subroutine of Module 1. (Only the baud rate needs to be changed.)

2. KCS receive-circuit description (Fig. 31-5*b*).

   a. The LM319 comparator converts low-level signals from the tape recorder output jack to logic-level signals. For a 101 pattern from the tape, what waveform would you expect to see on the output of the comparator?

   b. The 74123 is a dual, retriggerable monostable multivibrator. The first section of the 74123 is set to trigger on the falling edge and give an output pulse width of about 600 μs. For 2400 Hz it is retriggered before its *RC* time is up. Therefore, for a 2400-Hz input, the output of the first section is high. With a 1200-Hz input, the Q output of this section of the 74123 will fall low after 600 μs and stay low until retriggered by the next falling edge of the 1200-Hz signal.

   c. The second stage of the 74123 is set to trigger on an input falling edge and give an output pulse width of about 840 μs. When triggered by an input low then, the $\overline{Q}$ of this section will go low for 3.3 ms, which is the bit time for 300 baud. If this section is not triggered by an input low, the $\overline{Q}$ output will remain high.

   d. To clarify the operation of this circuit, for each stage Fig. 31-6 shows an output timing diagram for a KCS 101 pattern input from the comparator.

3. Building and testing the KCS receive circuit, using two microcomputers.

   a. Build the second section of the 74123 circuitry, and adjust its output pulse width to 840 μs.

   b. Build the first section of the 74123 circuitry, and adjust its output pulse so that with an 1800-Hz-input square wave, the Q output just barely stays high all the time.

   c. Connect the input of the 74123 circuit to the output of a microcomputer programmed with the KCS output program.

   d. The output of the second stage of the 74123 can be connected to the input of a microcomputer programmed with the TTY IN subroutine.

   e. Running both programs tests the complete transmit-receive process.

4. Completing and testing the KCS receive circuit, using a tape recorder.

   a. If a tape recorder is available, build the comparator section.

   b. Test it by applying a 1200-Hz, 100-mV rms sinewave input to the comparator and observing its output on an oscilloscope. You should obtain a TTL-level square-wave output from the comparator. What waveform should this produce on the second section of the 74123?

   c. When the comparator section works correctly, data can be sent from the microcomputer with the KCS program to a tape recorder microphone input.

   d. The headphone output of the tape recorder is connected to the comparator input, and the tape is played back.

   e. With these circuits and programs you can save long programs on tape and then reload them into RAM as needed.

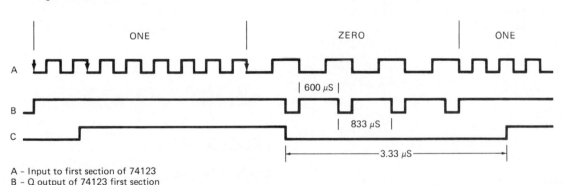

A – Input to first section of 74123
B – Q output of 74123 first section
C – $\overline{Q}$ output of 74123 second section

Fig. 31-6 Waveforms for KCS input circuitry.

USING AN LSI CLOCK CIRCUIT WITH A MICROCOMPUTER FOR A REAL-TIME REFERENCE

REFERENCES

Hall: page 360.

MM5314 data sheet (in appendix).

OBJECTIVES

At the conclusion of this laboratory exercise, you should be able to:

1. Demonstrate how an LSI clock IC can be interfaced with a microcomputer.
2. Create and test an assembly language subroutine to read in multiplexed data from an LSI clock circuit.
3. Write and test an assembly language subroutine to convert seven-segment code values for time to BCD or ASCII.
4. Devise and test an assembly language interrupt service routine to increment every 24 h a count of days kept in a register or memory location.

EQUIPMENT

1 Microcomputer with two 8-bit input ports
1 Oscilloscope
1 Sine wave signal generator with 10-V peak at 60 Hz
2 Power supplies with outputs of 5 and −12 V

MATERIALS

Clock module parts:
  1 MM5314 clock IC
  7 Common-anode LED displays
  7 2N3904 transistors
  6 2N2907 transistors
  1 1N914 diode (or equivalent)
  1 0.01-μF capacitor
  1 220-kΩ resistor

  1 100-kΩ resistor
 14 4.7-kΩ resistors
  6 2.2-kΩ resistors
  7 150-Ω resistors
Buffers and interrupt-circuitry parts:
  2 CD4049s (or equivalent)
  1 CD4050 (or equivalent)
  1 7430 eight-input NAND gate
  1 7474 dual D flip-flop
  1 74121 monostable multivibrator
  1 0.01-μF capacitor
  1 0.005-μF capacitor
  8 10-kΩ resistors
General parts:
  1 10-μF capacitor
  4 0.01-μF bypass capacitors
Assorted color-coded hookup wire

PROCEDURE

MODULE 1 Interfacing and operating a real-time clock with a microcomputer.

1. Many microcomputer applications require a seconds, minutes, and hours real-time reference. Experiment 25 shows how this can be accomplished on an interrupt basis by using the 60-Hz power line frequency as a reference. For applications where the time load of the interrupt method is not desirable, an external LSI clock circuit can be used to independently keep track of time. The time is then read in by the microcomputer only when required. A side benefit of this method is that the time can also be continuously displayed without any additional software load on the microcomputer.
2. Analyzing the MM5314 clock IC.
   a. Figure 32-1 shows a circuit for a clock using an MM5314 IC. The circuit requires only a 5-V sup-

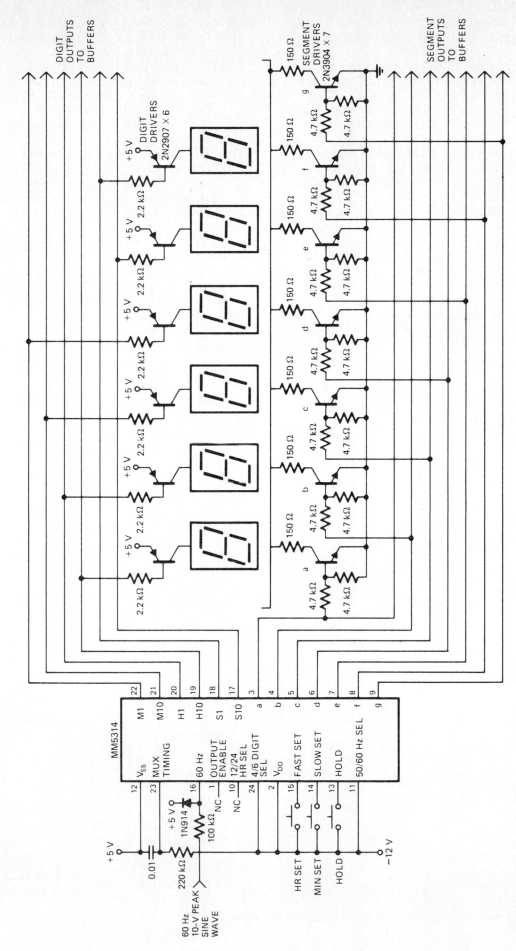

Fig. 32-1 A digital-clock circuit module using the MM5314.

ply, a −12-V supply, and a 60-Hz, 8- to 10-V-peak sine wave input. It displays seconds, minutes, and hours.

b. Read the data sheet in the appendix to learn the operation of the MM5314, and answer the following questions:

(1) To what logic family does the device belong?

(2) Are the segment outputs active high or active low?

(3) Are the digit outputs active high or active low?

(4) Which digit strobe is sent out first?

(5) Is the 5314 in Fig. 32-1 connected for 12- or 24-h format?

(6) For about what frequency is the multiplex oscillator set?

3. Building and testing the clock circuit module.

a. If this circuit is not already built as a laboratory module, first build and test the display section.

b. Then add the MM5314 circuitry and test it.

(1) Remember MOS handling precautions.

(2) The fast-set, slow-set, and hold inputs of the MM5314 can be used to set it to the correct time.

c. Figure 32-2 shows circuitry to level-shift and buffer the segment outputs and digit-driver outputs to TTL levels.

(1) Note that 10-kΩ resistors are used on the inputs of the digit drivers to prevent too much current from flowing through the input protection diodes of the CMOS 4049 when the 5314 digit outputs go low. The resistors are not needed on the segment outputs.

(2) Add these buffers if they are not already present.

d. Connect the outputs of the segment buffers, in order, to one input port of your microcomputer. Connect the outputs of the digit drivers, in order, to another input port.

e. For software convenience, connect unused input-port bits to ground.

f. The remainder of the circuit in Fig. 32-2, which consists of the 7430, 7474, 74121, and clock circuitry for the 7474, is described and added in Module 3.

4. Reading the clock.

a. Draw a flowchart for a program to read in the

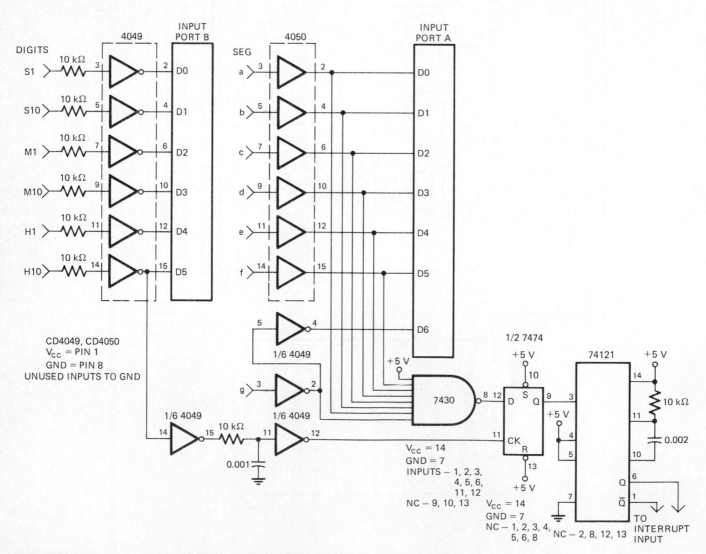

Fig. 32-2 Digit and segment buffers and the 24-h interrupt pulse circuitry for a digital clock.

seven-segment code for each time digit from the MM5314.

(1) The seven-segment codes should be put in six successive memory locations with seconds first.

(2) To shorten the program, think about how the strobe-detect, read-data process can be done as a loop. (*Hint:* Use a mask word to check for the presence of a strobe. Then rotate it and use it to check for the next strobe.)

b. Write and test the assembly language program for this flowchart.

c. How long does it take the microcomputer to read in the 6 data bytes (segment codes)? What is the major factor that determines this?

MODULE 2 Converting seven-segment code for time to BCD or ASCII.

1. One use of this real-time data might be to print out the time on some kind of time card. The printer most likely will require BCD or ASCII data, so the seven-segment code must be converted. A simple technique for doing this is described in Hall, pages 303–305.

   a. The seven-segment codes for 0 through 9 are put in a table in memory, in descending order.

   b. A register or memory location is loaded with the number of entries in the table.

   c. The byte to be converted is compared to the first table entry.

   (1) If they match, the register contains the correct code for the byte.

   (2) If they do not match, the register is decremented by 1 and the next value in the table is compared with the byte to be converted.

   d. The process is continued until a match is found. At this point the counter register will contain the desired BCD code.

2. Write and test an assembly language routine to convert the seven-segment codes for seconds, minutes, and hours, read in from the MM5314, to BCD code.

   a. The BCD code can replace the seven-segment code in the table into which it was loaded as it was read. Hall, Table 3-1, contains the seven-segment codes for BCD digits 0 through 9. Note that in this table the *a* segment is in the MSB position. How can the BCD code for 0 through 9 easily be converted to ASCII if required? [*Hint:* Look at the hexadecimal code for numbers 0 through 9 in Hall, Table 3-2.]

   b. When this routine works correctly, add it to the routine you wrote in Module 1 to read in the time from the MM5314. The sum of these two routines

produces a table of time values that can be easily accessed by a print routine.

3. If your microcomputer has a readily available display routine, use it to show the time on the LED displays of the microcomputer.

MODULE 3 Interrupt-based day counter.

1. The MM5314 clock IC chosen for this experiment is inexpensive and readily available, but it does not have the output for days.

   a. The 7430, 7474, and 74121 shown in Fig. 33-2 produce an interrupt pulse every 24 h. A count of these pulses can be kept in a memory location by an interrupt service routine. Determine and explain how these devices produce the pulse.

   b. If it is not already built, add this interrupt circuitry to your clock module circuit.

   c. Connect an output of this circuit to an interrupt input of your microcomputer.

   (1) Use the Q output of the 74121 for an active high interrupt input and the $\overline{Q}$ output of the 74121 for an active low interrupt input.

   (2) The 74121 pulse narrower is required so that the processor will not keep getting interrupted by the same pulse.

2. Write an assembly language interrupt service subroutine to increment the count in a memory location each time the interrupt input is pulsed. *Note:*

   a. The memory location chosen should immediately follow the hours code. It can then be easily accessed by a print routine.

   b. The count should be kept in BCD format.

   c. Flags and any registers used in the routine should be saved.

   d. What must be done to interrupts prior to a return to the main program?

3. Testing the interrupt routine.

   a. Write a program to initialize the stack pointer and ports, load a 0 in the memory location to be used as a day counter, and execute a HERE: JMP HERE instruction while waiting for an interrupt.

   b. Run this program.

   c. Instead of waiting 24 h to find out whether the routine works, connect the fast-set input of the MM5314 to V_{DD}. This speeds up the hours count. After the display shows that 2 or 3 days have passed, press RESET and check whether the day count in memory has been incremented.

4. If time permits, you can write a print routine to read the time values from the table and send them in serial format to a printer or CRT terminal.

A MICROCOMPUTER-CONTROLLED 2708 EPROM PROGRAMMER

REFERENCES

Hall: pages 365–377.

2708 data sheet (in appendix).

OBJECTIVES

At the conclusion of this laboratory exercise, you should be able to:

1. Build and test the hardware interface between a microcomputer and a 2708 to be programmed.
2. Write an assembly language program to read a 2708 and verify that it is fully erased.
3. Create an assembly language program to program a 2708 with data stored in system memory and then to verify that the programming was successful.

EQUIPMENT

1 Microcomputer with a latched 8-bit output port, a latched 6-bit output port, and an 8-bit port programmable as either input or output

4 Power supplies with outputs of 5, 12, 26, and −5 V

1 Oscilloscope

MATERIALS

Hardware-interface module parts:

1 7407 open-collector high-voltage output hex buffer

2 2N3906 transistors

2 2N3904 transistors

4 LEDs

2 0.005-μF capacitors

4 10-kΩ resistors

2 2.7-kΩ resistors

4 150-Ω resistors

2 51-Ω resistors

1 SPST switch

1 3PST switch

1 24-pin zero-insertion-force socket (optional)

PROCEDURE

INTRODUCTION As you write longer programs for a microcomputer, it is very helpful to have some means of storing them so that you do not have to hand-load them into RAM each time you want to run them. One storage option is magnetic tape; another is EPROMs. Now EPROMs have the advantage that the stored program is ready to run when the system is powered up.

Hall, pages 365–367, describes the hardware and software for a 2716 EPROM programmer. The 2716 is an excellent device that requires only a 5-V power supply. However, its cost is still quite high for general laboratory use. Therefore, the smaller but much less expensive 2708 was chosen for this experiment. Most microcomputer boards such as the MEK6800D2 and the SDK-85 can easily be adapted to interface to a 2708. In a laboratory environment, the 12-, 5-, and −5-V supplies required for normal read operation of the 2708 should not be a problem.

MODULE 1 Hardware interface for a 2708 EPROM programmer.

1. Carefully read the data sheet for the 2708 (in the appendix).
   a. How many data bytes can be stored in a 2708?
   b. How many address inputs does it have?
   c. How is a 2708 erased?
   d. What is the state of all bits when erased?
   e. What voltage levels are required on $\overline{\text{CS}}$/WE and PGM (program) during a read operation?
   f. What voltage levels are required on $\overline{\text{CS}}$/WE and PGM during programming?
   g. Are these levels static or pulsed?
   h. How is data sent to an address being programmed?

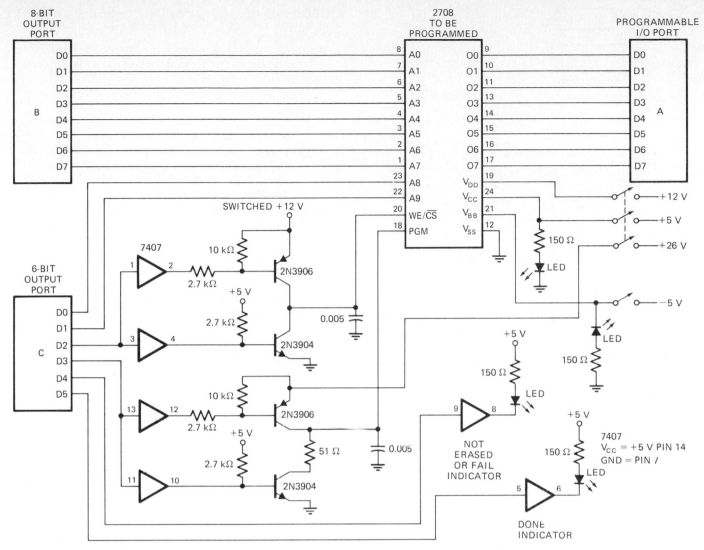

Fig. 33-1 Schematic for circuitry to interface a 2708 EPROM to a microcomputer for programming.

2. Figure 33-1 shows how a 2708 can be interfaced to three microcomputer output ports.

   a. Port A sends data to the 2708 or reads data from it.

   b. Port B is used to send the lower 8 address bits.

   c. Port C sends the upper 2 address bits, the control bits for the $\overline{CS}$/WE and program-driver circuits, and the control bits for two LED indicators.

   d. Intel recommends that ideally the -5-V V_{BB} should be turned on before the other supply voltages and turned off after they have been. This is the purpose of the switches on the right side of Fig. 33-1.

3. If this interface is not available as a laboratory module, build and test it.

   a. Are the control outputs from port C active high or active low?

   b. Connect a pulse source to the inputs of each pulse-driver circuit, and make sure the output voltage levels are correct.

   c. For the program pulse, also make sure the rise-times and falltimes are within the range specified on the data sheet.

   d. When these circuits work correctly, connect all lines to the microprocessor ports.

   e. Before writing the major programs for this experiment, write and test a short routine to initialize the ports and exercise each of the four control outputs of port C.

MODULE 2 A program to read and verify fully erased 2708 EPROM.

1. Figure 33-2 shows a flowchart for a program module to check whether a 2708 is fully erased. Write an assembly language program for this flowchart. Note that 2 address bits and 4 control bits must be sent to port C. These two parts can be combined into one word for sending, with an OR or an ADD instruction. Review Hall, Fig. 8-11, if necessary.

2. Test the program.

   a. First run the program without a 2708 in the socket and with the eight port A data input/outputs tied to 5 V with 1-kΩ resistors.

   b. Check that the correct voltage levels are present on $\overline{CS}$/WE and PGM.

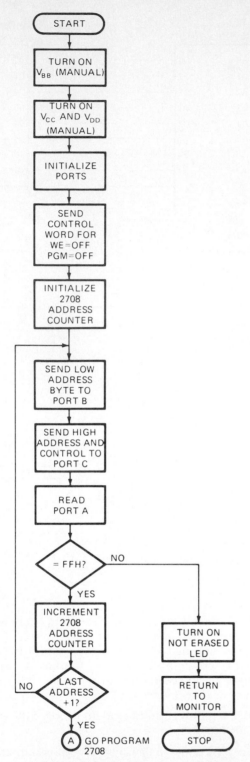

START

TURN ON
V_BB (MANUAL)

TURN ON
V_CC AND V_DD
(MANUAL)

INITIALIZE
PORTS

SEND
CONTROL
WORD FOR
WE=OFF
PGM=OFF

INITIALIZE
2708
ADDRESS
COUNTER

SEND LOW
ADDRESS
BYTE TO
PORT B

SEND HIGH
ADDRESS AND
CONTROL TO
PORT C

READ
PORT A

= FFH? —— NO

YES

INCREMENT
2708
ADDRESS
COUNTER

TURN ON
NOT ERASED
LED

NO — LAST
ADDRESS
+1?

RETURN
TO
MONITOR

YES

(A) GO PROGRAM
2708

STOP

Fig. 33-2 Flowchart for a program module to check whether a 2708 EPROM is completely erased.

c. If the program exits to the monitor without lighting the not-erased LED, tie one port B data input/output to ground and rerun the program. This time the not-erased LED should light.

d. If your program passes all these tests, try running it with a 2708 in the socket.

MODULE 3 Programming and verifying a 2708 EPROM.

1. Study the data sheet sections on programming to determine the sequence of signals that must be sent to a 2708 to program it.
   a. Note that programming is done a little bit at a time.
      (1) A location is addressed and pulsed with the desired value and a program pulse.
      (2) Then the next sequential location is addressed and written to, and a program pulse is sent.
      (3) The process is repeated until all 1024 locations have been addressed.
   b. A loop through all 1024 locations must be made between 100 and 1000 times, depending on the program pulse width.
   c. The number of loops N times the program pulse width T_{PW} must be greater than or equal to 100 ms.
   d. For $T_{PW} = 0.5$ ms, how many loops are required?
2. Writing a routine to program a 2708.
   a. Figure 33-3 shows a flowchart for a program to program a 2708 and verify that the programming was successful.
   b. Write an assembly language program for the section of this flowchart up to the end of the second decision box.
   c. Add a jump or branch-back-to-start instruction to make the program into an endless loop.
   d. Run this program loop with no 2708 in the socket.
   e. Check the $\overline{CS}$/WE level and the program pulse width with an oscilloscope.
   f. Adjust your delay constant so that the program pulse width is slightly more than 0.5 ms.
   g. Why does the first decision box in Fig. 33-3 check for the last address plus 1?
   h. How long does it take to program a 2708?
3. Writing the routine to verify 2708 programming.
   a. The verify section of the flowchart in Fig. 33-3 switches the 2708 back to read mode. It then reads a byte from the 2708 and compares it to the source byte in system RAM.
   b. Write an assembly language program for the verify section and add it to the program section in step 2.
   c. Run the combined program with no 2708 in the socket to make sure that $\overline{CS}$/WE and PGM are set to the right levels for read mode.
4. If all works well, put a 2708 in the socket and run the combined programs of Figs. 33-2 and 33-3.
   a. For a test, you might set the source pointer to the start of your system monitor program. When programmed, the 2708 should contain a copy of the monitor or at least the first 1024 bytes of it.
   b. Remember that all 1024 bytes of the 2708 must be looped through during a programming operation.
   c. Happiness is seeing the done-LED light come on after 2 or 3 min.
      (1) When you see this, turn off V_{DD}, V_P, and V_{CC}.
      (2) Then turn off V_{BB} and remove the 2708 from the socket.

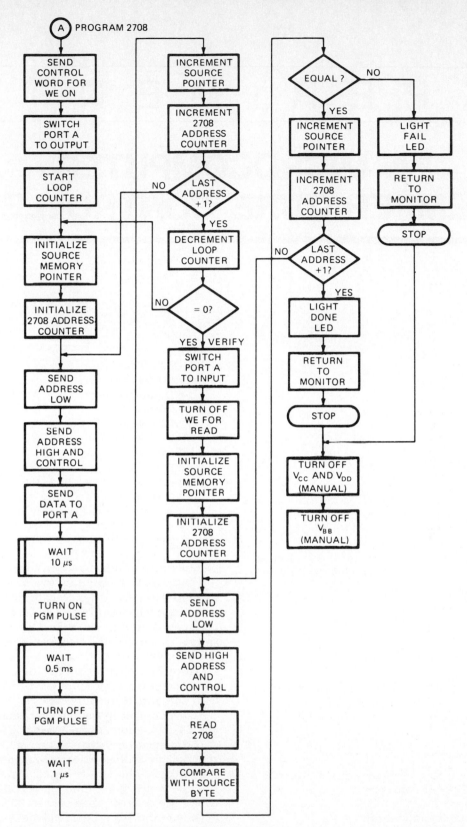

Fig. 33-3 Flowchart for a subroutine to program and verify a 2708 EPROM.

A MICROCOMPUTER-CONTROLLED 2708 EPROM PROGRAMMER

A MICROCOMPUTER
TEMPERATURE CONTROLLER

REFERENCES

Hall: pages 377–389.

OBJECTIVES

At the conclusion of this laboratory exercise, you should be able to:

1. Build and test circuitry to produce a voltage proportional to temperature and digitize this voltage.
2. Write an assembly language program to control an ADC0808 analog-to-digital converter.
3. Write an assembly language program to control the temperature of a water bath by varying the duty cycle of power applied to a heater.

EQUIPMENT

1 Microcomputer with two input ports and one output port
3 Power supplies with outputs of +5, +15, and −15 V
1 120-V ac hotplate or immersion heater
1 1-liter Pyrex beaker

MATERIALS

1 ADC0808 CMOS A/D converter
2 LM308 op amps
1 74121 monostable multivibrator
1 74C14 CMOS hex Schmitt-trigger inverter
2 LM329 voltage-reference diodes
1 LM335 temperature sensor
1 Solid-state relay with 0-V turn-on (Potter-Brumfield EOM1DB72)
1 10-μF tantalum capacitor
7 0.1-μF ceramic bypass capacitors
1 0.001-μF capacitor

1 0.002-μF capacitor
2 10-kΩ potentiometers
1 5-kΩ potentiometer
5 10-kΩ resistors
1 12-kΩ resistor
1 18-kΩ resistor
1 82-kΩ resistor
1 6-kΩ resistor
1 2-kΩ resistor
1 1-kΩ resistor

PROCEDURE

As described in the references, the temperature of a liquid bath can be brought up to a set point very precisely by controlling the duty cycle of the applied power. As the water bath temperature gets closer to the set point temperature, the duty cycle of the applied power is reduced, so that the water bath temperature does not overshoot the set point.

Figure 34-1 shows circuitry that can be added to a microcomputer to measure the temperature of a water bath and control the duty cycle of 120-V ac power delivered to a hotplate or immersion heater. The circuitry in Fig. 34-1 functions as follows:

The temperature sensor is an LM335. The LM335 is a zener diode with a linear temperature coefficient of +10 mV/°C. The low-drift LM308 amplifier amplifies this to 40 mV/°C for input to the A/D converter. This allows the desired range of 0 to 99°C to use a greater portion of the A/D range. Applying a negative reference voltage to the noninverting input of the amplifier allows the output to be adjusted to 0.0 V at 0.0°C. The LM335 is rated for operation over a temperature range of −10 to +100°C. A temperature probe can be made by sealing the LM335 in the end of a piece of $\frac{1}{4}$-in-diameter glass tubing with high-temperature silicon sealant.

Analog-to-digital conversion is done by a National ADC0808 data acquisition system. The heart of the

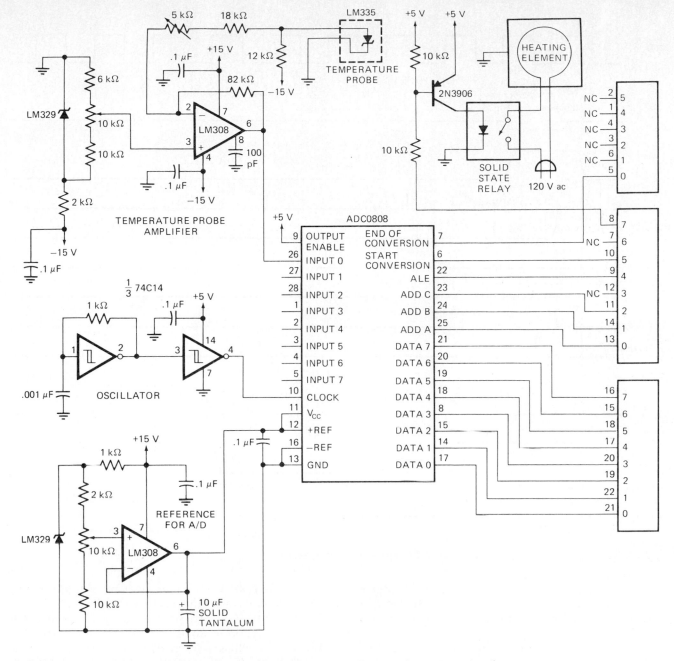

Fig. 34-1 Circuitry for temperature sensing, A/D conversion, and power control.

ADC0808 is an 8-bit binary output, successive-approximation A/D converter. On the input of the A/D converter is an eight-input multiplexer. The input channel being digitized by the A/D converter is determined by a 3-bit address on the ADD A, ADD B, and ADD C inputs. An eight-input data acquisition system was chosen so that eight variables could be monitored with the same A/D converter. A Schmitt-trigger oscillator produces a 300-kHz clock for the A/D converter. The voltage drop of an LM329 low-drift zener is buffered by an LM308 amplifier to produce a V_{CC} and V_{REF} of 5.12 V for the A/D converter. With this reference voltage, the A/D converter will have 256 steps of 20 mV each.

Figure 34-2 shows the timing waveforms and parameters for the ADC0808. Note the sequence in which signals must be sent to the device. First the address of the

desired channel is sent to the multiplexer address inputs. After 50 ns, address latch enable (ALE) is sent high. After another 2.5 μs the start-conversion signal is made high and then low, and ALE is made low. When the end-of-conversion signal goes high, data can be read from the A/D converter into a port.

The heater can be either a 120-V ac hotplate or a 120-V ac immersion heater such as those used to heat a single cup of water for coffee. A solid-state relay is used to switch the heater on and off. The microcomputer controls the heat output by pulsing the relay on and off for varying duty cycles.

The relay used is an optically isolated, zero-voltage-turn-on, zero-current-turn-off type. This type is a little more expensive, but it switches on and off rapidly, provides several thousand volts of electrical isolation be-

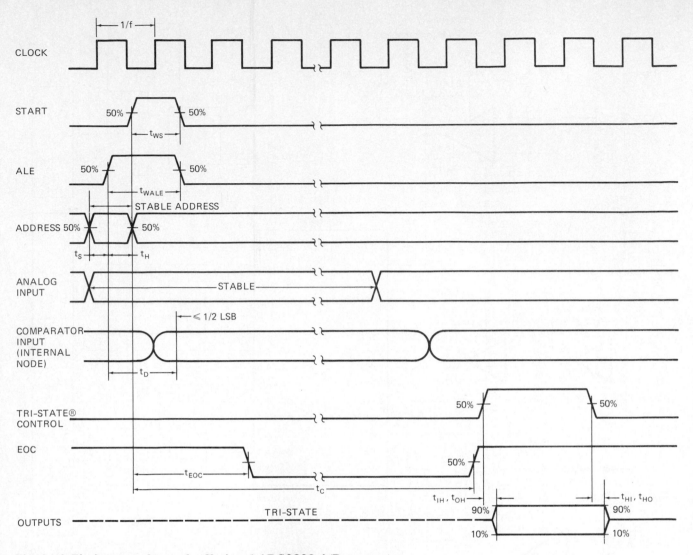

Fig. 34-2 Timing waveforms for National ADC0808 A/D converter.

tween control input and power output, and produces very little electromagnetic interference (EMI) because the power is always on for some integral number of half cycles of the ac line voltage.

A relay such as the Potter-Brumfield EOM1DB72 requires only 11 mA maximum at 5 V to turn it on, and with a proper heat sink it will control up to 25 A.

The driver transistor on the input of the relay serves three purposes. It supplies the drive for the relay, isolates the port pin from the relay, and holds the relay in the off position when power is first turned on. This is a good idea because the port pins are floating after a reset.

MODULE 1 Building and testing the hardware.

1. If the circuitry in Fig. 34-1 is not already built as a unit, build and test each part individually.

   a. Build the temperature probe and amplifier. The LM335 probe should be sealed in high-temperature silicon sealant so the leads do not short-circuit. With the probe in an ice and water mixture (0°C), adjust the 10-kΩ potentiometer so that the output of the amplifier reads 0.000 V. Then with the probe in boiling water (100°C) adjust the 5-kΩ potentiometer so that the output of the amplifier

reads 4.000 V. The circuit is then calibrated to produce a voltage output of 40 mV/°C.

2. Build the 74C14 Schmitt-trigger oscillator next. The output should be about a 300-kHz square wave.

3. Build the voltage reference for the A/D converter, and adjust the 10-kΩ potentiometer so that the output voltage is 5.12 V.

4. Build the solid-state relay-driver circuit, and test it. Since this circuit is useful for turning on many kinds of appliances with a microcomputer, you may want to wire in a standard 120-V ac outlet. You can then plug in a standard light and see whether your driver turns on the light when you ground its input.

5. Connect all the inputs and outputs to the ADC0808 A/D converter. To test the A/D converter, you must write a test program.

6. Look closely at the timing waveforms for the ADC0808 in Fig. 34-2 to determine the sequence of signals that must be sent to the ADC0808 to perform a conversion. Draw a flowchart or write a task list for this sequence.

7. Write an assembly language program to produce this sequence of signals to the ADC0808 and to read the 8-bit binary value for the temperature into the accumulator.

8. Enter the program in your microcomputer and run it. The binary value you get in the accumulator should be twice the actual temperature.

9. When the A/D converter program runs correctly, write and run a short test routine to turn the solid-state relay on for about 1 s and off for about 1 s. It is important to use software to test each part of the hardware before you try to write and run the main program.

MODULE 2 Writing the control program.

Overview Power delivered to the heater is determined by the duty cycle of a waveform with a 10-s period. The duty cycle is adjusted in increments of 100 ms. The number of increments that the heater is on during a period is called DCHI. The number of increments that the heater is off during a period is called DCLO. Initially, and after every 10 s, the program does an A/D conversion to find the current temperature of the bath. This temperature is compared to the set point temperature. If the actual temperature is at or above the set point, the program sets DCLO for maximum, 64H (100 decimal), and DCHI for minimum, 01H. Then the program counts off 10 s (100 increments × 100 ms per increment) with the heater off and loops back to recheck the water bath temperature.

If the water bath temperature is less than the set point temperature, then the program goes to a look-up table to get the appropriate value for DCLO. The value for DCHI is then found by subtracting DCLO from decimal 100 (64H). The heater is turned on and DCHI counted down with 100 ms for each count. The heater is then turned off, and DCLO is counted down with 100 ms for each count. After the 10 s required to count down DCHI and DCLO, the program loops back, does another A/D conversion to recheck the current temperature, and repeats the cycle.

1. Figure 34-3 shows a flowchart for the heater control program. Study this flowchart carefully to get an overview of the program you will be writing. Listed here are a few notes and hints concerning the program.

   a. The A/D conversion routine should have been already written for Module 1. The binary value returned from the A/D converter is actually twice the actual temperature. This can be divided by 2 by using instructions to rotate right and mask the MSB.

   b. If your microcomputer has a readily accessible display routine, you can convert the binary value for the temperature to BCD and display it on the data or address field LEDs. A binary-to-BCD algorithm is shown in the reference.

   c. The set point temperature is manually loaded into a memory location by the user before the program is run. The measured temperature from the A/D converter is subtracted from the set point temperature.

   d. To simplify program flow, if the bath temperature has reached the set point, 64H is loaded into an accumulator before the ΔT decision instructions.

   e. If the bath temperature has not reached the set point, then the value for DCLO is read from a

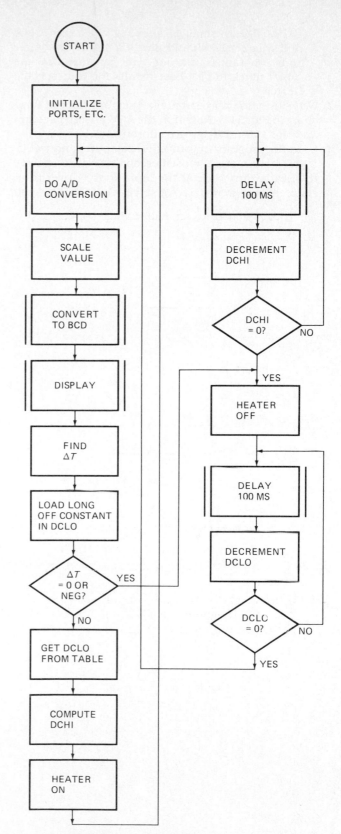

Fig. 34-3 Flowchart of program to control heater output by controlling the duty cycle.

table. This can be done by initializing a pointer to the start of the table and adding ΔT as an offset to point to the desired value for DCLO. This is the same technique used for code conversion in Experiment 27. Values in the table should range from

01H to 63H. A small ΔT should give a large DCLO, and a large ΔT should give a small DCLO. After your program is running, you can fine-tune the table values to give best results for your specific heater.

2. Write the assembly language program for the flowchart in Fig. 34-3. Note that the A/D converter section and the 100-ms delay are subroutines.

3. Load the program in your microcomputer and test it. If you have a storage oscilloscope, use it to observe the heater duty cycle at the input to the driver transistor. If you do not have a storage oscilloscope, you can connect a small neon pilot lamp in parallel with the heater to observe the change in duty cycle as the bath temperature approaches the set point temperature.

4. Plot a graph of temperature versus time for a set point temperature of 60°C. Does your controller overshoot the set point temperature? Does your controller hold the temperature within ±2°C? If not, experiment with different values in the table until it does. From this you should see that a microcomputer-controlled system can easily be customized by simply changing values in a table.

APPENDIX: DATA SHEETS

54/74 FAMILIES OF COMPATIBLE TTL CIRCUITS

PIN ASSIGNMENTS (TOP VIEWS)

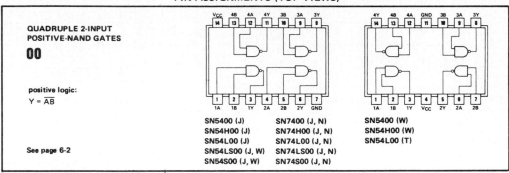

QUADRUPLE 2-INPUT POSITIVE-NAND GATES

00

positive logic:
$Y = \overline{AB}$

See page 6-2

SN5400 (J)   SN7400 (J, N)   SN5400 (W)
SN54H00 (J)   SN74H00 (J, N)   SN54H00 (W)
SN54L00 (J)   SN74L00 (J, N)   SN54L00 (T)
SN54LS00 (J, W)   SN74LS00 (J, N)
SN54S00 (J, W)   SN74S00 (J, N)

supply current¶

TYPE	I_{CCH} (mA) Total with outputs high		I_{CCL} (mA) Total with outputs low		I_{CC} (mA) Average per gate (50% duty cycle)
	TYP	MAX	TYP	MAX	TYP
'00	4	8	12	22	2
'04	6	12	18	33	2
'10	3	6	9	16.5	2
'20	2	4	6	11	2
'30	1	2	3	6	2
'H00	10	16.8	26	40	4.5
'H04	16	26	40	58	4.5
'H10	7.5	12.6	19.5	30	4.5
'H20	5	8.4	13	20	4.5
'H30	2.5	4.2	6.5	10	4.5
'L00	0.44	0.8	1.16	2.04	0.20
'L04	0.66	1.2	1.74	3.06	0.20
'L10	0.33	0.6	0.87	1.53	0.20
'L20	0.22	0.4	0.58	1.02	0.20
SN54L30	0.11	0.33	0.29	0.51	0.20
SN74L30	0.11	0.2	0.29	0.51	0.20
'LS00	0.8	1.6	2.4	4.4	0.4
'LS04	1.2	2.4	3.6	6.6	0.4
'LS10	0.6	1.2	1.8	3.3	0.4
'LS20	0.4	0.8	1.2	2.2	0.4
'LS30	0.35	0.5	0.6	1.1	0.48
'S00	10	16	20	36	3.75
'S04	15	24	30	54	3.75
'S10	7.5	12	15	27	3.75
'S20	5	8	10	18	3.75
'S30	3	5	5.5	10	4.25
'S133	3	5	5.5	10	4.25

switching characteristics at $V_{CC} = 5$ V, $T_A = 25°$C

TYPE	TEST CONDITIONS#	t_{PLH} (ns) Propagation delay time, low-to-high-level output			t_{PHL} (ns) Propagation delay time, high-to-low-level output		
		MIN	TYP	MAX	MIN	TYP	MAX
'00, '10	$C_L = 15$ pF, $R_L = 400\ \Omega$		11	22		7	15
'04, '20			12	22		8	15
'30			13	22		8	15
'H00	$C_L = 25$ pF, $R_L = 280\ \Omega$		5.9	10		6.2	10
'H04			6	10		6.5	10
'H10			5.9	10		6.3	10
'H20			6	10		7	10
'H30			6.8	10		8.9	12
'L00, 'L04, 'L10, L20	$C_L = 50$ pF, $R_L = 4$ kΩ		35	60		31	60
'L30			35	60		70	100
'LS00, 'LS04 'LS10, 'LS20	$C_L = 15$ pF, $R_L = 2$ kΩ		9	15		10	15
'LS30			8	15		13	20
'S00, 'S04	$C_L = 15$ pF, $R_L = 280\ \Omega$		3	4.5		3	5
'S10, 'S20	$C_L = 50$ pF, $R_L = 280\ \Omega$		4.5			5	
'S30, 'S133	$C_L = 15$ pF, $R_L = 280\ \Omega$		4	6		4.5	7
	$C_L = 50$ pF, $R_L = 280\ \Omega$		5.5			6.5	

#Load circuits and voltage waveforms are shown on pages 3-10 and 3-11.

¶Maximum values of I_{CC} are over the recommended operating ranges of V_{CC} and T_A; typical values are at $V_{CC} = 5$ V, $T_A = 25°$C.

schematics (each gate)

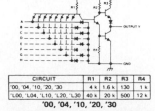

CIRCUIT	R1	R2	R3	R4
'00, '04, '10, '20, '30	4 k	1.6 k	130	1 k
'L00, 'L04, 'L10, 'L20, 'L30	40 k	20 k	500	12 k

'00, '04, '10, '20, '30
'L00, 'L04, 'L10, 'L20, 'L30, CIRCUITS
Input clamp diodes not on SN54L'/SN74L' circuits.

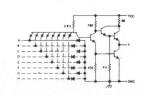

'H00, 'H04, 'H10, 'H20, 'H30 CIRCUITS

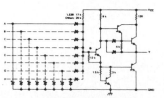

'LS00, 'LS04, 'LS10, 'LS20, 'LS30 CIRCUITS
*The 12-kΩ resistor is not on 'LS30.

Resistor values shown are nominal and in ohms.

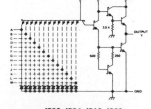

'S00, 'S04, 'S10, 'S20, 'S30, 'S133 CIRCUITS

Courtesy of Texas Instruments Incorporated.

113

POSITIVE-NAND GATES AND INVERTERS WITH TOTEM-POLE OUTPUTS

recommended operating conditions

		SERIES 54 / SERIES 74 '00, '04, '10, '20, '30			SERIES 54H / SERIES 74H 'H00, 'H04, 'H10, 'H20, 'H30			SERIES 54L / SERIES 74L 'L00, 'L04, 'L10, 'L20, 'L30			SERIES 54LS / SERIES 74LS 'LS00, 'LS04, 'LS10, 'LS20, 'LS30			SERIES 54S / SERIES 74S 'S00, 'S04, 'S10, 'S20, 'S133			UNIT
		MIN	NOM	MAX	MIN	NOM	MAX	MIN	NOM	MAX	MIN	NOM	MAX	MIN	NOM	MAX	
Supply voltage, V_{CC}	54 Family	4.5	5	5.5	4.5	5	5.5	4.5	5	5.5	4.5	5	5.5	4.5	5	5.5	V
	74 Family	4.75	5	5.25	4.75	5	5.25	4.75	5	5.25	4.75	5	5.25	4.75	5	5.25	
High-level output current, I_{OH}	54 Family		−400			−500			−100			−400			−1000		µA
	74 Family		−400			−500			−200			−400			−1000		
Low-level output current, I_{OL}	54 Family		16			20			2			4			20		mA
	74 Family		16			20			3.6			8			20		
Operating free-air temperature, T_A	54 Family	−55		125	−55		125	−55		125	−55		125	−55		125	°C
	74 Family	0		70	0		70	0		70	0		70	0		70	

electrical characteristics over recommended operating free-air temperature range (unless otherwise noted)

PARAMETER	TEST FIGURE	TEST CONDITIONS†		SERIES 54 / SERIES 74 '00, '04, '10, '20, '30			SERIES 54H / SERIES 74H 'H00, 'H04, 'H10, 'H20, 'H30			SERIES 54L / SERIES 74L 'L00, 'L04, 'L10, 'L20, 'L30			SERIES 54LS / SERIES 74LS 'LS00, 'LS04, 'LS10, 'LS20, 'LS30			SERIES 54S / SERIES 74S 'S00, 'S04, 'S10, 'S20, 'S133			UNIT
				MIN	TYP‡	MAX	MIN	TYP‡	MAX	MIN	TYP‡	MAX	MIN	TYP‡	MAX	MIN	TYP‡	MAX	
V_{IH} High-level input voltage	1, 2			2			2			2			2			2			V
V_{IL} Low-level input voltage	1, 2		54 Family			0.8			0.8			0.7			0.7			0.8	V
			74 Family			0.8			0.8			0.7			0.8			0.8	
V_{IK} Input clamp voltage	3	V_{CC} = MIN, I_I = §				−1.5			−1.5						−1.5			−1.2	V
V_{OH} High-level output voltage	1	V_{CC} = MIN, V_{IL} = V_{IL} max, I_{OH} = MAX	54 Family	2.4	3.4		2.4	3.5		2.4	3.3		2.5	3.4		2.5	3.4		V
			74 Family	2.4	3.4		2.4	3.5		2.4	3.2		2.7	3.4		2.7	3.4		
V_{OL} Low-level output voltage	2	V_{CC} = MIN, V_{IH} = 2 V, I_{OL} = MAX	54 Family		0.2	0.4		0.2	0.4		0.15	0.3		0.25	0.4			0.5	V
			74 Family		0.2	0.4		0.2	0.4		0.2	0.4		0.25	0.5			0.5	
		I_{OL} = 4 mA	Series 74LS												0.4				
I_I Input current at maximum input voltage	4	V_{CC} = MAX	V_I = 5.5 V			1			1			0.1						1	mA
			V_I = 7 V												0.1				
I_{IH} High-level input current	4	V_{CC} = MAX	V_{IH} = 2.4 V			40			50			10							µA
			V_{IH} = 2.7 V												20			50	
I_{IL} Low-level input current	5	V_{CC} = MAX	V_{IL} = 0.3 V									−0.18							mA
			V_{IL} = 0.4 V			−1.6			−2						−0.4				
			V_{IL} = 0.5 V															−2	
I_{OS} Short-circuit output current♦	6	V_{CC} = MAX	54 Family	−20		−55	−40		−100	−3		−15	−20		−100	−40		−100	mA
			74 Family	−18		−55	−40		−100	−3		−15	−20		−100	−40		−100	
I_{CC} Supply current	7	V_{CC} = MAX		See table on next page																mA

†For conditions shown as MIN or MAX, use the appropriate value specified under recommended operating conditions.

‡All typical values are at V_{CC} = 5 V, T_A = 25°C.

§ I_I = −12 mA for SN54'/SN74', −8 mA for SN54H'/SN74H', and −18 mA for SN54LS'/SN74LS' and SN54S'/SN74S'.

♦Not more than one output should be shorted at a time, and for SN54H'/SN74H', SN54LS'/SN74LS', and SN54S'/SN74S', duration of short-circuit should not exceed 1 second.

QUADRUPLE 2-INPUT
POSITIVE-NOR GATES

02

positive logic:
$Y = \overline{A+B}$

See page 6-8

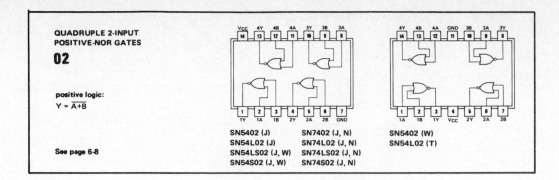

SN5402 (J)   SN7402 (J, N)   SN5402 (W)
SN54L02 (J)   SN74L02 (J, N)   SN54L02 (T)
SN54LS02 (J, W) SN74LS02 (J, N)
SN54S02 (J, W)   SN74S02 (J, N)

supply current¶

TYPE	I_{CCH} (mA) Total with outputs high		I_{CCL} (mA) Total with outputs low		I_{CC} (mA) Average per gate (50% duty cycle)
	TYP	MAX	TYP	MAX	TYP
'02	8	16	14	27	2.75
'25	8	16	10	19	2.25
'27	10	16	16	26	4.34
'L02	0.8	1.6	1.4	2.6	0.275
'LS02	1.6	3.2	2.8	5.4	0.55
'LS27	2.0	4	3.4	6.8	0.9
'S02	17	29	26	45	5.38
'S260	17	29	26	45	10.75

¶Maximum values of I_{CC} are over the recommended operating ranges of V_{CC} and T_A; typical values are at V_{CC} = 5 V, T_A = 25°C.

switching characteristics at V_{CC} = 5 V, T_A = 25°C

TYPE	TEST CONDITIONS#	t_{PLH} (ns) Propagation delay time, low-to-high-level output			t_{PHL} (ns) Propagation delay time, high-to-low-level output		
		MIN	TYP	MAX	MIN	TYP	MAX
'02			12	15		8	15
'25	C_L = 15 pF, R_L = 400 Ω		13	22		8	15
'27			10	15		7	11
'L02	C_L = 50 pF, R_L = 4 kΩ		31	60		35	60
'LS02, 'LS27	C_L = 15 pF, R_L = 2 kΩ		10	15		10	15
'S02	C_L = 15 pF, R_L = 280 Ω		3.5	5.5		3.5	5.5
	C_L = 50 pF, R_L = 280 Ω		5			5	
'S260	C_L = 15 pF, R_L = 280 Ω		4	5.5		4	6

#Load circuit and voltage waveforms are shown on pages 3-10 and 3-11.

schematics (each gate)

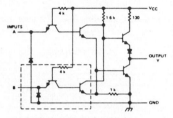

The portion of the schematic within the dashed lines is repeated for the C input of the '27.

'02, '27 CIRCUITS

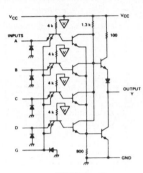

'25 CIRCUITS

Resistor values are nominal and in ohms.

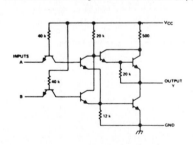

'L02 CIRCUITS

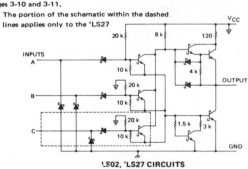

The portion of the schematic within the dashed lines applies only to the 'LS27

'LS02, 'LS27 CIRCUITS

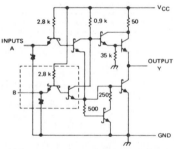

The portion of the schematic within the dashed lines is repeated for each additional input of the 'S260, and the 0.9-kΩ resistor is changed to 0.6 kΩ.

'S02, 'S260 CIRCUITS

POSITIVE-NOR GATES WITH TOTEM-POLE OUTPUTS

recommended operating conditions

	54 FAMILY / 74 FAMILY	SERIES 54 / SERIES 74 '02			SERIES 54 / SERIES 74 '25, '27			SERIES 54L / SERIES 74L 'L02			SERIES 54LS / SERIES 74LS 'LS02, 'LS27			SERIES 54S / SERIES 74S 'S02, 'S260			UNIT
		MIN	NOM	MAX	MIN	NOM	MAX	MIN	NOM	MAX	MIN	NOM	MAX	MIN	NOM	MAX	
Supply voltage, V_{CC}	54 Family	4.5	5	5.5	4.5	5	5.5	4.5	5	5.5	4.5	5	5.5	4.5	5	5.5	V
	74 Family	4.75	5	5.25	4.75	5	5.25	4.75	5	5.25	4.75	5	5.25	4.75	5	5.25	
High-level output current, I_{OH}	54 Family			−400			−800			−100			−400			−1000	μA
	74 Family			−400			−800			−200			−400			−1000	
Low-level output current, I_{OL}	54 Family			16			16			2			4			20	mA
	74 Family			16			16			3.6			8			20	
Operating free-air temperature, T_A	54 Family	−55		125	−55		125	−55		125	−55		125	−55		125	°C
	74 Family	0		70	0		70	0		70	0		70	0		70	

electrical characteristics over recommended operating free-air temperature range (unless otherwise noted)

PARAMETER		TEST FIGURE	TEST CONDITIONS†		SERIES 54 / SERIES 74 '02, '25, '27 MIN TYP‡ MAX			SERIES 54L / SERIES 74L 'L02 MIN TYP‡ MAX			SERIES 54LS / SERIES 74LS 'LS02 'LS27 MIN TYP‡ MAX			SERIES 54S / SERIES 74S 'S02, 'S260 MIN TYP‡ MAX			UNIT
V_{IH}	High-level input voltage	1, 2			2			2			2			2			V
V_{IL}	Low-level input voltage	1, 2		54 Family			0.8			0.7			0.7			0.8	V
				74 Family			0.8			0.7			0.8			0.8	
V_{IK}	Input clamp voltage	3	V_{CC} = MIN, I_I = §				−1.5						−1.5			−1.2	V
V_{OH}	High-level output voltage	1	V_{CC} = MIN, V_{IL} = V_{IL} max, I_{OH} = MAX	54 Family	2.4	3.4		2.4	3.3		2.5	3.4		2.5	3.4		V
				74 Family	2.4	3.4		2.4	3.2		2.7	3.4		2.7	3.4		
V_{OL}	Low-level output voltage	2	V_{CC} = MIN, V_{IH} = 2 V, I_{OL} = MAX	54 Family		0.2	0.4		0.15	0.3		0.25	0.4			0.5	V
				74 Family		0.2	0.4		0.2	0.4		0.35	0.5			0.5	
			I_{OL} = 4 mA	Series 74LS								0.25	0.4				
I_I	Input current at maximum input voltage	4	V_{CC} = MAX	V_I = 5.5 V			1			0.1						1	mA
				V_I = 7 V									0.1				
I_{IH}	High-level input current: Data inputs	4	V_{CC} = MAX	V_{IH} = 2.4 V			40			10							μA
	Strobe of '25						160										
	All inputs			V_{IH} = 2.7 V									20			50	
I_{IL}	Low-level input current: All inputs	5	V_{CC} = MAX	V_{IL} = 0.3 V						−0.18							mA
	Data inputs			V_{IL} = 0.4 V			−1.6						−0.4				
	Strobe of '25						−6.4										
	All inputs			V_{IL} = 0.5 V												−2	
I_{OS}	Short-circuit output current◆	6	V_{CC} = MAX	54 Family	−20		−55	−3		−15	−20		−100	−40		−100	mA
				74 Family	−18		−55	−3		−15	−20		−100	−40		−100	
I_{CC}	Supply current	7	V_{CC} = MAX					See table on next page									mA

†For conditions shown as MIN or MAX, use the appropriate value specified under recommended operating conditions.
‡All typical values are at V_{CC} = 5 V, T_A = 25°C.
§I_I = −12 mA for SN54'/SN74' and −18 mA for SN54LS'/SN74LS' and SN54S/SN74S'.
◆Not more than one output should be shorted at a time, and for SN54LS'/SN74LS' and SN54S/SN74S', duration of output short-circuit should not exceed one second.

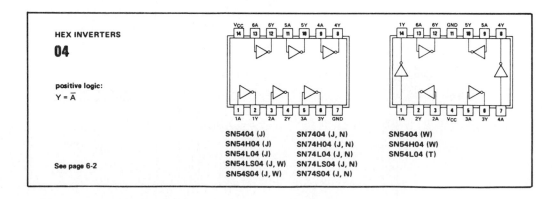

HEX INVERTERS
04

positive logic:
$Y = \overline{A}$

See page 6-2

SN5404 (J)	SN7404 (J, N)	SN5404 (W)
SN54H04 (J)	SN74H04 (J, N)	SN54H04 (W)
SN54L04 (J)	SN74L04 (J, N)	SN54L04 (T)
SN54LS04 (J, W)	SN74LS04 (J, N)	
SN54S04 (J, W)	SN74S04 (J, N)	

Courtesy of Texas Instruments Incorporated.

MC10102 QUAD 2-INPUT GATE

The MC10102 is a quad 2-input NOR gate. Input pulldown resistors eliminate the need to tie unused inputs to an external supply.

CIRCUIT SCHEMATIC

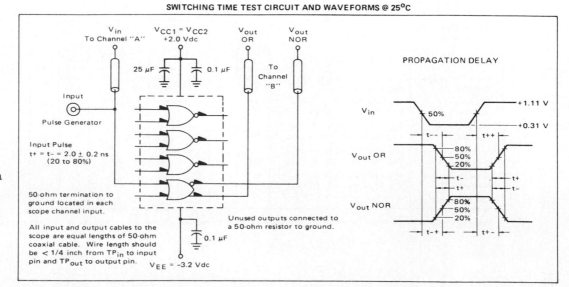

POSITIVE LOGIC | NEGATIVE LOGIC

V_{CC1} = Pin 1
V_{CC2} = Pin 16
V_{EE} = Pin 8

P_D = 25 mW typ/gate (No Load)
t_{pd} = 2.0 ns typ
Output Rise and Fall Time
- 3.5 ns typ (10% - 90%)
- 2.0 ns typ (20% - 80%)

ELECTRICAL CHARACTERISTICS

Each MECL 10,000 series has been designed to meet the dc specifications shown in the test table, after thermal equilibrium has been established. The circuit is in a test socket or mounted on a printed circuit board and transverse air flow greater than 500 linear fpm is maintained. Outputs are terminated through a 50-ohm resistor to -2.0 volts. Test procedures are shown for only one gate. The other gates are tested in the same manner.

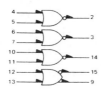

TEST VOLTAGE VALUES (Volts)

@ Test Temperature	$V_{IH\,max}$	$V_{IL\,min}$	$V_{IHA\,min}$	$V_{ILA\,max}$	V_{EE}
-30°C	-0.890	-1.890	-1.205	-1.500	-5.2
+25°C	-0.810	-1.850	-1.105	-1.475	-5.2
+85°C	-0.700	-1.825	-1.035	-1.440	5.2

MC10102 Test Limits

Characteristic	Symbol	Pin Under Test	-30°C Min	-30°C Max	+25°C Min	+25°C Typ	+25°C Max	+85°C Min	+85°C Max	Unit	$V_{IH\,max}$	$V_{IL\,min}$	$V_{IHA\,min}$	$V_{ILA\,max}$	V_{EE}	V_{CC} Gnd
											TEST VOLTAGE APPLIED TO PINS LISTED BELOW:					
Power Supply Drain Current	I_E	8				20	26	-	-	mAdc					8	1,16
Input Current	I_{inH}	12	-	-	-	-	265	-	-	µAdc	12				8	1,16
	I_{inL}	12	-	-	0.5		-	-	-	µAdc		12			8	1,16
Logic "1" Output Voltage	V_{OH}	9	-1.060	-0.890	-0.960		-0.810	-0.890	-0.700	Vdc	12	-			8	1,16
		9	-1.060	-0.890	-0.960		-0.810	-0.890	-0.700		13	-				
		15	-1.060	-0.890	-0.960		-0.810	-0.890	-0.700		-	-				
		15	-1.060	-0.890	-0.960		-0.810	-0.890	-0.700		-	-				
Logic "0" Output Voltage	V_{OL}	9	-1.890	-1.675	-1.850		-1.650	-1.825	-1.615	Vdc	-	-			8	1,16
		9	-1.890	-1.675	-1.850		-1.650	-1.825	-1.615		-	-				
		15	-1.890	-1.675	-1.850		-1.650	-1.825	-1.615		12	-				
		15	-1.890	-1.675	-1.850		-1.650	-1.825	-1.615		13	-				
Logic "1" Threshold Voltage	V_{OHA}	9	-1.080	-	-0.980			-0.910	-	Vdc			12		8	1,16
		9	-1.080	-	0.980			-0.910	-				13			
		15	-1.080	-	-0.980			-0.910	-					12		
		15	-1.080	-	-0.980			-0.910	-					13		
Logic "0" Threshold Voltage	V_{OLA}	9		-1.655	-		-1.630		-1.595	Vdc				12	8	1,16
		9		-1.655	-		-1.630		-1.595					13		
		15		-1.655	-		-1.630		-1.595				12			
		15		-1.655	-		-1.630		-1.595				13			
Switching Times (50-ohm load)											Pulse In	Pulse Out	-3.2 V	+2.0 V		
Propagation Delay	t_{12+15+}	15	1.0	3.1	1.0	2.0	2.9	1.0	3.3	ns	-	12	15		8	1,16
	t_{12-15+}	15									-		15			
	t_{12+9+}	9									-		9			
	t_{12-9-}	9									-		9			
Rise Time (20 to 80%)	t_{15+}	15	1.1	3.6	1.1		3.3	1.1	3.7		-		15			
	t_{9+}	9									-		9			
Fall Time (20 to 80%)	t_{15-}	15									-		15			
	t_{9-}	9									-		9			

SWITCHING TIME TEST CIRCUIT AND WAVEFORMS @ 25°C

V_{in} To Channel "A"

$V_{CC1} = V_{CC2}$ +2.0 Vdc

V_{out} OR

V_{out} NOR

25 µF   0.1 µF

To Channel "B"

Input
Pulse Generator

Input Pulse
$t+ = t- = 2.0 \pm 0.2$ ns
(20 to 80%)

50-ohm termination to ground located in each scope channel input.

All input and output cables to the scope are equal lengths of 50-ohm coaxial cable. Wire length should be < 1/4 inch from TP_{in} to input pin and TP_{out} to output pin.

0.1 µF

Unused outputs connected to a 50-ohm resistor to ground.

V_{EE} = -3.2 Vdc

PROPAGATION DELAY

V_{in} 50%   +1.11 V   +0.31 V

$t--$ $t++$

V_{out} OR   80% 50% 20%

$t-$ $t+$ $t-$ $t+$

V_{out} NOR   80% 50% 20%

$t-+$ $t+-$

CD4001M/CD4001C quadruple 2-input NOR gate

general description

The CD4001M/CD4001C is a monolithic complementary MOS (CMOS) quadruple two-input NOR gate integrated circuit. N and P-channel enhancement mode transistors provide a symmetrical circuit with output swings essentially equal to the supply voltage. This results in high noise immunity over a wide supply voltage range. No dc power other than that caused by leakage current is consumed during static conditions.

All inputs are protected against static discharge and latching conditions.

features

- Wide supply voltage range — 3V to 15V
- Low power — 10 nW (typ)
- High noise immunity — 0.45 V_{DD} (typ)

schematic and connection diagrams

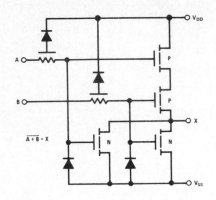

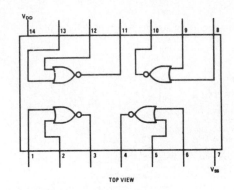

TOP VIEW

absolute maximum ratings

Voltage at Any Pin (Note 1) — $V_{SS} - 0.3V$ to $V_{DD} + 0.3V$
Operating Temperature Range
  CD4001M — $-55°C$ to $+125°C$
  CD4001C — $-40°C$ to $+85°C$
Storage Temperature Range — $-65°C$ to $+150°C$
Package Dissipation — 500 mW
Operating V_{DD} Range — $V_{SS} + 3.0V$ to $V_{SS} + 15V$
Lead Temperature (Soldering, 10 seconds) — $300°C$

dc electrical characteristics CD4001C

PARAMETER	CONDITIONS	-40°C			25°C			85°C			UNITS
		MIN	TYP	MAX	MIN	TYP	MAX	MIN	TYP	MAX	
Quiescent Device	$V_{DD} = 5V$			0.5		0.005	0.5			15	μA
Current (I_L)	$V_{DD} = 10V$			5		0.005	5			30	μA
Quiescent Device Dissi-	$V_{DD} = 5V$			2.5		0.025	2.5			75	μW
pation/Package (P_D)	$V_{DD} = 10V$			50		0.05	50			300	μW
Output Voltage Low	$V_{DD} = 5V$, $V_I = V_{DD}$, $I_O = 0A$			0.01		0	0.01			0.05	V
Level (V_{OL})	$V_{DD} = 10V$, $V_I = V_{DD}$, $I_O = 0A$			0.01		0	0.01			0.05	V
Output Voltage High	$V_{DD} = 5V$, $V_I = V_{SS}$, $I_O = 0A$	4.99			4.99	5		4.95			V
Level (V_{OH})	$V_{DD} = 10V$, $V_I = V_{SS}$, $I_O = 0A$	9.99			9.99	10		9.95			V
Noise Immunity	$V_{DD} = 5V$, $V_O = 3.6V$, $I_O = 0A$	1.5			1.5	2.25		1.4			V
(V_{NL}) (All Inputs)	$V_{DD} = 10V$, $V_O = 7.2V$, $I_O = 0A$	3			3	4.5		2.9			V
Noise Immunity	$V_{DD} = 5V$, $V_O = 0.95V$, $I_O = 0A$	1.4			1.5	2.25		1.5			V
(V_{NH}) (All Inputs)	$V_{DD} = 10V$, $V_O = 2.9V$, $I_O = 0A$	2.9			3	4.5		3			V
Output Drive Current	$V_{DD} = 5V$, $V_O = 0.4V$, $V_I = V_{DD}$	0.35			0.3	1		0.24			mA
N-Channel (I_DN)	$V_{DD} = 10V$, $V_O = 0.5V$, $V_I = V_{DD}$	0.72			0.6	2.5		0.48			mA
Output Drive Current	$V_{DD} = 5V$, $V_O = 2.5V$, $V_I = V_{SS}$	-0.35			-0.3	-2		-0.24			mA
P-Channel (I_DP)	$V_{DD} = 10V$, $V_O = 9.5V$, $V_I = V_{SS}$	-0.3			-0.25	-1		-0.2			mA
Input Current (I_I)						10					pA

Note 1: This device should not be connected to circuits with the power on because high transient voltages may cause permanent damage.

ac electrical characteristics CD4001C

$T_A = 25°C$ and $C_L = 15$ pF and input rise and fall times = 20 ns. Typical temperature coefficient for all values of $V_{DD} = 0.3\%/°C$.

PARAMETER	CONDITIONS	MIN	TYP	MAX	UNITS
Propagation Delay Time High to Low Level (t_{PHL})	$V_{DD} = 5V$		35	80	ns
	$V_{DD} = 10V$		25	55	ns
Propagation Delay Time Low to High Level (t_{PLH})	$V_{DD} = 5V$		35	120	ns
	$V_{DD} = 10V$		25	65	ns
Transition Time High to Low Level (t_{THL})	$V_{DD} = 5V$		65	200	ns
	$V_{DD} = 10V$		35	115	ns
Transition Time Low to High Level (t_{TLH})	$V_{DD} = 5V$		65	300	ns
	$V_{DD} = 10V$		35	125	ns
Input Capacitance (C_I)	Any Input		5		pF

Courtesy of National Semiconductor Corporation.

54/74 FAMILIES OF COMPATIBLE TTL CIRCUITS

PIN ASSIGNMENTS (TOP VIEWS)

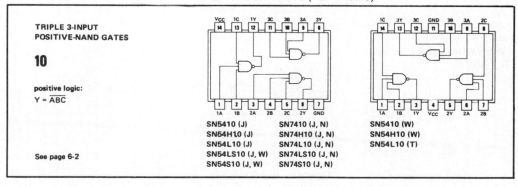

TRIPLE 3-INPUT POSITIVE-NAND GATES

10

positive logic:
$Y = \overline{ABC}$

See page 6-2

SN5410 (J)   SN7410 (J, N)   SN5410 (W)
SN54H10 (J)   SN74H10 (J, N)   SN54H10 (W)
SN54L10 (J)   SN74L10 (J, N)   SN54L10 (T)
SN54LS10 (J, W)   SN74LS10 (J, N)
SN54S10 (J, W)   SN74S10 (J, N)

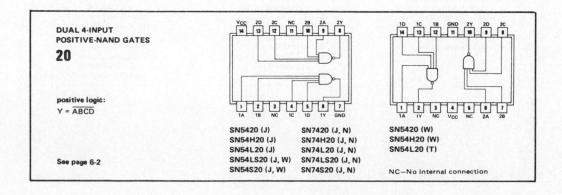

DUAL 4-INPUT POSITIVE-NAND GATES

20

positive logic:
$Y = \overline{ABCD}$

See page 6-2

SN5420 (J)   SN7420 (J, N)   SN5420 (W)
SN54H20 (J)   SN74H20 (J, N)   SN54H20 (W)
SN54L20 (J)   SN74L20 (J, N)   SN54L20 (T)
SN54LS20 (J, W)   SN74LS20 (J, N)
SN54S20 (J, W)   SN74S20 (J, N)

NC—No internal connection

National Semiconductor

Analog Switches/Multiplexers

CD4051BM/CD4051BC Single 8-Channel Analog Multiplexer/Demultiplexer
CD4052BM/CD4052BC Dual 4-Channel Analog Multiplexer/Demultiplexer
CD4053BM/CD4053BC Triple 2-Channel Analog Multiplexer/Demultiplexer

general description

These analog multiplexers/demultiplexers are digitally controlled analog switches having low "ON" impedance and very low "OFF" leakage currents. Control of analog signals up to 15 Vp-p can be achieved by digital signal amplitudes of 3 - 15 V. For example, if V_{DD} = 5 V, V_{SS} = 0 V and V_{EE} = –5 V, analog signals from –5 V to +5 V can be controlled by digital inputs of 0 - 5 V. The multiplexer circuits dissipate extremely low quiescent power over the full V_{DD} – V_{SS} and V_{DD} – V_{EE} supply voltage ranges, independent of the logic state of the control signals. When a logical "1" is present at the inhibit input terminal all channels are "OFF."

CD4051BM/CD4051BC is a single 8-channel multiplexer having three binary control inputs, A, B and C, and an inhibit input. The three binary signals select 1 of 8 channels to be turned "ON" and connect the input to the output.

CD4052BM/CD4052BC is a differential 4-channel multiplexer having two binary control inputs, A and B, and an inhibit input. The two binary input signals select 1 of 4 pairs of channels to be turned on and connect the differential analog inputs to the differential outputs.

CD4053BM/CD4053BC is a triple 2-channel multiplexer having three separate digital control inputs, A, B and C, and an inhibit input. Each control input selects one of a pair of channels which are connected in a single-pole double-throw configuration.

features

- Wide range of digital and analog signal levels: digital 3 - 15 V, analog to 15 Vp-p
- Low "ON" resistance: 80 Ω (typ) over entire 15 Vp-p signal-input range for V_{DD} – V_{EE} = 15 V
- High "OFF" resistance: channel leakage of ±10 pA (typ) at V_{DD} – V_{EE} = 10 V
- Logic level conversion for digital addressing signals of 3 - 15 V (V_{DD} – V_{SS} = 3 - 15 V) to switch analog signals to 15 Vp-p (V_{DD} – V_{EE} = 15 V)
- Matched switch characteristics: ΔR_{ON} = 5 Ω (typ) for V_{DD} – V_{EE} = 15 V
- Very low quiescent power dissipation under all digital-control input and supply conditions: 1 μW (typ) at V_{DD} – V_{SS} = V_{DD} – V_{EE} = 10 V
- Binary address decoding on chip

connection diagrams

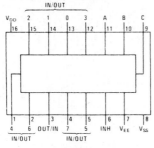

TOP VIEW

Order Number CD4051BMD
or CD4051BCD
See NS Package D16A
Order Number CD4051BMF
or CD4051BCF
See NS Package F16A
Order Number CD4051BMJ
or CD4051BCJ
See NS Package J16A

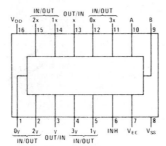

TOP VIEW

Order Number CD4052BMD
or CD4052BCD
See NS Package D16A
Order Number CD4052BMJ
or CD4052BCJ
See NS Package J16A
Order Number CD4052BMN
or CD4052BCN
See NS Package N16A
Order Number CD4052BMW
or CD4052BCW
See NS Package W16A

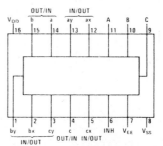

TOP VIEW

Order Number CD4053BMD
or CD4053BCD
See NS Package D16A
Order Number CD4053BMF
or CD4053BCF
See NS Package F16A
Order Number CD4053BMJ
or CD4053BCJ
See NS Package J16A
Order Number CD4053BMW
or CD4053BCW
See NS Package W16A

TYPES SN54150, SN54151A, SN54152A, SN54LS151, SN54LS152, SN54S151, SN74150, SN74151A, SN74LS151, SN74S151
DATA SELECTORS/MULTIPLEXERS
BULLETIN NO. DL-S 7611819, DECEMBER 1972—REVISED OCTOBER 1976

- '150 Selects One-of-Sixteen Data Sources
- Others Select One-of-Eight Data Sources
- Performs Parallel-to-Serial Conversion
- Permits Multiplexing from N Lines to One Line
- Also For Use as Boolean Function Generator
- Input-Clamping Diodes Simplify System Design
- Fully Compatible with Most TTL and DTL Circuits

TYPE	TYPICAL AVERAGE PROPAGATION DELAY TIME DATA INPUT TO W OUTPUT	TYPICAL POWER DISSIPATION
'150	11 ns	200 mW
'151A	8 ns	145 mW
'152A	8 ns	130 mW
'LS151	11 ns†	30 mW
'LS152	11 ns†	28 mW
'S151	4.5 ns	225 mW

†Tentative data

description

These monolithic data selectors/multiplexers contain full on-chip binary decoding to select the desired data source. The '150 selects one-of-sixteen data sources; the '151A, '152A, 'LS151, 'LS152, and 'S151 select one-of-eight data sources. The '150, '151A, 'LS151, and 'S151 have a strobe input which must be at a low logic level to enable these devices. A high level at the strobe forces the W output high, and the Y output (as applicable) low.

The '151A, 'LS151, and 'S151 feature complementary W and Y outputs whereas the '150, '152A, and 'LS152 have an inverted (W) output only.

The '151A and '152A incorporate address buffers which have symmetrical propagation delay times through the complementary paths. This reduces the possibility of transients occurring at the output(s) due to changes made at the select inputs, even when the '151A outputs are enabled (i.e., strobe low).

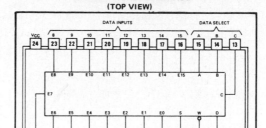

SN54150 ... J OR W PACKAGE
SN74150 ... J OR N PACKAGE
(TOP VIEW)

positive logic: see function table

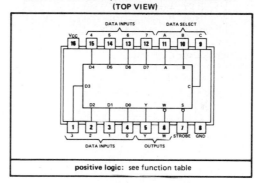

SN54151A, SN54LS151, SN54S151 ... J OR W PACKAGE
SN74151A SN74LS151, SN74S151 ... J OR N PACKAGE
(TOP VIEW)

positive logic: see function table

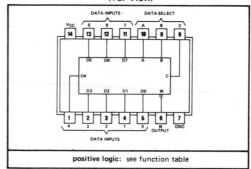

SN54152A, SN54LS152 ... W PACKAGE
(TOP VIEW)

positive logic: see function table

REVISED OCTOBER 1976

logic

'150
FUNCTION TABLE

INPUTS					OUTPUT
SELECT				STROBE	W
D	C	B	A	S	
X	X	X	X	H	H
L	L	L	L	L	$\overline{E0}$
L	L	L	H	L	$\overline{E1}$
L	L	H	L	L	$\overline{E2}$
L	L	H	H	L	$\overline{E3}$
L	H	L	L	L	$\overline{E4}$
L	H	L	H	L	$\overline{E5}$
L	H	H	L	L	$\overline{E6}$
L	H	H	H	L	$\overline{E7}$
H	L	L	L	L	$\overline{E8}$
H	L	L	H	L	$\overline{E9}$
H	L	H	L	L	$\overline{E10}$
H	L	H	H	L	$\overline{E11}$
H	H	L	L	L	$\overline{E12}$
H	H	L	H	L	$\overline{E13}$
H	H	H	L	L	$\overline{E14}$
H	H	H	H	L	$\overline{E15}$

'151A, 'LS151, 'S151
FUNCTION TABLE

INPUTS				OUTPUTS	
SELECT			STROBE	Y	W
C	B	A	S		
X	X	X	H	L	H
L	L	L	L	D0	$\overline{D0}$
L	L	H	L	D1	$\overline{D1}$
L	H	L	L	D2	$\overline{D2}$
L	H	H	L	D3	$\overline{D3}$
H	L	L	L	D4	$\overline{D4}$
H	L	H	L	D5	$\overline{D5}$
H	H	L	L	D6	$\overline{D6}$
H	H	H	L	D7	$\overline{D7}$

'152A, 'LS152
FUNCTION TABLE

SELECT INPUTS			OUTPUT
C	B	A	W
L	L	L	$\overline{D0}$
L	L	H	$\overline{D1}$
L	H	L	$\overline{D2}$
L	H	H	$\overline{D3}$
H	L	L	$\overline{D4}$
H	L	H	$\overline{D5}$
H	H	L	$\overline{D6}$
H	H	H	$\overline{D7}$

H = high level, L = low level, X = irrelevant
$\overline{E0}$, $\overline{E1}$ . . . $\overline{E15}$ = the complement of the level of the respective E input
D0, D1 . . . D7 = the level of the D respective input

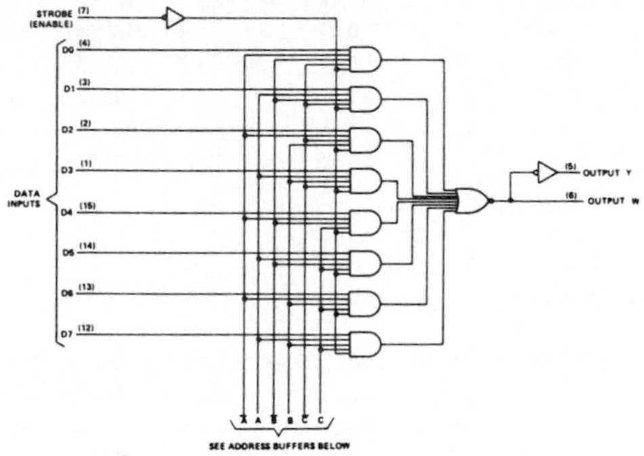

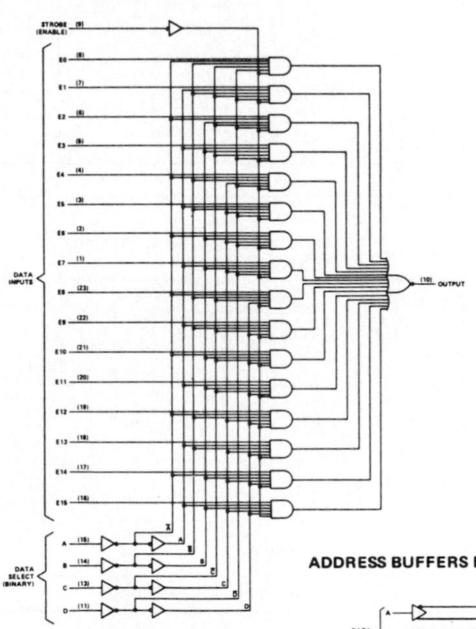

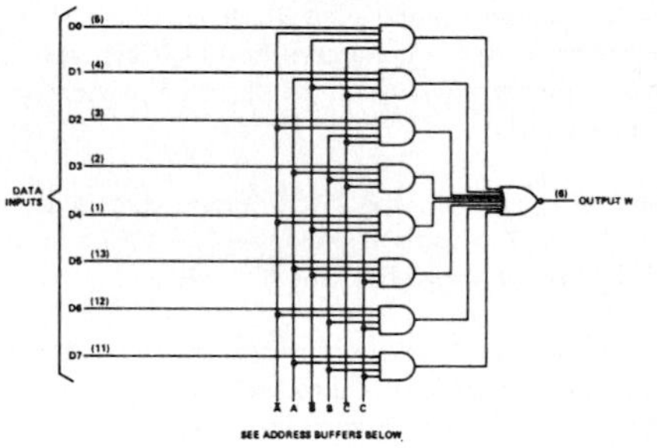

functional block diagrams

'151A, 'LS151, 'S151

'150

'152A, 'LS152

ADDRESS BUFFERS FOR '151A, '152A

ADDRESS BUFFERS FOR 'LS151, 'S151, 'LS152

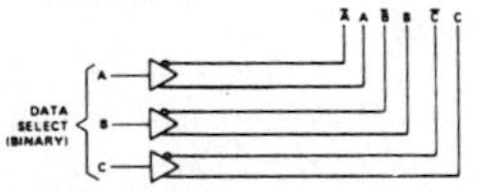

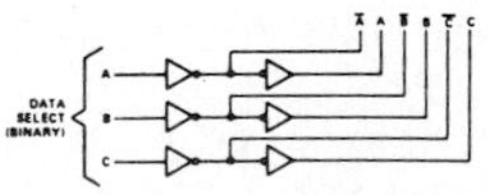

Courtesy of Texas Instruments Incorporated.

Red Single Digit Reflector

PART NUMBER	CHARACTER HEIGHT (INCHES)	POLARITY	DESCRIPTION	LIGHT OUTPUT (MCD) SEGMENT AVERAGE @ 20 mA		FORWARD VOLTAGE SEGMENT (V) I_F = 20 mA		CONTINUOUS FORWARD CURRENT PER SEGMENT (mA) MAX	DIMENSIONS & PINOUTS	
				TYP	MIN	TYP	MAX		PAGE	DWG
DL-500		Common Cathode	7 Segment Decimal Point Right						38	73
▲ DL-501	.50	Common	± 1 Polarity Overflow						38	74
DL-507		Anode	7 Segment Decimal Point Right	.4	.14	1.7	2.0	30	38	73

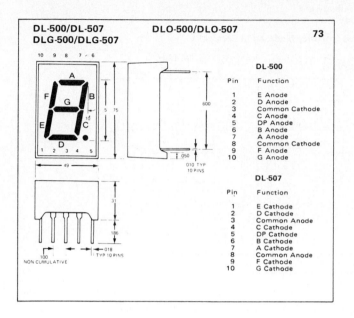

DL-500/DL-507
DLG-500/DLG-507   DLO-500/DLO-507   73

DL-500

Pin	Function
1	E Anode
2	D Anode
3	Common Cathode
4	C Anode
5	DP Anode
6	B Anode
7	A Anode
8	Common Cathode
9	F Anode
10	G Anode

DL-507

Pin	Function
1	E Cathode
2	D Cathode
3	Common Anode
4	C Cathode
5	DP Cathode
6	B Cathode
7	A Cathode
8	Common Anode
9	F Cathode
10	G Cathode

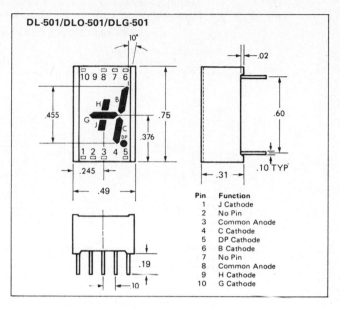

DL-501/DLO-501/DLG-501

Pin	Function
1	J Cathode
2	No Pin
3	Common Anode
4	C Cathode
5	DP Cathode
6	B Cathode
7	No Pin
8	Common Anode
9	H Cathode
10	G Cathode

TYPES SN5446A, '47A, '48, '49, SN54L46, 'L47, SN54LS47, 'LS48, 'LS49, SN7446A, '47A, '48, SN74L46, 'L47, SN74LS47, 'LS48, 'LS49
BCD-TO-SEVEN-SEGMENT DECODERS/DRIVERS
BULLETIN NO. DL-S 7611811, MARCH 1974—REVISED OCTOBER 1976

'46A, '47A, 'L46, 'L47, 'LS47 feature	'48, 'LS48 feature	'49, 'LS49 feature
• Open-Collector Outputs Drive Indicators Directly	• Internal Pull-Ups Eliminate Need for External Resistors	• Open-Collector Outputs
• Lamp-Test Provision	• Lamp-Test Provision	• Blanking Input
• Leading/Trailing Zero Suppression	• Leading/Trailing Zero Suppression	

• **All Circuit Types Feature Lamp Intensity Modulation Capability**

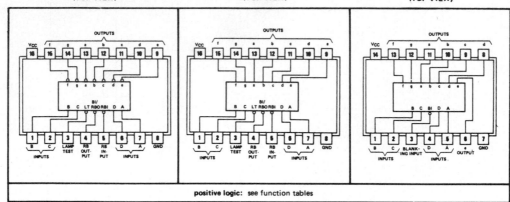

positive logic: see function tables

electrical characteristics over recommended operating free-air temperature range (unless otherwise noted)

PARAMETER		TEST CONDITIONS†		MIN	TYP‡	MAX	UNIT
V_{IH}	High-level input voltage			2			V
V_{IL}	Low-level input voltage					0.8	V
V_{IK}	Input clamp voltage	V_{CC} = MIN, I_I = −12 mA				−1.5	V
V_{OH}	High-level output voltage	BI/RBO	V_{CC} = MIN, V_{IH} = 2 V, V_{IL} = 0.8 V, I_{OH} = −200 µA	2.4	3.7		V
V_{OL}	Low-level output voltage	BI/RBO	V_{CC} = MIN, V_{IH} = 2 V, V_{IL} = 0.8 V, I_{OL} = 8 mA		0.27	0.4	V
$I_{O(off)}$	Off-state output current	a thru g	V_{CC} = MAX, V_{IH} = 2 V, V_{IL} = 0.8 V, $V_{O(off)}$ = MAX			250	µA
$V_{O(on)}$	On-state output voltage	a thru g	V_{CC} = MIN, V_{IH} = 2 V, V_{IL} = 0.8 V, $I_{O(on)}$ = 40 mA		0.3	0.4	V
I_I	Input current at maximum input voltage	Any input except BI/RBO	V_{CC} = MAX, V_I = 5.5 V			1	mA
I_{IH}	High-level input current	Any input except BI/RBO	V_{CC} = MAX, V_I = 2.4 V			40	µA
I_{IL}	Low-level input current	Any input except BI/RBO	V_{CC} = MAX, V_I = 0.4 V			−1.6	mA
		BI/RBO				−4	
I_{OS}	Short-circuit output current	BI/RBO	V_{CC} = MAX			−4	mA
I_{CC}	Supply current		V_{CC} = MAX, See Note 2	SN54'		64	85	mA
				SN74'		64	103	

†For conditions shown as MIN or MAX, use the appropriate value specified under recommended operating conditions.
‡All typical values are at V_{CC} = 5 V, T_A = 25°C.
NOTE 2: I_{CC} is measured with all outputs open and all inputs at 4.5 V.

description

The '46A, 'L46, '47A, 'L47, and 'LS47 feature active-low outputs designed for driving common-anode VLEDs or incandescent indicators directly, and the '48, '49, 'LS48, 'LS49 feature active-high outputs for driving lamp buffers or common-cathode VLEDs. All of the circuits except '49 and 'LS49 have full ripple-blanking input/output controls and a lamp test input. The '49 and 'LS49 circuits incorporate a direct blanking input. Segment identification and resultant displays are shown below. Display patterns for BCD input counts above 9 are unique symbols to authenticate input conditions.

The '46A, '47A, '48, 'L46, 'L47, 'LS47, and 'LS48 circuits incorporate automatic leading and/or trailing-edge zero-blanking control (RBI and RBO). Lamp test (LT) of these types may be performed at any time when the BI/RBO node is at a high level. All types (including the '49 and 'LS49) contain an overriding blanking input (BI) which can be used to control the lamp intensity by pulsing or to inhibit the outputs. Inputs and outputs are entirely compatible for use with TTL or DTL logic outputs.

The SN54246/SN74246 through '249 and the SN54LS247/SN74LS247 through 'LS249 compose the 6 and the 9 with tails and have been designed to offer the designer a choice between two indicator fonts. The SN54249/SN74249 and SN54LS249/SN74LS249 are 16-pin versions of the 14-pin SN5449 and 'LS49. Included in the '249 circuit and 'LS249 circuits are the full functional capability for lamp test and ripple blanking, which is not available in the '49 or 'LS49 circuit.

NUMERICAL DESIGNATIONS AND RESULTANT DISPLAYS

SEGMENT IDENTIFICATION

'46A, '47A, 'L46, 'L47, 'LS47 FUNCTION TABLE

DECIMAL OR FUNCTION	INPUTS						BI/RBO†	OUTPUTS							NOTE
	LT	RBI	D	C	B	A		a	b	c	d	e	f	g	
0	H	H	L	L	L	L	H	ON	ON	ON	ON	ON	ON	OFF	
1	H	X	L	L	L	H	H	OFF	ON	ON	OFF	OFF	OFF	OFF	
2	H	X	L	L	H	L	H	ON	ON	OFF	ON	ON	OFF	ON	
3	H	X	L	L	H	H	H	ON	ON	ON	ON	OFF	OFF	ON	
4	H	X	L	H	L	L	H	OFF	ON	ON	OFF	OFF	ON	ON	
5	H	X	L	H	L	H	H	ON	OFF	ON	ON	OFF	ON	ON	
6	H	X	L	H	H	L	H	OFF	OFF	ON	ON	ON	ON	ON	
7	H	X	L	H	H	H	H	ON	ON	ON	OFF	OFF	OFF	OFF	
8	H	X	H	L	L	L	H	ON	ON	ON	ON	ON	ON	ON	1
9	H	X	H	L	L	H	H	ON	ON	ON	OFF	OFF	ON	ON	
10	H	X	H	L	H	L	H	OFF	OFF	OFF	ON	ON	OFF	ON	
11	H	X	H	L	H	H	H	OFF	OFF	ON	ON	OFF	OFF	ON	
12	H	X	H	H	L	L	H	OFF	ON	OFF	OFF	OFF	ON	ON	
13	H	X	H	H	L	H	H	ON	OFF	OFF	ON	OFF	ON	ON	
14	H	X	H	H	H	L	H	OFF	OFF	OFF	ON	ON	ON	ON	
15	H	X	H	H	H	H	H	OFF	OFF	OFF	OFF	OFF	OFF	OFF	
BI	X	X	X	X	X	X	L	OFF	OFF	OFF	OFF	OFF	OFF	OFF	2
RBI	H	L	L	L	L	L	L	OFF	OFF	OFF	OFF	OFF	OFF	OFF	3
LT	L	X	X	X	X	X	H	ON	ON	ON	ON	ON	ON	ON	4

H = high level, L = low level, X = irrelevant

NOTES: 1. The blanking input (BI) must be open or held at a high logic level when output functions 0 through 15 are desired. The ripple-blanking input (RBI) must be open or high if blanking of a decimal zero is not desired.

2. When a low logic level is applied directly to the blanking input (BI), all segment outputs are off regardless of the level of any other input.

3. When ripple-blanking input (RBI) and inputs A, B, C, and D are at a low level with the lamp test input high, all segment outputs go off and the ripple-blanking output (RBO) goes to a low level (response condition).

4. When the blanking input/ripple blanking output (BI/RBO) is open or held high and a low is applied to the lamp-test input, all segment outputs are on.

†BI/RBO is wire-AND logic serving as blanking input (BI) and/or ripple-blanking output (RBO).

Courtesy of Texas Instruments Incorporated.

TTL
MSI

**TYPES SN54147, SN54148, SN54LS147, SN54LS148,
SN74147, SN74148 (TIM9907),SN74LS147, SN74LS148
10-LINE-TO-4-LINE AND 8-LINE-TO-3-LINE PRIORITY ENCODERS**
BULLETIN NO. DL-S 7711727, OCTOBER 1976—REVISED AUGUST 1977

'147, 'LS147

- Encodes 10-Line Decimal to 4-Line BCD

- Applications Include:

    Keyboard Encoding
    Range Selection

'148, 'LS148

- Encodes 8 Data Lines to 3-Line Binary (Octal)

- Applications Include:

    N-Bit Encoding
    Code Converters and Generators

TYPE	TYPICAL DATA DELAY	TYPICAL POWER DISSIPATION
'147	10 ns	225 mW
'148	10 ns	190 mW
'LS147	15 ns	60 mW
'LS148	15 ns	60 mW

description

These TTL encoders feature priority decoding of the inputs to ensure that only the highest-order data line is encoded. The '147 and 'LS147 encode nine data lines to four-line (8-4-2-1) BCD. The implied decimal zero condition requires no input condition as zero is encoded when all nine data lines are at a high logic level. The '148 and 'LS148 encode eight data lines to three-line (4-2-1) binary (octal). Cascading circuitry (enable input EI and enable output EO) has been provided to allow octal expansion without the need for external circuitry. For all types, data inputs and outputs are active at the low logic level. All inputs are buffered to represent one normalized Series 54/74 or 54LS/74LS load, respectively.

functional block diagrams

'148, 'LS148

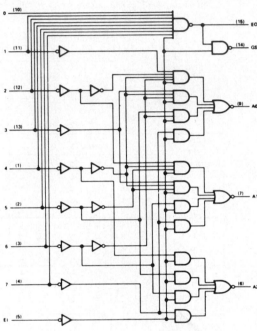

SN54148, SN54LS148 . . . J OR W PACKAGE
SN74148, SN74LS148 . . . J OR N PACKAGE
(TOP VIEW)

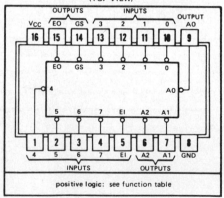

positive logic: see function table

**'148, 'LS148
FUNCTION TABLE**

INPUTS									OUTPUTS				
EI	0	1	2	3	4	5	6	7	A2	A1	A0	GS	EO
H	X	X	X	X	X	X	X	X	H	H	H	H	H
L	H	H	H	H	H	H	H	H	H	H	H	H	L
L	X	X	X	X	X	X	X	L	L	L	L	L	H
L	X	X	X	X	X	X	L	H	L	L	H	L	H
L	X	X	X	X	X	L	H	H	L	H	L	L	H
L	X	X	X	X	L	H	H	H	L	H	H	L	H
L	X	X	X	L	H	H	H	H	H	L	L	L	H
L	X	X	L	H	H	H	H	H	H	L	H	L	H
L	X	L	H	H	H	H	H	H	H	H	L	L	H
L	L	H	H	H	H	H	H	H	H	H	H	L	H

Courtesy of Texas Instruments Incorporated.

PIN ASSIGNMENTS (TOP VIEWS)

74
DUAL D-TYPE POSITIVE-EDGE-TRIGGERED FLIP-FLOPS WITH PRESET AND CLEAR

FUNCTION TABLE

INPUTS				OUTPUTS	
PRESET	CLEAR	CLOCK	D	Q	Q̄
L	H	X	X	H	L
H	L	X	X	L	H
L	L	X	X	H*	H*
H	H	↑	H	H	L
H	H	↑	L	L	H
H	H	L	X	Q₀	Q̄₀

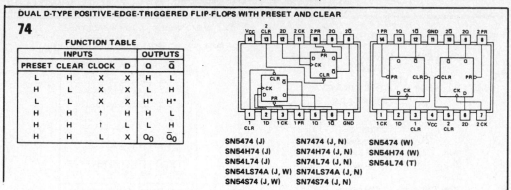

SN5474 (J)   SN7474 (J, N)   SN5474 (W)
SN54H74 (J)   SN74H74 (J, N)   SN54H74 (W)
SN54L74 (J)   SN74L74 (J, N)   SN54L74 (T)
SN54LS74A (J, W) SN74LS74A (J, N)
SN54S74 (J, W)   SN74S74 (J, N)

description

These latches are ideally suited for use as temporary storage for binary information between processing units and input/output or indicator units. Information present at a data (D) input is transferred to the Q output when the enable (G) is high and the Q output will follow the data input as long as the enable remains high. When the enable goes low, the information (that was present at the data input at the time the transition occurred) is retained at the Q output until the enable is permitted to go high.

4-BIT BISTABLE LATCHES

75

FUNCTION TABLE
(Each Latch)

INPUTS		OUTPUTS	
D	G	Q	Q̄
L	H	L	H
H	H	H	L
X	L	Q₀	Q̄₀

H = high level, L = low level, X = irrelevant
Q₀ = the level of Q before the high-to-low transistion of G

SN5475, SN54LS75 . . . J OR W PACKAGE
SN54L75 . . . J PACKAGE
SN7475, SN74L75, SN74LS75 . . . J OR N PACKAGE
(TOP VIEW)

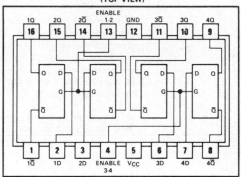

DUAL J-K FLIP-FLOPS WITH PRESET AND CLEAR

76

'76, 'H76 FUNCTION TABLE

INPUTS					OUTPUTS	
PRESET	CLEAR	CLOCK	J	K	Q	Q̄
L	H	X	X	X	H	L
H	L	X	X	X	L	H
L	L	X	X	X	H*	H*
H	H	⊓	L	L	Q₀	Q̄₀
H	H	⊓	H	L	H	L
H	H	⊓	L	H	L	H
H	H	⊓	H	H	TOGGLE	

'LS76A FUNCTION TABLE

INPUTS					OUTPUTS	
PRESET	CLEAR	CLOCK	J	K	Q	Q̄
L	H	X	X	X	H	L
H	L	X	X	X	L	H
L	L	X	X	X	H*	H*
H	H	↓	L	L	Q₀	Q̄₀
H	H	↓	H	L	H	L
H	H	↓	L	H	L	H
H	H	↓	H	H	TOGGLE	
H	H	H	X	X	Q₀	Q̄₀

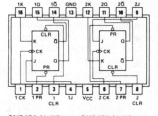

SN5476 (J, W)   SN7476 (J, N)
SN54H76 (J, W)   SN74H76 (J, N)
SN54LS76A (J, W)   SN74LS76A (J, N)

*This configuration is nonstable; that is, it will not persist when preset and clear inputs return to their inactive (high) level.

QUAD D-TYPE FLIP-FLOPS

175
COMPLEMENTARY OUTPUTS
COMMON DIRECT CLEAR

FUNCTION TABLE
(EACH FLIP-FLOP)

INPUTS			OUTPUTS	
CLEAR	CLOCK	D	Q	Q̄†
L	X	X	L	H
H	↑	H	H	L
H	↑	L	L	H
H	L	X	Q₀	Q̄₀

H = high level (steady state)
L = low level (steady state)
X = irrelevant
↑ = transition from low to high level
Q₀ = the level of Q before the indicated steady-state input conditions were established.
† = '175, 'LS175, and 'S175 only

SN54175, SN54LS175, SN54S175 . . . J OR W PACKAGE
SN74175, SN74LS175, SN74S175 . . . J OR N PACKAGE
(TOP VIEW)

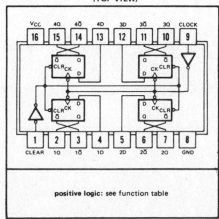

positive logic: see function table

Courtesy of Texas Instruments Incorporated.

TTL MSI

TYPES SN5490A, SN5492A, SN5493A, SN54L90, SN54L93, SN54LS90, SN54LS92, SN54LS93, SN7490A, SN7492A, SN7493A, SN74L90, SN74L93, SN74LS90, SN74LS92, SN74LS93 DECADE, DIVIDE-BY-TWELVE, AND BINARY COUNTERS

BULLETIN NO. DL-S 7611807, MARCH 1974—REVISED OCTOBER 1976

'90A, 'L90, 'LS90 . . . DECADE COUNTERS

'92A, 'LS92 . . . DIVIDE-BY-TWELVE COUNTERS

'93A, 'L93, 'LS93 . . . 4-BIT BINARY COUNTERS

TYPES	TYPICAL POWER DISSIPATION
'90A	145 mW
'L90	20 mW
'LS90	45 mW
'92A, '93A	130 mW
'LS92, 'LS93	45 mW
'L93	16 mW

description

Each of these monolithic counters contains four master-slave flip-flops and additional gating to provide a divide-by-two counter and a three-stage binary counter for which the count cycle length is divide-by-five for the '90A, 'L90, and 'LS90, divide-by-six for the '92A and 'LS92, and divide-by-eight for the '93A, 'L93, and 'LS93.

All of these counters have a gated zero reset and the '90A, 'L90, and 'LS90 also have gated set-to-nine inputs for use in BCD nine's complement applications.

To use their maximum count length (decade, divide-by-twelve, or four-bit binary) of these counters, the B input is connected to the Q_A output. The input count pulses are applied to input A and the outputs are as described in the appropriate function table. A symmetrical divide-by-ten count can be obtained from the '90A, 'L90, or 'LS90 counters by connecting the Q_D output to the A input and applying the input count to the B input which gives a divide-by-ten square wave at output Q_A.

Courtesy of Texas Instruments Incorporated.

SN54', SN54LS' . . . J OR W PACKAGE
SN54L' . . . J OR T PACKAGE
SN54', SN74L', SN74LS' . . . J OR N PACKAGE

'90A, 'L90, 'LS90 (TOP VIEW)

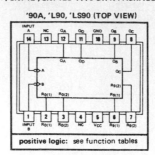

'92A, 'LS92, (TOP VIEW)

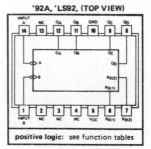

'93A, 'LS93 (TOP VIEW)

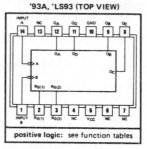

'L93 (TOP VIEW)

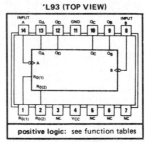

NC—No internal connection

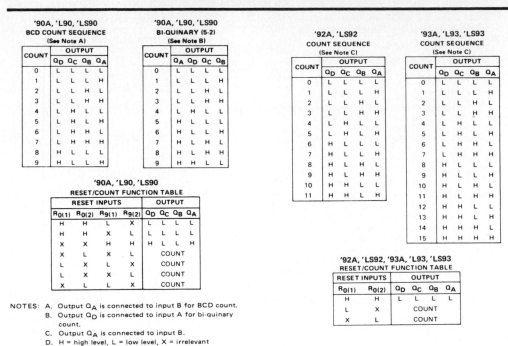

'90A, 'L90, 'LS90 BCD COUNT SEQUENCE (See Note A)

COUNT	Q_D	Q_C	Q_B	Q_A
0	L	L	L	L
1	L	L	L	H
2	L	L	H	L
3	L	L	H	H
4	L	H	L	L
5	L	H	L	H
6	L	H	H	L
7	L	H	H	H
8	H	L	L	L
9	H	L	L	H

'90A, 'L90, 'LS90 BI-QUINARY (5-2) (See Note B)

COUNT	Q_A	Q_D	Q_C	Q_B
0	L	L	L	L
1	L	L	L	H
2	L	L	H	L
3	L	L	H	H
4	L	H	L	L
5	H	L	L	L
6	H	L	L	H
7	H	L	H	L
8	H	L	H	H
9	H	H	L	L

'92A, 'LS92 COUNT SEQUENCE (See Note C)

COUNT	Q_D	Q_C	Q_B	Q_A
0	L	L	L	L
1	L	L	L	H
2	L	L	H	L
3	L	L	H	H
4	L	H	L	L
5	L	H	L	H
6	H	L	L	L
7	H	L	L	H
8	H	L	H	L
9	H	L	H	H
10	H	H	L	L
11	H	H	L	H

'93A, 'L93, 'LS93 COUNT SEQUENCE (See Note C)

COUNT	Q_D	Q_C	Q_B	Q_A
0	L	L	L	L
1	L	L	L	H
2	L	L	H	L
3	L	L	H	H
4	L	H	L	L
5	L	H	L	H
6	L	H	H	L
7	L	H	H	H
8	H	L	L	L
9	H	L	L	H
10	H	L	H	L
11	H	L	H	H
12	H	H	L	L
13	H	H	L	H
14	H	H	H	L
15	H	H	H	H

'90A, 'L90, 'LS90 RESET/COUNT FUNCTION TABLE

$R_{0(1)}$	$R_{0(2)}$	$R_{9(1)}$	$R_{9(2)}$	Q_D	Q_C	Q_B	Q_A
H	H	L	X	L	L	L	L
H	H	X	L	L	L	L	L
X	X	H	H	H	L	L	H
X	L	X	L	COUNT			
L	X	L	X	COUNT			
L	X	X	L	COUNT			
X	L	L	X	COUNT			

'92A, 'LS92, '93A, 'L93, 'LS93 RESET/COUNT FUNCTION TABLE

$R_{0(1)}$	$R_{0(2)}$	Q_D	Q_C	Q_B	Q_A
H	H	L	L	L	L
L	X	COUNT			
X	L	COUNT			

NOTES: A. Output Q_A is connected to input B for BCD count.
B. Output Q_D is connected to input A for bi-quinary count.
C. Output Q_A is connected to input B.
D. H = high level, L = low level, X = irrelevant

functional block diagrams

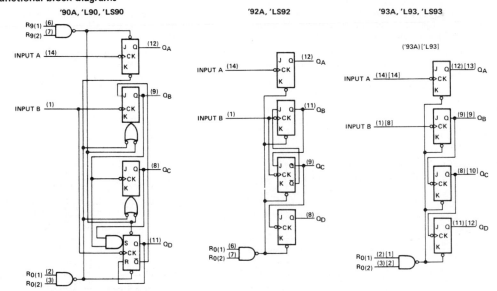

'90A, 'L90, 'LS90   '92A, 'LS92   '93A, 'L93, 'LS93

The J and K inputs shown without connection are for reference only and are functionally at a high level.

Courtesy of Texas Instruments Incorporated.

- Cascading Circuitry Provided Internally
- Synchronous Operation
- Individual Preset to Each Flip-Flop
- Fully Independent Clear Input

TYPES	TYPICAL MAXIMUM COUNT FREQUENCY	TYPICAL POWER DISSIPATION
'192, '193	32 MHz	325 mW
'L192, 'L193	7 MHz	43 mW
'LS192, 'LS193	32 MHz	95 mW

SN54', SN54LS' . . . J OR W PACKAGE
SN54L' . . . J PACKAGE
SN74', SN74L', SN74LS' . . . J OR N PACKAGE
(TOP VIEW)

logic: Low input to load sets $Q_A = A$,
$Q_B = B$, $Q_C = C$, and $Q_D = D$

description

These monolithic circuits are synchronous reversible (up/down) counters having a complexity of 55 equivalent gates. The '192, 'L192, and 'LS192 circuits are BCD counters and the '193, 'L193 and 'LS193 are 4-bit binary counters. Synchronous operation is provided by having all flip-flops clocked simultaneously so that the outputs change coincidently with each other when so instructed by the steering logic. This mode of operation eliminates the output counting spikes which are normally associated with asynchronous (ripple-clock) counters.

The outputs of the four master-slave flip-flops are triggered by a low-to-high-level transition of either count (clock) input. The direction of counting is determined by which count input is pulsed while the other count input is high.

All four counters are fully programmable; that is, each output may be preset to either level by entering the desired data at the data inputs while the load input is low. The output will change to agree with the data inputs independently of the count pulses. This feature allows the counters to be used as modulo-N dividers by simply modifying the count length with the preset inputs.

A clear input has been provided which forces all outputs to the low level when a high level is applied. The clear function is independent of the count and load inputs. The clear, count, and load inputs are buffered to lower the drive requirements. This reduces the number of clock drivers, etc., required for long words.

These counters were designed to be cascaded without the need for external circuitry. Both borrow and carry outputs are available to cascade both the up- and down-counting functions. The borrow output produces a pulse equal in width to the count-down input when the counter underflows. Similarly, the carry output produces a pulse equal in width to the count-up input when an overflow condition exists. The counters can then be easily cascaded by feeding the borrow and carry outputs to the count-down and count-up inputs respectively of the succeeding counter.

recommended operating conditions

	SN54192 SN54193			SN74192 SN74193			UNIT
	MIN	NOM	MAX	MIN	NOM	MAX	
Supply voltage, V_{CC}	4.5	5	5.5	4.75	5	5.25	V
High-level output current, I_{OH}			−400			−400	μA
Low-level output current, I_{OL}			16			16	mA
Clock frequency, f_{clock}	0		25	0		25	MHz
Width of any input pulse, t_w	20			20			ns
Data setup time, t_{su} (see Figure 1)	20			20			ns
Data hold time, t_h	0			0			ns
Operating free-air temperature, T_A	−55		125	0		70	°C

Courtesy of Texas Instruments Incorporated.

typical clear, load, and count sequences

Illustrated below is the following sequence:

1. Clear outputs to zero.
2. Load (preset) to binary thirteen.
3. Count up to fourteen, fifteen, carry, zero, one, and two.
4. Count down to one, zero, borrow, fifteen, fourteen, and thirteen.

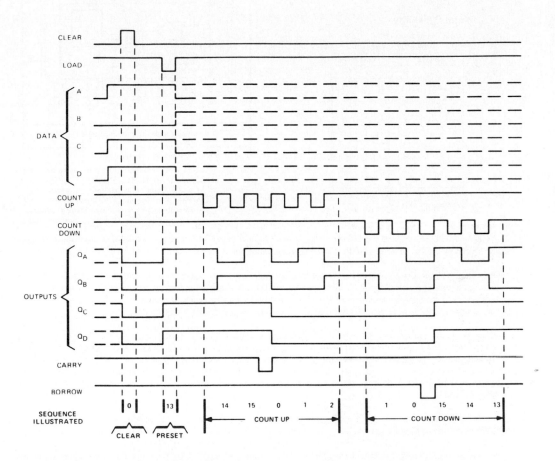

NOTES: A. Clear overrides load, data, and count inputs.

B. When counting up, count-down input must be high; when counting down, count-up input must be high.

switching characteristics, $V_{CC} = 5$ V, $T_A = 25°C$

PARAMETER¶	FROM INPUT	TO OUTPUT	TEST CONDITIONS	MIN	TYP	MAX	UNIT
f_{max}				25	32		MHz
t_{PLH}	Count-up	Carry			17	26	ns
t_{PHL}					16	24	
t_{PLH}	Count-down	Borrow	$C_L = 15$ pF,		16	24	ns
t_{PHL}			$R_L = 400$ Ω,		16	24	
t_{PLH}	Either Count	Q	See Figures 1 and 2		25	38	ns
t_{PHL}					31	47	
t_{PLH}	Load	Q			27	40	ns
t_{PHL}					29	40	
t_{PHL}	Clear	Q			22	35	ns

¶$f_{max} \equiv$ maximum clock frequency

$t_{PLH} \equiv$ propagation delay time, low-to-high-level output

$t_{PHL} \equiv$ propagation delay time, high-to-low-level output

TYPES SN54121, SN54L121, SN74121, SN74L121
MONOSTABLE MULTIVIBRATORS
WITH SCHMITT-TRIGGER INPUTS

- **Programmable Output Pulse Width**
  With R_{int} ... 35 ns Typ
  With R_{ext}/C_{ext} ... 40 ns to 28 Seconds

- **Internal Compensation for Virtual
  Temperature Independence**

- **Jitter-Free Operation up to 90%
  Duty Cycle**

- **Inhibit Capability**

SN54121 ... J OR W PACKAGE
SN54L121 ... J OR T PACKAGE
SN74121, SN74L121 ... J OR N PACKAGE

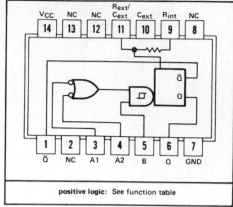

positive logic: See function table

NC—No internal connection

NOTES: 1. An external capacitor may be connected between
C_{ext} (positive) and R_{ext}/C_{ext}.

2. To use the internal timing resistor, connect R_{int}
to V_{CC}. For improved pulse width accuracy and
repeatability, connect an external resistor between
R_{ext}/C_{ext} and V_{CC} with R_{int} open-circuited.

FUNCTION TABLE

INPUTS			OUTPUTS	
A1	A2	B	Q	$\overline{Q}$
L	X	H	L	H
X	L	H	L	H
X	X	L	L	H
H	H	X	L	H
H	↓	H	⊓	⊔
↓	H	H	⊓	⊔
↓	↓	H	⊓	⊔
L	X	↑	⊓	⊔
X	L	↑	⊓	⊔

For explanation of function table
symbols, see page 3-8.

description

These multivibrators feature dual negative-transition-triggered inputs and a single positive-transition-triggered input
which can be used as an inhibit input. Complementary output pulses are provided.

Pulse triggering occurs at a particular voltage level and is not directly related to the transition time of the input pulse.
Schmitt-trigger input circuitry (TTL hysteresis) for the B input allows jitter-free triggering from inputs with transition
rates as slow as 1 volt/second, providing the circuit with an excellent noise immunity of typically 1.2 volts. A high
immunity to V_{CC} noise of typically 1.5 volts is also provided by internal latching circuitry.

Once fired, the outputs are independent of further transitions of the inputs and are a function only of the timing
components. Input pulses may be of any duration relative to the output pulse. Output pulse length may be varied from
40 nanoseconds to 28 seconds by choosing appropriate timing components. With no external timing components
(i.e., R_{int} connected to V_{CC}, C_{ext} and R_{ext}/C_{ext} open), an output pulse of typically 30 or 35 nanoseconds is achieved
which may be used as a d-c triggered reset signal. Output rise and fall times are TTL compatible and independent of
pulse length.

Pulse width stability is achieved through internal compensation and is virtually independent of V_{CC} and temperature.
In most applications, pulse stability will only be limited by the accuracy of external timing components.

Jitter-free operation is maintained over the full temperature and V_{CC} ranges for more than six decades of timing
capacitance (10 pF to 10 μF) and more than one decade of timing resistance (2 kΩ to 30 kΩ for the
SN54121/SN54L121 and 2 kΩ to 40 kΩ for the SN74121/SN74L121). Throughout these ranges, pulse width is
defined by the relationship $t_{w(out)} = C_{ext}R_T\ln2 \approx 0.7\ C_{ext}R_T$. In circuits where pulse cutoff is not critical, timing
capacitance up to 1000 μF and timing resistance as low as 1.4 kΩ may be used. Also, the range of jitter-free output
pulse widths is extended if V_{CC} is held to 5 volts and free-air temperature is 25°C. Duty cycles as high as 90% are
achieved when using maximum recommended R_T. Higher duty cycles are available if a certain amount of pulse-width
jitter is allowed.

recommended operating conditions

		54 FAMILY 74 FAMILY	SN54121 SN74121			SN54L121 SN74L121			UNIT
			MIN	NOM	MAX	MIN	NOM	MAX	
Supply voltage, V_{CC}		54 Family	4.5	5	5.5	4.5	5	5.5	V
		74 Family	4.75	5	5.25	4.75	5	5.25	
High-level output current, I_{OH}					−400			−200	μA
Low-level output current, I_{OL}					16			8	mA
Rate of rise or fall of input pulse, dv/dt	Schmitt input, B			1			1		V/s
	Logic inputs, A1, A2			1			1		V/μs
Input pulse width, $t_{w(in)}$				50			100		ns
External timing resistance, R_{ext}		54 Family	1.4		30	1.4		30	kΩ
		74 Family	1.4		40	1.4		40	
External timing capacitance, C_{ext}			0		1000	0		1000	μF
Duty cycle	$R_T = 2 kΩ$				67			67	%
	$R_T = MAX\ R_{ext}$				90			90	
Operating free-air temperature, T_A		54 Family	−55		125	−55		125	°C
		74 Family	0		70	0		70	

Courtesy of Texas Instruments Incorporated.

TYPES SN54122, SN54123, SN54L122, SN54L123, SN54LS122, SN54LS123, SN74122, SN74123, SN74L122, SN74L123, SN74LS122, SN74LS123
RETRIGGERABLE MONOSTABLE MULTIVIBRATORS

- D-C Triggered from Active-High or Active-Low Gated Logic Inputs
- Retriggerable for Very Long Output Pulses, Up to 100% Duty Cycle
- Overriding Clear Terminates Output Pulse
- Compensated for V_{CC} and Temperature Variations
- '122, 'L122, 'LS122 Have Internal Timing Resistors

SN54122, SN54LS122 . . . J OR W
SN54L122 . . . J OR T
SN74122, SN74L122, SN74LS122 . . . J OR N
(TOP VIEW) (SEE NOTES 1 THRU 4)

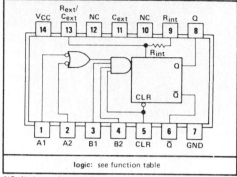

logic: see function table

NC—No internal connection.

'122, 'L122, 'LS122 FUNCTION TABLE

INPUTS					OUTPUTS	
CLEAR	A1	A2	B1	B2	Q	Q̄
L	X	X	X	X	L	H
X	H	H	X	X	L	H
X	X	X	L	X	L	H
X	X	X	X	L	L	H
H	L	X	↑	H	⊓	⊔
H	L	X	H	↑	⊓	⊔
H	X	L	↑	H	⊓	⊔
H	X	L	H	↑	⊓	⊔
H	H	↓	H	H	⊓	⊔
H	↓	↓	H	H	⊓	⊔
H	↓	H	H	H	⊓	⊔
↑	L	X	H	H	⊓	⊔
↑	X	L	H	H	⊓	⊔

'123, 'L123, 'LS123 FUNCTION TABLE

INPUTS			OUTPUTS	
CLEAR	A	B	Q	Q̄
L	X	X	L	H
X	H	X	L	H
X	X	L	L	H
H	L	↑	⊓	⊔
H	↓	H	⊓	⊔
↑	L	H	⊓	⊔

See explanation of function tables on page 3-8.

description

These d-c triggered multivibrators feature output pulse width control by three methods. The basic pulse time is programmed by selection of external resistance and capacitance values (see typical application data). The '122, 'L122, and 'LS122 have internal timing resistors that allow the circuits to be used with only an external capacitor, if so desired. Once triggered, the basic pulse width may be extended by retriggering the gated low-level-active (A) or high-level-active (B) inputs, or be reduced by use of the overriding clear. Figure 1 illustrates pulse control by retriggering and early clear.

The 'LS122 and 'LS123 are provided enough Schmitt hysteresis to ensure jitter-free triggering from the B input with transition rates as slow as 0.1 millivolt per nanosecond.

SN54123, SN54LS123 . . . J OR W
SN54L123 . . . J
SN74123, SN74L123, SN74LS123 . . . J OR N
(TOP VIEW) (SEE NOTES 1 THRU 4)

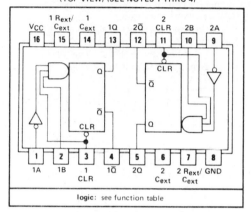

logic: see function table

NOTES: 1. An external timing capacitor may be connected between C_{ext} and R_{ext}/C_{ext} (positive).
2. To use the internal timing resistor of '122, 'L122 or 'LS122, connect R_{int} to V_{CC}.
3. For improved pulse width accuracy and repeatability, connect an external resistor between R_{ext}/C_{ext} and V_{CC} with R_{int} open-circuited.
4. To obtain variable pulse widths, connect an external variable resistance between R_{int} or R_{ext}/C_{ext} and V_{CC}.

recommended operating conditions

	SN54'			SN74'			UNIT
	MIN	NOM	MAX	MIN	NOM	MAX	
Supply voltage, V_{CC}	4.5	5	5.5	4.75	5	5.25	V
High-level output current, I_{OH}			−800			−800	μA
Low-level output current, I_{OL}			16			16	mA
Pulse width, t_w	40			40			ns
External timing resistance, R_{ext}	5		25	5		50	kΩ
External capacitance, C_{ext}	No restriction			No restriction			
Wiring capacitance at R_{ext}/C_{ext} terminal			50			50	pF
Operating free-air temperature, T_A	−55		125	0		70	°C

TYPICAL APPLICATION DATA FOR '122, '123, 'L122, 'L123

For pulse widths when $C_{ext} \leqslant 1000$ pF, See Figures 4 and 5.

The output pulse is primarily a function of the external capacitor and resistor. For $C_{ext} > 1000$ pF, the output pulse width (t_W) is defined as:

$$t_W = K \cdot R_T \cdot C_{ext} \left(1 + \frac{0.7}{R_T} \right)$$

where

K is 0.32 for '122, 0.28 for '123, 0.37 for 'L122, 0.33 for 'L123

R_T is in kΩ (internal or external timing resistance.

C_{ext} is in pF

t_W is in nanoseconds

To prevent reverse voltage across C_{ext}, it is recommended that the method shown in Figure 2 be employed when using electrolytic capacitors and in applications utilizing the clear function. In all applications using the diode, the pulse width is:

$$t_W = K_D \cdot R_T \cdot C_{ext} \left(1 + \frac{0.7}{R_T} \right)$$

K_D is 0.28 for '122, 0.25 for '123, 0.33 for 'L122, 0.29 for 'L123

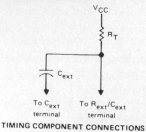

TIMING COMPONENT CONNECTIONS
FIGURE 3

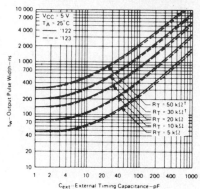

'122, '123
TYPICAL OUTPUT PULSE WIDTH vs EXTERNAL TIMING CAPACITANCE
FIGURE 4

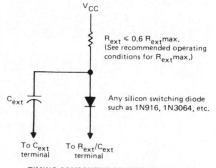

$R_{ext} \leqslant 0.6\ R_{ext}$max. (See recommended operating conditions for R_{ext}max.)

Any silicon switching diode such as 1N916, 1N3064, etc.

TIMING COMPONENT CONNECTIONS WHEN $C_{ext} > 1000$ pF AND CLEAR IS USED
FIGURE 2

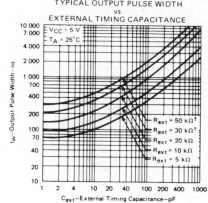

'L122
TYPICAL OUTPUT PULSE WIDTH vs EXTERNAL TIMING CAPACITANCE
FIGURE 5

†These values of resistance exceed the maximum recommended for use over the full temperature range of the SN54' and SN54L' circuits.

Applications requiring more precise pulse widths (up to 28 seconds) and not requiring the clear feature can best be satisfied with the '121 or 'L121.

Courtesy of Texas Instruments Incorporated.

TTL
MSI

TYPES SN54194, SN54LS194A, SN54S194, SN74194, SN74LS194A, SN74S194
4-BIT BIDIRECTIONAL UNIVERSAL SHIFT REGISTERS
BULLETIN NO. DL-S 7611866, MARCH 1974—REVISED OCTOBER 1976

- Parallel Inputs and Outputs
- Four Operating Modes:
  - Synchronous Parallel Load
  - Right Shift
  - Left Shift
  - Do Nothing
- Positive Edge-Triggered Clocking
- Direct Overriding Clear

TYPE	TYPICAL MAXIMUM CLOCK FREQUENCY	TYPICAL POWER DISSIPATION
'194	36 MHz	195 mW
'LS194A	36 MHz	75 mW
'S194	105 MHz	425 mW

SN54194, SN54LS194A, SN54S194 . . . J OR W PACKAGE
SN74194, SN74LS194A, SN74S194 . . . J OR N PACKAGE
(TOP VIEW)

```
        Vcc  QA  QB  QC  QD CLOCK S1  S0
        16   15  14  13  12  11   10   9

             QA  QB  QC  QD   CLOCK  S1
          CLEAR                       S0
             R   A   B   C   D   L

         1   2   3   4   5   6   7   8
       CLEAR SHIFT  A   B   C   D SHIFT GND
             RIGHT               LEFT
             SERIAL PARALLEL INPUTS SERIAL
             INPUT              INPUT
```

positive logic: see function table

description

These bidirectional shift registers are designed to incorporate virtually all of the features a system designer may want in a shift register. The circuit contains 46 equivalent gates and features parallel inputs, parallel outputs, right-shift and left-shift serial inputs, operating-mode-control inputs, and a direct overriding clear line. The register has four distinct modes of operation, namely:

Parallel (broadside) load
Shift right (in the direction Q_A toward Q_D)
Shift left (in the direction Q_D toward Q_A)
Inhibit clock (do nothing)

Synchronous parallel loading is accomplished by applying the four bits of data and taking both mode control inputs, S0 and S1, high. The data are loaded into the associated flip-flops and appear at the outputs after the positive transition of the clock input. During loading, serial data flow is inhibited.

Shift right is accomplished synchronously with the rising edge of the clock pulse when S0 is high and S1 is low. Serial data for this mode is entered at the shift-right data input. When S0 is low and S1 is high, data shifts left synchronously and new data is entered at the shift-left serial input.

Clocking of the flip-flop is inhibited when both mode control inputs are low. The mode controls of the SN54194/SN74194 should be changed only while the clock input is high.

FUNCTION TABLE

CLEAR	MODE S1	MODE S0	CLOCK	SERIAL LEFT	SERIAL RIGHT	PARALLEL A	PARALLEL B	PARALLEL C	PARALLEL D	Q_A	Q_B	Q_C	Q_D
L	X	X	X	X	X	X	X	X	X	L	L	L	L
H	X	X	L	X	X	X	X	X	X	Q_{A0}	Q_{B0}	Q_{C0}	Q_{D0}
H	H	H	↑	X	X	a	b	c	d	a	b	c	d
H	L	H	↑	X	H	X	X	X	X	H	Q_{An}	Q_{Bn}	Q_{Cn}
H	L	H	↑	X	L	X	X	X	X	L	Q_{An}	Q_{Bn}	Q_{Cn}
H	H	L	↑	H	X	X	X	X	X	Q_{Bn}	Q_{Cn}	Q_{Dn}	H
H	H	L	↑	L	X	X	X	X	X	Q_{Bn}	Q_{Cn}	Q_{Dn}	L
H	L	L	X	X	X	X	X	X	X	Q_{A0}	Q_{B0}	Q_{C0}	Q_{D0}

H = high level (steady state)
L = low level (steady state)
X = irrelevant (any input, including transitions)
↑ = transition from low to high level
a, b, c, d = the level of steady-state input at inputs A, B, C, or D, respectively.
Q_{A0}, Q_{B0}, Q_{C0}, Q_{D0} = the level of Q_A, Q_B, Q_C, or Q_D, respectively, before the indicated steady-state input conditions were established.
Q_{An}, Q_{Bn}, Q_{Cn}, Q_{Dn} = the level of Q_A, Q_B, Q_C, respectively, before the most-recent ↑ transition of the clock.

TEXAS INSTRUMENTS
INCORPORATED
POST OFFICE BOX 5012 • DALLAS, TEXAS 75222

 **MOTOROLA**

Specifications and Applications Information

EIGHT-BIT MULTIPLYING DIGITAL-TO-ANALOG CONVERTER

. . . designed for use where the output current is a linear product of an eight-bit digital word and an analog input voltage.

- Eight-Bit Accuracy Available in Both Temperature Ranges
  Relative Accuracy: ±0.19% Error maximum
  (MC1408L8, MC1408P8, MC1508L8)
- Seven and Six-Bit Accuracy Available with MC1408 Designated by 7 or 6 Suffix after Package Suffix
- Fast Settling Time — 300 ns typical
- Noninverting Digital Inputs are MTTL and CMOS Compatible
- Output Voltage Swing — +0.4 V to -5.0 V
- High-Speed Multiplying Input
  Slew Rate 4.0 mA/μs
- Standard Supply Voltages: +5.0 V and -5.0 V to -15 V

MC1408
MC1508

EIGHT-BIT MULTIPLYING DIGITAL-TO-ANALOG CONVERTER

SILICON MONOLITHIC INTEGRATED CIRCUIT

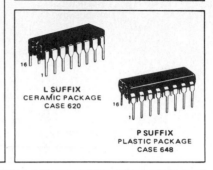

L SUFFIX
CERAMIC PACKAGE
CASE 620

P SUFFIX
PLASTIC PACKAGE
CASE 648

FIGURE 1 – D-to-A TRANSFER CHARACTERISTICS

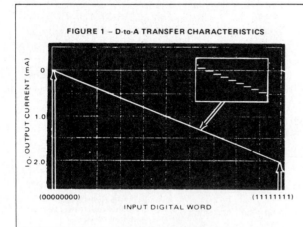

FIGURE 2 – BLOCK DIAGRAM

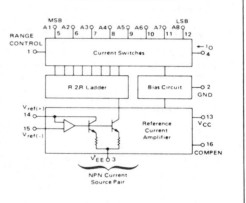

TYPICAL APPLICATIONS

- Tracking A-to-D Converters
- Successive Approximation A-to-D Converters
- 2 1/2 Digit Panel Meters and DVM's
- Waveform Synthesis
- Sample and Hold
- Peak Detector
- Programmable Gain and Attenuation
- CRT Character Generation

- Audio Digitizing and Decoding
- Programmable Power Supplies
- Analog-Digital Multiplication
- Digital-Digital Multiplication
- Analog-Digital Division
- Digital Addition and Subtraction
- Speech Compression and Expansion
- Stepping Motor Drive

Courtesy of Motorola Incorporated.

MC1408, MC1508

MAXIMUM RATINGS (T_A = +25°C unless otherwise noted.)

Rating	Symbol	Value	Unit
Power Supply Voltage	V_{CC} V_{EE}	+5.5 -16.5	Vdc
Digital Input Voltage	V_5 thru V_{12}	0 to +5.5	Vdc
Applied Output Voltage	V_O	+0.5, -5.2	Vdc
Reference Current	I_{14}	5.0	mA
Reference Amplifier Inputs	V_{14}, V_{15}	V_{CC}, V_{EE}	Vdc

Operating Temperature Range
    MC1508
    MC1408 Series
	T_A	
		-55 to +125
		0 to +75
			°C

Storage Temperature Range	T_{stg}	-65 to +150	°C

ELECTRICAL CHARACTERISTICS (V_{CC} = +5.0 Vdc, V_{EE} = -15 Vdc, $\frac{V_{ref}}{R14}$ = 2.0 mA, MC1508L8: T_A = -55°C to +125°C.
MC1408L Series: T_A = 0 to +75°C unless otherwise noted. All digital inputs at high logic level.)

Characteristic	Figure	Symbol	Min	Typ	Max	Unit

Relative Accuracy (Error relative to full scale I_O)
  MC1508L8, MC1408L8, MC1408P8
  MC1408P7, MC1408L7, See Note 1
  MC1408P6, MC1408L6, See Note 1
	4	E_r	
			—
			—
			—
				
				—
				—
				—
					
					±0.19
					±0.39
					±0.78
						%

Settling Time to within ±1/2 LSB [includes t_{PLH}] (T_A=+25°C) See Note 2	5	t_S	—	300	—	ns
Propagation Delay Time T_A = +25°C	5	t_{PLH}, t_{PHL}	—	30	100	ns
Output Full Scale Current Drift		TCI_O	—	-20	—	PPM/°C

Digital Input Logic Levels (MSB)
  High Level, Logic "1"
  Low Level, Logic "0"
	3	
		V_{IH}
		V_{IL}
			
			2.0
			—
				
				—
				—
					
					—
					0.8
						Vdc

Digital Input Current (MSB)
  High Level, V_{IH} = 5.0 V
  Low Level, V_{IL} = 0.8 V
	3	
		I_{IH}
		I_{IL}
			
			—
			—
				
				0
				-0.4
					
					0.04
					-0.8
						mA

Reference Input Bias Current (Pin 15)	3	I_{15}	—	-1.0	-5.0	µA

Output Current Range
  V_{EE} = -5.0 V
  V_{EE} = -15 V, T_A = 25°C
	3	I_{OR}	
			0
			0
				
				2.0
				2.0
					
					2.1
					4.2
						mA

Output Current V_{ref} = 2.000 V, R14 = 1000 Ω	3	I_O	1.9	1.99	2.1	mA
Output Current (All bits low)	3	$I_{O(min)}$	—	0	4.0	µA

Output Voltage Compliance ($E_r \leq$ 0.19% at T_A = +25°C)
  Pin 1 grounded
  Pin 1 open, V_{EE} below -10 V
	3	V_O	
			—
			—
				
				—
				—
					
					-0.55, +0.4
					-5.0, +0.4
						Vdc

Reference Current Slew Rate	6	SR I_{ref}	—	4.0	—	mA/µs
Output Current Power Supply Sensitivity		PSRR(−)	—	0.5	2.7	µA/V
Power Supply Current (All bits low)	3	I_{CC} I_{EE}	— —	+13.5 -7.5	+22 -13	mA
Power Supply Voltage Range (T_A = +25°C)	3	V_{CCR} V_{EER}	+4.5 -4.5	+5.0 -15	+5.5 -16.5	Vdc

Power Dissipation
  All bits low
    V_{EE} = -5.0 Vdc
    V_{EE} = -15 Vdc
  All bits high
    V_{EE} = -5.0 Vdc
    V_{EE} = -15 Vdc
	3	P_D	
			
			—
			—
			
			—
			—
				
				105
				190
				
				90
				160
					
					170
					305
					
					—
					—
						mW

Note 1. All current switches are tested to guarantee at least 50% of rated output current.
Note 2. All bits switched.

SC-01 SPEECH SYNTHESIZER

DATA SHEET

A Division of Federal Screw Works
500 Stephenson Highway
Troy, Michigan 48084

Votrax® CMOS Phoneme Speech Synthesizer

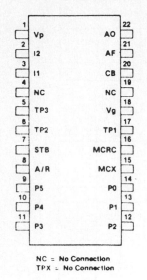

Pin			Pin
1	Vp	AO	22
2	I2	AF	21
3	I1	CB	20
4	NC	NC	19
5	TP3	Vg	18
6	TP2	TP1	17
7	STB	MCRC	16
8	A/R	MCX	15
9	P5	P0	14
10	P4	P1	13
11	P3	P2	12

NC = No Connection
TPX = No Connection

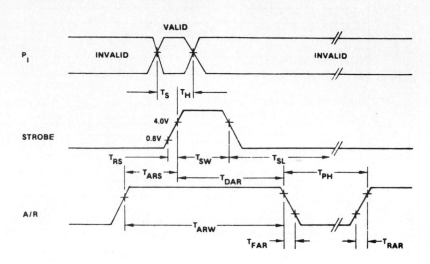

Timing Specifications

CHARACTERISTIC	SYMBOL	MIN	TYP	MAX	UNIT
Input Setup Time (P$_I$ to STB)	T$_S$	450			NS
Input Hold Time (P$_I$ to STB)	T$_H$	0			NS
Rise Time of STB Edge (.8V to 4V)	T$_{RS}$			100	NS
A/R Width ($\overline{A}$/R Connected to STB) +	T$_{ARW}$	1	1.3	2	µs
STB Width	T$_{SW}$	200			NS
STB Low*	T$_{SL}$	*			NS
Propagation Delay (STB to A/R after T$_{ARW}$)	T$_{DAR}$			500	NS
A/R Rise Time (Capacitive load = 30pf)	T$_{RAR}$			100	NS
A/R Fall Time (Capacitive load = 30pf)	T$_{FAR}$			100	NS
Time from $\overline{A}$/R Request to STB Service)	T$_{ARS}$	0		500	µs
Time of Phoneme Duration +	T$_{PH}$	47	107	250	MS

+ *Dependent on Master Clock frequency : 720kHz*

Copyright Votrax® 1980

* Strobe must remain low (72x Master Clock Period) before rising edge

Votrax® reserves the right to alter its product line at any time, or change specifications or design without notice and without obligation.

Phoneme Code	Phoneme Symbol	Duration (ms)	Example Word
00	EH3	59	jacket
01	EH2	71	enlist
02	EH1	121	heavy
03	PA0	47	no sound
04	DT	47	butter
05	A2	71	made
06	A1	103	made
07	ZH	90	azure
08	AH2	71	honest
09	I3	55	inhibit
0A	I2	80	inhibit
0B	I1	121	inhibit
0C	M	103	mat
0D	N	80	sun
0E	B	71	bag
0F	V	71	van
10	CH*	71	chip
11	SH	121	shop
12	Z	71	zoo
13	AW1	146	lawful
14	NG	121	thing
15	AH1	146	father
16	OO1	103	looking
17	OO	185	book
18	L	103	land
19	K	80	trick
1A	J*	47	judge
1B	H	71	hello
1C	G	71	get
1D	F	103	fast
1E	D	55	paid
1F	S	90	pass

Phoneme Code	Phoneme Symbol	Duration (ms)	Example Word
20	A	185	day
21	AY	65	day
22	Y1	80	yard
23	UH3	47	mission
24	AH	250	mop
25	P	103	past
26	O	185	cold
27	I	185	pin
28	U	185	move
29	Y	103	any
2A	T	71	tap
2B	R	90	red
2C	E	185	meet
2D	W	80	win
2E	AE	185	dad
2F	AE1	103	after
30	AW2	90	salty
31	UH2	71	about
32	UH1	103	uncle
33	UH	185	cup
34	O2	80	for
35	O1	121	aboard
36	IU	59	you
37	U1	90	you
38	THV	80	the
39	TH	71	thin
3A	ER	146	bird
3B	EH	185	get
3C	E1	121	be
3D	AW	250	call
3E	PA1	185	no sound
3F	STOP	47	no sound

/T/ must precede /CH/ to produce CH sound.
/D/ must precede /J/ to produce J sound.

Phoneme   Categories   According   to   Production   Features

Voiced					'Voiced' Fricat.	'Voiced' Stop	Fricative Stop	Fricative	Nasal	No Sound
E	EH	AE	UH	OO1	Z	B	T	S	M	PA0
E1	EH1	AE1	UH1	R	ZH	D	DT	SH	N	PA1
Y	EH2	AH	UH2	ER	J	G	K	CH	NG	STOP
Y1	EH3	AH1	UH3	L	V		P	TH		
I	A	AH2	O	IU	THV			F		
I1	A1	AW	O1	U				H		
I2	A2	AW1	O2	U1						
I3	AY	AW2	OO	W						

Analog Output Specifications

CHARACTERISTIC	MIN	MAX	UNIT
Output Voltage (AH Phoneme)	.18 x Vp	.26 x Vp	Vp-p
Output Bias Current ** (.6V < CB < Vp)	3.5	7.3	mA

ELECTRICAL CHARACTERISTICS: T_o = 0 to 70°C, Vp = 7 to 14 V_{DC}

CHARACTERISTIC	MIN	TYP	MAX	UNIT
Digital Input Impedance	1 meg.			Ohm
Input Capacitance (P_I, STB)			3	pf
Input Capacitance (I1, I2, MCX)			8	pf
Digital Input Logic "0" (except I1, I2, MCX)	V_G - 0.5		V_G + 0.8	V_{DC}
Digital Input Logic "0" (MCX)			V_G + 1.0	V_{DC}
Digital Input Logic "0" (I1, I2)			.2 x Vp	V_{DC}
Digital Input Logic "1" (except I1, I2, MCX)	V_G + 4.0		Vp + 0.5	V_{DC}
Digital Input Logic "1" (I1, I2)	.8 x Vp			V_{DC}
Digital Input Logic "1" (MCX)	4.6			V_{DC}
Digital Output Logic "0" (I sink = 0.8mA)			V_G + 0.5	V_{DC}
Digital Output Logic "1" (I source = 0.5mA)	Vp − 0.5			V_{DC}
Power Supply Current Vp = 9V		9.1		mA
Vp = 9V**		11	18	mA
Vp = 14V**		18	27	mA
*Master Clock Frequency		720K		Hz
MCX Input Duty Cycle	60:40		40:60	%
Master Clock Resistor Value (MCRC)***	6.5k			Ohm
Master Clock Capacitor Value (MCRC)***			300	pf

*Variable

**With CB, AF, AO connected for Class B audio amplifier (see APPLICATION NOTES)

***Frequency of Master Clock $\simeq$ 1.25 / RC

Note: TP1, TP2 must be left open for normal operation.

Copyright Votrax® 1980

Clocks

For additional application information, see AN-143 at the end of this section.

MM5309, MM5311, MM5312, MM5313, MM5314, MM5315 digital clocks

general description

These digital clocks are monolithic MOS integrated circuits utilizing P-channel low-threshold, enhancement mode and ion implanted. depletion mode devices. The devices provide all the logic required to build several types of clocks. Two display modes (4 or 6-digits) facilitate end-product designs of varied sophistication. The circuits interface to LED and gas discharge displays with minimal additional components, and require only a single power supply. The timekeeping function operates from either a 50 or 60 Hz input, and the display format may be either 12 hours (with leading-zero blanking) or 24 hours. Outputs consist of multiplexed display drives ($\overline{BCD}$ and 7-segment) and digit enables. The devices operate over a power supply range of 11V to 19V and do not require a regulated supply. These clocks are packaged in dual-in-line packages.

features

- 50 or 60 Hz operation
- 12 or 24-hour display format
- Leading-zero blanking (12-hour format)
- 7-segment outputs
- Single power supply
- Fast and slow set controls
- Internal multiplex oscillator
- For features of individual clocks, see Table I

applications

- Desk clocks
- Automobile clocks
- Industrial clocks
- Interval Timers

TABLE I.

FEATURES	MM5309	MM5311	MM5312	MM5313	MM5314	MM5315
$\overline{BCD}$ Outputs	X	X	X	X		X
4/6-Digit Display Mode	X	X		X	X	X
Hold Count Control		X		X	X	X
1 Hz Output			X	X		
Output Enable Control	X	X			X	
Reset	X					X

connection diagrams (Dual-In-Line Packages)

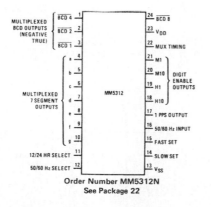

Order Number MM5312N
See Package 22

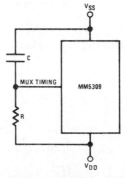

FIGURE 4a. Relaxation Oscillator

1-2

Courtesy of National Semiconductor Corporation.

absolute maximum ratings

Voltage at Any Pin $V_{SS} + 0.3$ to $V_{SS} - 20V$
Operating Temperature $-25°C$ to $+70°C$
Storage Temperature $-65°C$ to $+150°C$
Lead Temperature (Soldering, 10 seconds) $300°C$

electrical characteristics
T_A within operating range, $V_{SS} = 11V$ to $19V$, $V_{DD} = 0V$, unless otherwise specified.

PARAMETER	CONDITIONS	MIN	TYP	MAX	UNITS
Power Supply Voltage	V_{SS} ($V_{DD} = 0V$)	11		19	V
Power Supply Current	$V_{SS} = 14V$, (No Output Loads)			10	mA
50/60 Hz Input Frequency		dc	50 or 60	60k	Hz
50/60 Hz Input Voltage					
Logical High Level		$V_{SS}-1$	V_{SS}	V_{SS}	V
Logical Low Level		V_{DD}	V_{DD}	$V_{SS}-10$	V
Multiplex Frequency	Determined by External R & C	0.100	1.0	60	kHz
All Logic Inputs	Driven by External Timebase	dc		60	kHz
Logical High Level	Internal Depletion Device to V_{SS}	$V_{SS}-1$	V_{SS}	V_{SS}	V
Logical Low Level		V_{DD}	V_{DD}	$V_{SS}-10$	V
$\overline{BCD}$ and 7-Segment Outputs					
Logical High Level	Loaded 2 kΩ to V_{DD}	2.0		20	mA source
Logical Low Level				0.01	mA source
Digital Enable Outputs					
Logical High Level				0.3	mA source
Logical Low Level	Loaded 100 Ω to V_{SS}	5.0		25	mA sink

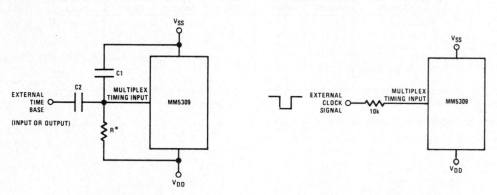

FIGURE 4b. External Time Base   FIGURE 4c. External Clock

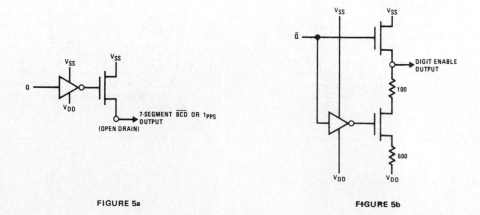

FIGURE 5a   FIGURE 5b

FIGURE 5. Output Circuits

functional description

A block diagram of the MM5309 digital clock is shown in *Figure 1*. MM5311, MM5312, MM5313, MM5314 and MM5315 clocks are bonding options of MM5309 clock. Table I shows the pin-outs for these clocks.

50 or 60 Hz Input: This input is applied to a Schmitt Trigger shaping circuit which provides approximately 5V of hysteresis and allows using a filtered sinewave input. A simple RC filter such as shown in *Figure 10* should be used to remove possible line voltage transients that could either cause the clock to gain time or damage the device. The shaper output drives a counter chain which performs the timekeeping function.

50 or 60 Hz Select Input: This input programs the prescale counter to divide by either 50 or 60 to obtain a 1 Hz timebase. The counter is programmed for 60 Hz operation by connecting this input to V_{DD}. An internal depletion device is common to this pin; simply leaving this input unconnected programs the clock for 50 Hz operation. As shown in *Figure 1*, the prescale counter provides both 1 Hz and 10 Hz signals, which can be brought out as bonding options.

Time Setting Inputs: Both fast and slow setting inputs, as well as a hold input, are provided. Internal depletion devices provide the normal timekeeping function. Switching any of these inputs (one at a time) to V_{DD} results in the desired time setting function.

The three gates in the counter chain *(Figure 1)* are used for setting time. During normal operation, gate A connects the shaper output to a prescale counter ($\div 50$ or $\div 60$); gates B and C cascade the remaining counters. Gate A is used to inhibit the input to the counters for the duration of slow, fast or hold time-setting input activity. Gate B is used to connect the shaper output directly to a seconds counter ($\div 60$), the condition for slow advance. Likewise, gate C connects the shaper output directly to a minutes counter ($\div 60$) for fast advance.

Fast set then, advances hours information at one hour per second and slow set advances minutes information at one minute per second.

12 or 24-Hour Select Input: This input is used to program the hours counter to divide by either 12 or 24, thereby providing the desired display format. The 12-hour display format is selected by connecting this input to V_{DD}; leaving the input unconnected (internal depletion device) selects the 24-hour format.

Output Multiplexer Operation: The seconds, minutes, and hours counters continuously reflect the time of day. Outputs from each counter (indicative of both units and tens of seconds, minutes, and hours) are time-division multiplexed to provide digit-sequential access to the time data. Thus, instead of requiring 42 leads to interconnect a 6-digit clock and its display (7 segments per digit), only 13 output leads are required. The multiplexer is addressed by a multiplex divider decoder, which is driven by a multiplex oscillator. The oscillator and external timing components set the frequency of the multiplexing function and, as controlled by the 4 or 6-digit select input, the divider determines whether data will be output for 4 or 6 digits. A zero-blanking circuit suppresses the zero that would otherwise sometimes appear in the tens-of-hours display; blanking is effective only in the 12-hour format. The multiplexer addresses also become the display digit-enable outputs. The multiplexer outputs are applied to a decoder which is used to address a programmable (code converting) ROM. This ROM generates the final output codes, i.e., $\overline{BCD}$ and 7-segment. The sequential output order is from digit 6 (unit seconds) through digit 1 (tens of hours).

Multiplex Timing Input: The multiplex oscillator is shown in *Figure 2*. Adding an external resistor and capacitor to this circuit via the multiplex timing input (as shown in *Figure 4a*) produces a relaxation oscillator. The waveform at this input is a quasi-sawtooth that is squared by the shaping action of the Schmitt Trigger in *Figure 2*. *Figure 3* provides guidelines for selecting the external components relative to desired multiplex frequency.

Figure 4 also illustrates two methods of synchronizing the multiplex oscillator to an external timebase. The external RC timing components may be omitted and this input may be driven by an external timebase; the required logic levels are the same as 50 or 60 Hz input.

Reset: Applying V_{DD} to this input resets the counters to 0:00:00.00 in 12-hour format and 00:00:00.00 in 24-hour formats leaving the input unconnected (internal depletion pull-up) selects normal operation.

4 or 6-Digit Select Input: Like the other control inputs, this input is provided with an internal depletion pull-up device. With no input connection the clock outputs data for a 4-digit display. Applying V_{DD} to this input provides a 6-digit display.

Output Enable Input: With this pin unconnected the $\overline{BCD}$ and 7-segment outputs are enabled (via an internal depletion pull-up). Switching V_{DD} to this input inhibits these outputs. (Not applicable to MM5312, MM5313, and MM5315 clocks.)

Output Circuits: *Figure 5a* illustrates the circuit used for the $\overline{BCD}$ and 7-segment outputs. *Figure 5b* shows the digit enable output circuit. *Figure 6* illustrates interfacing these outputs to standard and low power TTL. *Figures 7 and 8* illustrate methods of interfacing these outputs to common anode and common cathode LED displays, respectively. A method of interfacing these clocks to gas discharge display tubes is shown in *Figure 9*. When driving gas discharge displays which enclose more than one digit in a common gas envelope, it is necessary to inhibit the segment drive voltage(s) during inter-digit transitions. *Figure 9* also illustrates a method of generating a voltage for application to the output enable input to accomplish the required inter-digit blanking.

functional description (Continued)

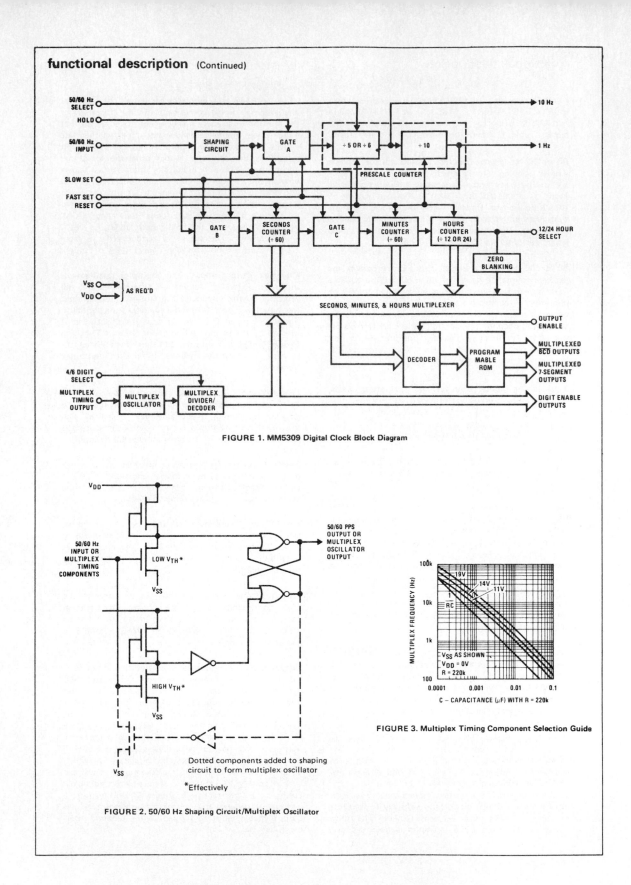

FIGURE 1. MM5309 Digital Clock Block Diagram

FIGURE 3. Multiplex Timing Component Selection Guide

Dotted components added to shaping circuit to form multiplex oscillator

*Effectively

FIGURE 2. 50/60 Hz Shaping Circuit/Multiplex Oscillator

2708/8708*
8K AND 4K UV ERASABLE PROM

	Max. Power	Max. Access	Organization
2708	800 mW	450 ns	1K × 8
2708L	425 mW	450 ns	1K × 8
2708-1	800 mW	350 ns	1K × 8
2704	800 mW	450 ns	512 × 8

- **Low Power Dissipation — 425 mW Max. (2708L)**

- **Fast Access Time — 350 ns Max. (2708-1)**

- **Pin Compatible to Intel® 2308 ROM**

- **Static — No Clocks Required**

- **Data Inputs and Outputs TTL Compatible during both Read and Program Modes**

- **Three-State Outputs — OR-Tie Capability**

The Intel® 2708 is a 8192-bit ultraviolet light erasable and electrically reprogrammable EPROM, ideally suited where fast turnaround and pattern experimentation are important requirements. All data inputs and outputs are TTL compatible during both the read and program modes. The outputs are three-state, allowing direct interface with common system bus structures. A pin-for-pin mask programmed ROM, the Intel® 2308, is available for large volume production runs of systems initially using the 2708.

The 2708L at 425 mW is available for systems requiring lower power dissipation than from the 2708. A power dissipation savings of over 50%, without any sacrifice in speed, is obtained with the 2708L. The 2708L has high input noise immunity and is specified at 10% power supply tolerance. A high-speed 2708-1 is also available at 350 ns for microprocessors requiring fast access times. For smaller size systems there is the 4096-bit 2704 which is organized as 512 words by 8 bits. All these devices have the same programming and erasing specifications of the 2708. The 2704 electrical specifications are the same as the 2708.

The 2708 family is fabricated with the N-channel silicon gate FAMOS technology and is available in a 24-pin dual in-line package.

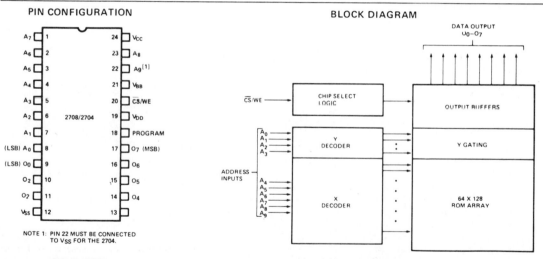

PIN CONFIGURATION

NOTE 1: PIN 22 MUST BE CONNECTED TO V_{SS} FOR THE 2704.

PIN NAMES

A_0-A_9	ADDRESS INPUTS
O_1-O_8	DATA OUTPUTS/INPUTS
$\overline{CS}$/WE	CHIP SELECT/WRITE ENABLE INPUT

BLOCK DIAGRAM

PIN CONNECTION DURING READ OR PROGRAM

	PIN NUMBER							
MODE	DATA I/O 9-11, 13-17	ADDRESS INPUTS 1-8, 22, 23	V_{SS} 12	PROGRAM 18	V_{DD} 19	$\overline{CS}$/WE 20	V_{BB} 21	V_{CC} 24
READ	D_{OUT}	A_{IN}	GND	GND	+12	V_{IL}	-5	+5
DESELECT	HIGH IMPEDANCE	DON'T CARE	GND	GND	+12	V_{IH}	-5	+5
PROGRAM	D_{IN}	A_{IN}	GND	PULSED 26V	+12	V_{IHW}	-5	+5

*All 8708 specifications are identical to the 2708 specifications.

Courtesy of Intel Corporation.

PROGRAMMING

The programming specifications are described in the PROM/ROM Programming Instructions on page 4-83.

Absolute Maximum Ratings*

Temperature Under Bias	$-25°C$ to $+85°C$
Storage Temperature	$-65°C$ to $+125°C$
V_{DD} With Respect to V_{BB}	+20V to -0.3V
V_{CC} and V_{SS} With Respect to V_{BB}	+15V to -0.3V
All Input or Output Voltages With Respect to V_{BB} During Read	+15V to -0.3V
$\overline{CS}$/WE Input With Respect to V_{BB} During Programming	+20V to -0.3V
Program Input With Respect to V_{BB}	+35V to -0 3V
Power Dissipation	1.5W

*COMMENT

Stresses above those listed under "Absolute Maximum Ratings" may cause permanent damage to the device. This is a stress rating only and functional operation of the device at these or any other conditions above those indicated in the operational sections of this specification is not implied. Exposure to absolute maximum rating conditions for extended periods may affect device reliability.

DC and AC Operating Conditions During Read

	2708	2708-1	2708L
Temperature Range	$0°C - 70°C$	$0°C - 70°C$	$0°C - 70°C$
V_{CC} Power Supply	5V ± 5%	5V ± 5%	5V ± 10%
V_{DD} Power Supply	12V ± 5%	12V ± 5%	12V ± 10%
V_{BB} Power Supply	-5V ± 5%	-5V ± 5%	-5V ± 10%

READ OPERATION
D.C. and Operating Characteristics

Symbol	Parameter	2708, 2708-1 Limits			2708L Limits			Units	Test Conditions
		Min.	Typ.[2]	Max.	Min.	Typ.[2]	Max.		
I_{LI}	Address and Chip Select Input Sink Current		1	10		1	10	μA	$V_{IN} = 5.25V$ or $V_{IN} = V_{IL}$
I_{LO}	Output Leakage Current		1	10		1	10	μA	$V_{OUT} = 5.5V$, $\overline{CS}$/WE = 5V
I_{DD}[3]	V_{DD} Supply Current		50	65		21	28	mA	Worst Case Supply Currents[4]
I_{CC}[3]	V_{CC} Supply Current		6	10		2	4	mA	All Inputs High,
I_{BB}[3]	V_{BB} Supply Current		30	45		10	14	mA	$\overline{CS}$/WE = 5V; $T_A = 0$ C
V_{IL}	Input Low Voltage	V_{SS}		0.65	V_{SS}		0.65	V	
V_{IH}	Input High Voltage	3.0		V_{CC}+1	2.2		V_{CC}+1	V	
V_{OL}	Output Low Voltage			0.45			0.4	V	I_{OL} 1.6mA (2708, 2708-1); I_{OL} 2mA (2708L)
V_{OH1}	Output High Voltage	3.7			3.7			V	$I_{OH} = -100 \mu A$
V_{OH2}	Output High Voltage	2.4			2.4			V	$I_{OH} = -1$ mA
PD	Power Dissipation			800			325	mW	T_A 70 C
							425	mW	$T_A = 0$ C

NOTES: 1. V_{BB} must be applied prior to V_{CC} and V_{DD}. V_{BB} must also be the last power supply switched off.
2. Typical values are for $T_A = 25$ C and nominal supply voltages.
3. The total power dissipation is not calculated by summing the various currents (I_{DD}, I_{CC}, and I_{BB}) multiplied by their respective voltages since current paths exist between the various power supplies and V_{SS}. The I_{DD}, I_{CC}, and I_{BB} currents should be used to determine power supply capacity only.
4. I_{BB} for the 2708L is specified in the programmed state and is 18 mA maximum in the unprogrammed state.

ERASURE CHARACTERISTICS

The erasure characteristics of the 2708 are such that erasure begins to occur when exposed to light with wavelengths shorter than approximately 4000 Angstroms (Å). It should be noted that sunlight and certain types of fluorescent lamps have wavelengths in the 3000—4000Å range. Data show that constant exposure to room level fluorescent lighting could erase the typical 2708 in approximately 3 years, while it would take approximatley 1 week to cause erasure when exposed to direct sunlight. If the 2708 is to be exposed to these types of lighting conditions for extended periods of time, opaque labels are available from Intel which should be placed over the 2708 window to prevent unintentional erasure.

The recommended erasure procedure (see page 3-55) for the 2708 is exposure to shortwave ultraviolet light which has a wavelength of 2537 Angstroms (Å). The integrated dose (i.e., UV intensity X exposure time) for erasure should be a minimum of 15 W-sec/cm². The erasure time with this dosage is approximately 15 to 20 minutes using an ultraviolet lamp with a 12000 $\mu W/cm^2$ power rating. The 2708 should be placed within 1 inch of the lamp tubes during erasure. Some lamps have a filter on their tubes which should be removed before erasure.

C. 2708/2704 Family Programming

Initially, and after each erasure, all 8192/4096 bits of the 2708/2704 are in the "1" state (output high). Information is introduced by selectively programming "0" into the desired bit locations. A programmed "0" can only be changed to a "1" by UV erasure.

The circuit is set up for programming operation by raising the CS/WE input (pin 20) to +12V. The word address is selected in the same manner as in the read mode. Data to be programmed are presented, 8 bits in parallel, to the data output lines (O_1–O_8). Logic levels for address and data lines and the supply voltages are the same as for the read mode. After address and data set up, one program pulse per address is applied to the program input (pin 18). One pass through all addresses is defined as a program loop. The number of loops (N) required is a function of the program pulse width (t_{PW}) according to N x t_{PW} ≥ 100 ms.

The width of the program pulse is from 0.1 to 1 ms. The number of loops (N) is from a minimum of 100 (t_{PW} = 1 ms) to greater than 1000 (t_{PW} = 0.1 ms). There must be N successive loops throuhg all 1024 addresses. *It is not permitted to apply N program pulses to an address and then change to the next address to be programmed.* Caution should be observed regarding the end of a program sequence. The CS/WE falling edge transition must occur before the first address transition when changing from a program to a read cycle. The program pin should also be pulled down to V_{ILP} with an active instead of a passive device. This pin will source a small amount of current (I_{ILL}) when CS/WE is at V_{IHW} (12V) and the program pulse is at V_{ILP}.

Programming Examples (Using N x t_{PW} ≥ 100 ms)

Example 1:   All 8096 bits are to be programmed with a 0.5 ms program pulse width.

   The minimum number of program loops is 200. One program loop consists of words 0 to 1023.

Example 2:   Words 0 to 100 and 500 to 600 are to be programmed. All other bits are "don't care". The program pulse width is 0.75 ms.

   The minimum number of program loops is 133. One program loop consists of words 0 to 1023. The data entered into the "don't care" bits should be all 1's.

Example 3:   Same requirements as example 2, but the PROM is now to be *updated* to include data for words 750 to 770.

   The minimum number of program loops is 133. One program loop consists of words 0 to 1023. The data entered into the "don't care" bits should be all 1's. Addresses 0 to 100 and 500 to 600 must be re-programmed with their original data pattern.

2704, 2708 Family
PROGRAM CHARACTERISTICS

T_A = 25°C, V_{CC} = 5V ±5%, V_{DD} = +12V ±5%, V_{BB} = –5V ±5%, V_{SS} = 0V, Unless Otherwise Noted.

D.C. Programming Characteristics

Symbol	Parameter		Min.	Typ.	Max.	Units	Test Conditions
I_{LI}	Address and CS/WE Input Sink Current				10	µA	V_{IN} = 5.25V
I_{IPL}	Program Pulse Source Current				3	mA	
I_{IPH}	Program Pulse Sink Current				20	mA	
I_{DD}	V_{DD} Supply Current	2708, 2704		50	65	mA	
		2708L		21	28	mA	Worst Case Supply
I_{CC}	V_{CC} Supply Current	2708, 2704		6	10	mA	Currents[1]:
		2708L		2	4	mA	All Inputs High
I_{BB}	V_{BB} Supply Current	2708, 2704		30	45	mA	CS/WE = 5V; T_A = 0°C
		2708L		10	14	mA	
V_{IL}	Input Low Level (except Program)		V_{SS}		0.65	V	
V_{IH}	Input High Level For all Addresses and Data	2708, 2704	3.0		V_{CC} + 1	V	
		2708L	2.2		V_{CC} + 1	V	
V_{IHW}	CS/WE Input High Level		11.4		12.6	V	Referenced to V_{SS}
V_{IHP}	Program Pulse High Level		25		27	V	Referenced to V_{SS}
V_{ILP}	Program Pulse Low Level		V_{SS}		1	V	V_{IHP} – V_{ILP} 25V min.

Note 1. I_{BB} for the 2708L is specified in the programmed state and is 18 mA maximum in the unprogrammed state.

A.C. Programming Characteristics

Symbol	Parameter	Min.	Typ.	Max.	Units
t_{AS}	Address Setup Time	10			μs
t_{CSS}	$\overline{CS}$/WE Setup Time	10			μs
t_{DS}	Data Setup Time	10			μs
t_{AH}	Address Hold Time	1			μs
t_{CH}	$\overline{CS}$/WE Hold Time	.5			μs
t_{DH}	Data Hold Time	1			μs
t_{DF}	Chip Deselect to Output Float Delay	0		120	ns
t_{DPR}	Program To Read Delay			10	μs
t_{PW}	Program Pulse Width	.1		1.0	ms
t_{PR}	Program Pulse Rise Time	.5		2.0	μs
t_{PF}	Program Pulse Fall Time	.5		2.0	μs

NOTE: Intel's standard product warranty applies only to devices programmed to specifications described herein.

2704, 2708 Family
Programming Waveforms

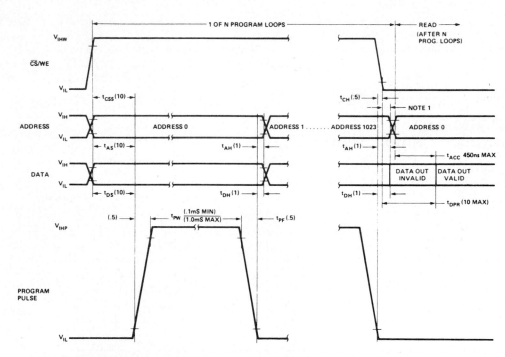

NOTE 1. THE $\overline{CS}$/WE TRANSITION MUST OCCUR AFTER THE PROGRAM PULSE TRANSITION AND BEFORE THE ADDRESS TRANSITION.

NOTE 2. NUMBERS IN ( ) INDICATE MINIMUM TIMING IN μS UNLESS OTHERWISE SPECIFIED.

Absolute Maximum Ratings (Notes 1 and 2)

Voltage at Any Pin Except Control Inputs	−0.3V to V_{CC} + 0.3V
Voltage at Control Inputs	−0.3V to + 15V
(Start, TRI-STATE, Clock, ALE, ADD A, ADD B, ADD C)	
Operating Temperature Range	
ADC0808CCN, ADC0809CCN	−40°C to +85°C
ADC0808CD	−55°C to +125°C
Storage Temperature Range	−65°C to +150°C
Package Dissipation (at 25°C)	500 mW
Operating V_{CC} Range	4.5V to 6V
Absolute Maximum V_{CC}	6.5V
Lead Temperature (Soldering, 10 seconds)	300°C

DC Electrical Characteristics

ADC0808CCN, ADC0809CCN
4.75V $\leq V_{CC} \leq$ 5.25V, −40°C $\leq T_A \leq$ +85°C unless otherwise noted, (Note 2)
ADC0808CD
4.5V $\leq V_{CC} \leq$ 5.5V, −55°C $\leq T_A \leq$ +125°C unless otherwise noted, (Note 2)

PARAMETER		CONDITIONS	MIN	TYP	MAX	UNITS
$V_{IN(1)}$	Logical "1" Input Voltage	V_{CC} = 5V	V_{CC}−1.5			V
$V_{IN(0)}$	Logical "0" Input Voltage	V_{CC} = 5V			1.5	V
$V_{OUT(1)}$	Logical "1" Output Voltage	I_O = −360 μA @ T_A = 85°C	V_{CC}−0.4			V
		I_O = −300 μA @ T_A = 125°C				
$V_{OUT(0)}$	Logical "0" Output Voltage	I_O = 1.6 mA			0.45	V
$V_{OUT(0)}$	Logical "0" Output Voltage EOC	I_O = 1.2 mA			0.45	V
$I_{IN(1)}$	Logical "1" Input Current (The Control Inputs)	V_{IN} = 15V			1.0	μA
$I_{IN(0)}$	Logical "0" Input Current (The Control Inputs)	V_{IN} = 0	−1.0			μA
I_{CC}	Supply Current	Clock Frequency = 500 kHz				
		@ T_A = 85°C		300	1000	μA
		@ T_A = 125°C			3000	μA
I_{OUT}	TRI-STATE Output Current	V_O = 5V			3	μA
		V_O = 0	−3			μA

Note 1: "Absolute Maximum Ratings" are those values beyond which the safety of the device cannot be guaranteed. Except for "Operating Temperature Range" they are not meant to imply that the devices should be operated at these limits. The table of "Electrical Characteristics" provides conditions for actual device operation.

Note 2: All voltages measured with respect to GND unless otherwise specified.